D0699145

Nations of Immigrants

Nations of Immigrants

Australia, the United States, and International Migration

Edited by GARY P. FREEMAN and JAMES JUPP

Melbourne
OXFORD UNIVERSITY PRESS
Oxford Auckland New York

OXFORD UNIVERSITY PRESS AUSTRALIA

Oxford New York Toronto
Delhi Bombay Calcutta Madras Karachi
Kuala Lumpur Singapore Hong Kong Tokyo
Nairobi Dar es Salaam Cape Town
Melbourne Auckland

and associated companies in
Berlin Ibadan

First published 1992

National Library of Australia
Cataloguing-in-Publication data:

Nations of immigrants: Australia, the United States, and international migration

Bibliography.
Includes index.
ISBN 0 19 553483 2.

1. Australia—Emigration and immigration—Government policy. 2. Australia—Emigration and immigration. 3. United States—Emigration and immigration—Government policy. 4. United States—Emigration and immigration. I. Freeman, Gary P. II. Jupp, James, 1932–

325.94

Edited by Kaye Quittner
Typeset by Syarikat Seng Teik Sdn. Bhd., Malaysia
Printed in Hong Kong
Published by Oxford University Press,
253 Normanby Road, South Melbourne, Australia

The writing of this book was made possible by grants from:

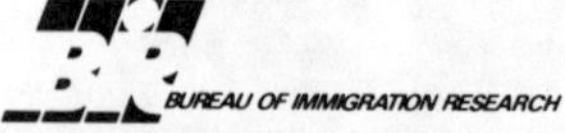

Center for Australian Studies, University of Texas at Austin

Centre for Immigration and Multicultural Studies, Australian National University

CONTENTS

PREFACE

Australia and the United States are nations of immigrants, drawing the great majority of their settlers from overseas in mass movements of population over the past two or three centuries. Their indigenous peoples have been reduced to small and disadvantaged minorities. While many simply see themselves as 'Americans' or 'Australians', most are easily able to trace an ancestor who migrated from elsewhere. One in five Australians, but only one in twenty Americans, were born overseas. The United States has a more varied ethnic history than Australia, with large numbers descended from African slaves or from Spanish Americans, and with much less of a recent tradition of drawing its people from the British Isles. While, proportionately, far more Australians have come directly from overseas, it is often easier for Americans to think of themselves as a 'nation of immigrants'.

The historic experience of these two English-speaking societies has been quite different in many ways. Australia looked to Britain far more recently than did the United States, which was a world power in its own right even before the disappearance of the British Empire of which Australia was for so long a willing member. The sheer size of the United States has meant that there is far less concern about being swamped by immigrants than has periodically surfaced in Australia. The entire population of Australia approximates that of Texas and is much less than that of California. The ethnic variety of the United States has meant that there is less of a tendency to define as 'real' Americans only those of British origin, although such a tendency was apparent in the fairly recent past. The administrative traditions of Australia are more interventionist than those of the United States, and the role of the trade union and labour movement is quite different.

These similarities and differences have only rarely been explored and have never been analysed in the important field of immigration policy. The United States has always been the greatest magnet for international migrants. What it decides has an immediate impact on

Australian immigration. The reverse is scarcely the case. However, because Australia has developed a more coherent immigration and settlement policy and more elaborate control mechanisms, it has something to offer American policy makers. The population movements which sweep towards America also lap the shores of Australia. The ethnic issues which arise in the United States have always influenced Australian perceptions of social harmony.

This book is a response to these converging and diverging experiences. It is jointly sponsored by the Bureau of Immigration Research in Melbourne and the Center for Australian Studies at the University of Texas in Austin. It has been edited through the Texas Center and the Centre for Immigration and Multicultural Studies at the Australian National University in Canberra. Seminars that brought the contributors together were held in Melbourne in June 1990 and in Austin in April 1991. The joint editors, Gary P. Freeman and James Jupp, exchanged visits to each other's universities and there were other personal interchanges between some of the Australian and American contributors. The result is something more than the conventional collected volume, because far more personal contact and group interchange has been possible than is normally the case.

All three of the collaborating institutions are of recent foundation, which indicates a growing interest in immigration studies in Australia and in Australian studies in the United States. The Center for Australian Studies at the University of Texas was established in June 1988. It was hoped that 'the endowment of this Center will assure the academic community at large of the sustained commitment of the University to the support of research and study of a country with which the University has maintained long and close ties'. The Centre for Immigration and Multicultural Studies was set up at the Australian National University in the same year. Like the Texas Center it arose from the interest generated by the Australian bicentennial celebrations. The Bureau of Immigration Research, which is a publicly funded but autonomous institution, was created in May 1989. It is 'an independent, professional research body within the Department of Immigration, Local Government and Ethnic Affairs, to conduct, commission and promote research into immigration and population issues'.

Contributing authors were chosen for their expert knowledge of immigration issues. Where a comparison between societies was required there was co-operation between authors drawn from Australia and the United States. Nine are resident in the United States and eight in Australia, though several have had professional experience in more than one society. Most have been engaged in consultancy or research work for government as well as in teaching and research at universities. They focus here on entry and control, the economics of immigration, settlement policy and issues arising in multicultural democracies. These issues are of obvious interest outside the United States and Australia, notably in Canada, Britain and western Europe.

The viewpoints of the authors differ on some issues. No orthodoxy was sought; nor would it be useful to seek one. International migration has been a fact of modern life for at least two centuries and neither the United States nor Australia could have been created without it. At different times the two countries have sought expansion or limitation of entry. They have attempted to control the ethnic, occupational and educational character of those allowed to settle. They have attracted settlers from different parts of the world at different times and for different reasons. Their common and differing experiences are of great significance for understanding current and future trends in developed and developing societies. This unique study aims at broadening understanding of one of the major social forces of modern times and to illuminate its impact on two comparable democracies which share many values, institutions and practices.

Dr John Nieuwenhuysen
Director, Bureau of Immigration Research, Melbourne

Dr John Higley
Director, Center for Australian Studies, University of Texas at Austin

Dr James Jupp
Director, Centre for Immigration and Multicultural Studies,
Australian National University, Canberra

January 1992

CONTRIBUTORS

Robert L. Bach is Associate Professor of Sociology and Director of the Institute for Research on Multiculturalism and International Labor at the State University of New York in Binghamton.

Frank D. Bean is Ashbel Smith Professor of Sociology at the University of Texas at Austin and was director of the Program for Research on Immigration Policy and the Population Studies Center at the Urban Institute in Washington.

Katharine Betts is a senior lecturer in social and political studies at the Swinburne Institute of Technology in Melbourne.

Robert Birrell is a reader in sociology at Monash University, Melbourne, and a member of the Australian National Population Council.

Stephen Castles is Director of the Centre for Multicultural Studies at the University of Wollongong.

Peter Dawkins is Director of the Western Australian Labour Market Research Centre in Perth.

Rodolfo de la Garza is Mike Hogg Professor in Community Affairs at the University of Texas at Austin and was previously director of the Center for Mexican American Studies.

Louis DeSipio is a doctoral candidate in government at the University of Texas at Austin.

Michael Fix is a lawyer and a senior research associate at the Urban Institute in Washington.

William Foster is a senior economic consultant to the Bureau of Immigration Research, Melbourne.

Gary P. Freeman is Associate Professor of Government at the University of Texas at Austin.

James Jupp is Director of the Centre for Immigration and Multicultural Studies at the Australian National University, Canberra.

Lindsay Lowell is a research demographer with the United States Department of Labor in Washington.

Mark Miller is Associate Professor of Political Science at the University of Delaware and assistant editor of the *International Migration Review*.

Demetrios Papademetriou is Director of the Immigration Policy Group at the United States Department of Labor in Washington.

Michael Webber is Professor of Geography at the University of Melbourne.

Glenn Withers is Professor of Economics at La Trobe University, Melbourne, and a co-Chair of the Australian National Population Council.

1

COMPARING IMMIGRATION POLICY IN AUSTRALIA AND THE UNITED STATES

Gary P. Freeman and James Jupp

Among the industrial countries of the world only Australia, Canada, and the United States are accepting large-scale new immigration for permanent settlement as a matter of official policy. They are, therefore, deviant cases in what otherwise is a strong pattern of restrictiveness in the immigration policies of the rich democracies.

The pursuit of these immigration policies occurs at a time when people are on the move on an enormous scale, either 'voluntarily' for economic reasons, or because they have been displaced by war, political repression, or natural calamity (Dowty 1987; Salt 1989; Zolberg 1989). Moreover, global demographic trends promise to exacerbate these pressures. Natural population growth in developed countries is approaching zero. In both the United States and Australia fertility rates have fallen below replacement. Developing countries, however, are projected to add nearly 1.2 billion people by 2001 and a further 4.7 billion during the next century (Demeny, 1988; Bourgeois-Pichat 1989, p. 65). All of this suggests that the demand for migration, for whichever reason, is likely to be stable at best and escalate dramatically at worst in the next decade. The pressures that led the European states to halt immigration (from the Mediterranean, Asia, and Africa) will probably also make them unlikely to respond to greater demands for refugee status (Messina 1990). In the densely populated countries of western Europe the arguments against immigration undoubtedly appear more plausible and have more political effect than in North America and Australia.

This chapter provides a basis for understanding and predicting the responses of Australia and the United States to these contemporary pressures through a historical and comparative analysis of their experiences with immigration since their founding. First, however, the following brief historical overview of immigration policies in the two countries will provide for those readers unfamiliar with the cases the minimal background necessary to evaluate the more detailed studies in the chapters to follow.

IMMIGRATION AND POLICY: AN OVERVIEW

Australia

The Australian people are predominantly drawn from the British Isles, with those of English and Welsh ancestry making up 45 per cent of the 1986 Census population, those of Irish 17 per cent, and those of Scottish 13 per cent. The remaining quarter are derived from a wide variety of backgrounds and include the indigenous Aborigines and Torres Strait Islanders, who numbered about 350 000 at the time of first British settlement in 1788 (though other estimates go higher). Those of non-British ancestry mainly represent recent immigrants and their children. Most of these fall into an official category known as non-English-speaking background (NESB). Overseas born of English-speaking background come mainly from the United Kingdom, New Zealand, the United States, Canada, and South Africa. While no racial statistics have been kept since 1966 (in the sense of physical inheritances), a reasonable estimate is that 1.5 per cent of Australians are of indigenous origin; 94 per cent of broadly European origin, and 4.5 per cent of non-European (predominantly Asian) origin. The 1991 Census shows that about 1.4 per cent are of Chinese ancestry. Thus Australia is still very much a 'White' society though much less of a 'British' society than it was 50 years ago.

Significant levels of immigration have been maintained over the past 200 years with two major exceptions—from 1890 to 1905 and from 1929 to 1947. These both correspond to periods of severe economic depression, coupled with wartime in the second instance. Different parts of Australia have attracted immigrants at different times, with Tasmania most consistently showing an emigrant loss over the past century. These differences reflect economic conditions and public policy. Queensland attracted more immigrants in the 1880s than ever before or since, but fewer in the 1920s and 1950s than other areas. Western Australia did not start to attract mass immigration until the 1890s, when much of it was from within Australia, but was the last colony to dispense with convict recruitment (in 1868). Any generalization about immigration should be qualified by noting these regional and temporal disparities.

Publicly Funded Migration

Convict transportation began in 1788 and lasted in eastern Australia until 1852, with a distinct Western Australian intake between 1850 and 1868, which was exclusively male. During this period about 170 000 convicts were sent to New South Wales, Tasmania, and Queensland, and about 10 000 to Western Australia. The great majority were English or Irish, though many were sent from throughout the British Empire, including some non-Europeans.

The ending of slavery in the British Empire and local and British agitation against the convict system led to its replacement by assisted immigration. Previous free settlers had mainly arrived as capitalist agricultural entrepreneurs, bringing their labourers with them. This was the basis for the first settlement of Western Australia in 1829 and of South Australia in 1836. Similar enterprises were launched in New South Wales from the 1790s and in Tasmania in the 1820s. Scottish agriculturalists were important in these colonizations, as they were in Victoria in the 1830s. This system, however, put a strain on the purses of employers and did not solve growing shortages of labour. Between 1831 and 1982 the most important single device for attracting immigrants was the extension of assisted passages to British subjects (including Irish even after independence in 1921). Only rarely were assisted passages extended to non-British, most notably to Germans and Scandinavians going to Queensland from the late 1870s. This exclusion of aliens caused the ending of a short-lived attempt to import Americans to New South Wales in 1879. Until the admission of Displaced Persons in 1947, this exclusion of non-British was general everywhere except Queensland (and after 1914 there as well).

The assisted passage system brought 1 068 000 immigrants to Australia between 1831 and 1947, and a further 2 168 500 until 1982 who were no longer exclusively British. Various schemes were operated, including completely free passages, loans, nomination by employers, partial assistance with passage and grants of lands in exchange for passage costs. These schemes had various advantages: they allowed British, and later Australian, authorities to choose the kind of immigrant in terms of nationality, occupation, health, employability, and any other criteria thought relevant; they were used to redress the gender imbalance caused by free migration but more seriously by the convict system; they could be suspended at times of economic decline and expanded to meet new demands for labor; they overcame the disincentive of high fares and distance in the face of competition from North America; and they brought out large numbers of settlers who could not possibly have financed themselves, especially agricultural workers. The numbers of British assisted immigrants brought out over 150 years were such that they can be fairly described as the 'foundation stone' of the native-born population.

Unassisted Immigration

The first free settlers arrived in New South Wales in 1793, and they were particularly important in the colonization of Western Australia,

South Australia and Victoria. By far the largest numbers arrived in the 1850s in response to the Victorian gold rush, when the Australian population trebled within a decade. There was little immigration control, especially for British subjects. Thus free settlers included many Germans, Chinese, Americans, and a variety of other nationalities. Figures for the unassisted are less accurate than for convicts and the assisted, who had to be accounted for. The great majority were British in the nineteenth century and the English were more preponderant than Scots or Irish among unassisted settlers. There were, however, large alien elements at various stages, usually causing restrictive immigration laws to be passed. The first major group to be legislated against were the Chinese, of whom 25 400 were recorded in Victoria in 1857. Eventually all non-Europeans were effectively excluded by the Commonwealth *Immigration Restriction Act* of 1901 which implemented the so-called White Australia Policy. European aliens began arriving in 1838, with German Lutheran settlement in South Australia. They did not cause any concern until southern Europeans became more prominent from the late 1880s. Quota restrictions were imposed in the 1920s, mainly against southern Europeans who had diverted to Australia after restrictive United States legislation.

Until 1947 assisted passages were overwhelmingly given only to British subjects. Until 1973 such subjects (if of European descent and with some exceptions for the Maltese) were virtually free to settle in Australia without restriction provided they had no known criminal record. This reinforced previous tendencies for the British (and increasingly the English) component of the population to be maintained.

Alien White Immigration

With the effective exclusion of non-Europeans by 1901, the main non-British element in immigration were those who came unassisted to Australia as a small and peripheral part of the mass European migrations of this century. The most important components prior to 1947 were from Italy, Greece, Yugoslavia, Malta, Poland, Lebanon, and Germany (who were augmented by Jewish refugees in 1938–39). These were often subjected to temporary restrictions but a general system of entry permit for aliens was not instituted until the *Migration Act* of 1958. They were not officially welcomed though some, such as Italian cane-cutters in North Queensland, had been deliberately recruited by employers. The arrival of Polish and, later, German Jews in Melbourne and Sydney between the wars caused some hostile comment, leading post-war immigration authorities to restrict the numbers of Jews admitted on any one ship. Distance and lack of knowledge kept European immigration down, and during and after the Depression of the 1930s it was virtually non-existent.

Mass assisted non-British White migration began in 1947 and continued to 1982 when assisted passages were ended for all but refugees. In 1949 Australia adopted its own citizenship distinct from the British, but British subjects continued to be more favourably received than were aliens until 1973 in terms of assistance and citizenship rights. Alien immigration took three forms: refugee, assisted, and unassisted. Refugee arrivals under agreement with the United Nations International Refugee Organisation began in 1947, and over 170 000 arrived in the next five years. This was the largest planned intake of non-British in Australian history, and most subsequent policy has been based on experience with this group. Additional intakes under separate arrangements were made from Hungary in 1956 and Czechoslovakia in 1968. Refugees were housed in camps and directed to employment for two years. The great majority came from eastern European societies, which previously had little or no representation in Australia.

Assisted European migration was arranged under a series of government-to-government agreements, such as with Malta (1948); Italy and The Netherlands (1951); West Germany, Austria, and Greece (1952); Spain (1958); Turkey (1967); and Yugoslavia (1970). The agreements detailed the forms of assistance, numbers, and services to be rendered on arrival. Large numbers arrived from these sources in the 1950s and 1960s, being drawn especially to manufacturing industry and to Melbourne, Adelaide, Sydney, Wollongong, and Geelong. Large numbers of British migrants also arrived under agreement with the British Government from 1946. This form of agreement no longer operates, and there was a sharp reduction in European immigration in the early 1970s, partly imposed by the Labor government (1972–75).

Unassisted immigration continued from countries with which there were no agreements, and included some people who were not of pure European descent (particularly from India, Burma, and Sri Lanka), or from states such as Lebanon, France, or Portugal with which agreements were not signed. Some migration also took place from Canada and the United States, although the prohibition on non-European migration made it difficult to recruit officially in the USA.

Non-European Immigration

The effective exclusion of non-Europeans lasted until 1966 and was not officially repudiated until 1973. It was administratively rather than legally enforced, but was even more effective because of that. Racial appearance was the important criterion rather than country of origin or culture, and exceptions were made for Asians of 'predominantly European heritage and appearance'. Since 1973 non-European immigrants have increased to a level of at least 40 per cent of intake from backgrounds which were previously excluded. New Zealand Maoris, like all other New Zealanders, were never subject to restrictions, and there are about 20 000 currently in Australia. Settlement opportunities were never extended, however, to indigenous Papua New Guineans, even when they were Australian-protected persons prior to independence.

The great majority of non-Europeans in Australia at present are post-1975 refugees and unassisted immigrants or their children. Of ancestries recorded in the 1986 Census, the most important include Chinese, Vietnamese, Indian, Filipino, and Malay/Indonesian. Many Australians also regard Arabs as Asians, despite the fact that they have never been totally excluded from Australia and that the majority are Christians. Although there is a wide variety of Asian origins and languages represented in Australia, the above six ethnic backgrounds are currently preponderant.

The United States

Immigration in the modern era to what is now the United States can be usefully categorized into five distinct periods (Archdeacon 1983): 1607–1790—The colonial era; 1790–1890—The old immigration; 1890–1930—The new immigration; 1930–1965—The Depression, World War II, and the cold war; and 1965– —Third World immigration. These demarcations are arbitrary, dictated partly by changes in the immigration flows, partly by regime changes or shifts in official policy.

The Colonial Era

North America was founded by European colonial powers—the Dutch, the French, the Spanish, and the British. Of these the British were most successful and eventually attained dominance over the territory that was to become the United States, especially with respect to language and in the political sphere where English law and constitutional practice were adopted. But British hegemony was never complete and by 1790, when the present style of government of the United States was established, persons of Anglo-Irish stock made up only about 49 per cent of the total population and 61 per cent of all Whites. The next largest White ethnic category was German (7 per cent), followed by Dutch (2.6), French (1.4) and Swedish (.05). Almost 20 per cent of the population was Black, with an untold number of indigenous Indians uncounted (Archdeacon 1983, p. 25).

Immigration policy did not exist in the eighteenth century. The various colonies took on their own ethnic and religious character, alternately soliciting and discouraging settlers of a particular sort. Roman Catholics were the most controversial group. The legend of the founding of America by refugees earnestly seeking religious freedom is, as with all such stories, only half true, and those who were genuine religious refugees were not normally inclined to extend tolerance to other groups once they had settled. Out of this discordant and unsystematic process, some four million souls, Black and White, were living in the United States when it attained independence from the Crown (Fairchild 1920, pp. 50–1).

The Old Immigration

In the next 100 years Americans settled the entire continent (the frontier was officially closed in 1890), and swelled the population to 62 947 714, some 15 million of this growth coming from immigrants and their offspring (Archdeacon 1983, p. 27). In 1890 well over a third of the White population was either first or second generation immigrant. The Government did not sit idly by while all this was taking place. One of the first acts of the new congress in 1790 was to pass a liberal naturalization act making citizenship available to settlers after only two years of residence. Over the next eight years, however, this was gradually extended to 14 years of residence. Moreover, in 1798 the Federalists began what was to become a well-honoured tradition, passing legislation that linked immigration to national security. The *Alien Enemies Acts* of 1798 and 1812 permitted the arrest, imprisonment, and deportation during time of war of immigrant males from enemy nations who were over 14 and were not citizens. This period also saw the rise of nativist opposition groups whose ire was directed most frequently against Roman Catholics. A host of regulatory laws (having to do with sabbatarianism, drinking, and religious observances in the schools) were devised by Protestants to impose their own cultural values on the society. This period was marked, then, by a fairly pervasive campaign of Americanization, which did not extend, however, to the Indians and Blacks.

The New Immigration

The 70 years between 1860 and 1930 saw unprecedented numbers of immigrants land on American shores. The majority of these were drawn from nationalities new to America (Poles, Czechs, Russian Jews, etc.) and were young and predominantly male. These new immigrants often saw their visit as temporary, and they were overwhelmingly working class in origin. They provided the hands to run the burgeoning industrial machine that was springing up in the East and Midwest. Between 1830 and 1860 the USA had received 4.7 million immigrants; in the next 30 years 10 million arrived; and in the next three decades 18.2 million more. For nearly a century immigration regulation was firmly in the hands of the states, in practice in the hands of those states (New York, Massachusetts, Pennsylvania, Louisiana, and California) that contained major ports of entry (Bernard 1950, p. 6). In 1849, however, the US Supreme Court held that the Congress alone had the power to control immigration under Article 1 of the Constitution. Congress began to exercise its powers in 1875 with the first of a series of laws excluding various categories of undesirables (prostitutes, felons, lunatics, the indigent, contract labourers, persons with certain diseases, etc.). In 1891 the *Immigration Act* required ship commanders to pay the return fares of those not admitted and set up an office of Superintendent of Immigration in the Treasury. The Act asserted the federal prerogative to screen all newcomers and in 1892 the Ellis Island facility in New York harbour was opened. Finally, in 1880 Congress began an incremental process of excluding Asians, a step that became complete and permanent in 1904 (Hutchison 1981, pp. 544–57; Bernard 1950, p. 7).

The massive influx of foreigners in the first decade of the twentieth century, the newly exercised federal regulatory powers, and strong nativist agitation culminated in the early 1920s in broad legislation controlling both the numbers and the ethnicity of immigrants. The Johnson–Reed *Immigration Act* (1924) created the framework for an admissions policy favouring those countries in western and northern Europe which had provided the bulk of the immigrants before 1860, by means of a complex national origins quota system. It went into effect in 1927 (Bernard 1950, pp. 23–6).

The Depression and War

The period from 1930 to 1965 must be seen as an interlude in the normal pattern of immigration. Depression, war, and the global struggle against communism disrupted normal immigration pressures and made the USA a less hospitable and desirable destination. At home it was a period of consolidation when immigrants were slowly transformed into ethnics. It was the time of the 'melting pot', a perhaps premature celebration of turning a great diversity of nationality groups into a cohesive social formation. Major immigration legislation became law in 1952. The *McCarran–Walter Act* was very much a product of the cold war. It continued the national origins quota system, but incorporated Asia into the scheme for the first time, allotting 100 visas annually to each nation in the region and setting aside an additional 100 for an area known as the Asia–Pacific triangle.

The 1924 and 1952 legislation marked a historic turning point in American immigration experience. The numbers of entrants fell dramatically—only 1 873 479 arrived between 1925 and 1948. As numbers declined and immigrant communities aged, America became much less an immigrant nation towards the middle of the century. Emphasis on assimilation and Americanization increased, and many believed that the melting pot would become a reality.

Third World Immigration

Events since 1965 have dampened these expectations. Quite by accident, immigration reforms adopted in 1965 to eliminate racial and national discrimination in the language of the law opened the way for significant new immigration of persons quite different from those who had come in earlier periods. The new law set an overall limit on immigration from the eastern hemisphere, but withdrew all national distinctions save that no more than 20 000 could be admitted annually from a single country; it also capped entries from the western hemisphere for the first time, but with no individual country limits. The 1965 amendments pushed policy in the direction of favouring family reunification in the selection of immigrants, and they liberalized refugee law, retaining for the Attorney-General the power to admit refugees in emergencies or in the national interest through the procedure known as 'parole'. This power was used to admit 30 000 Hungarians, 650 000 Cubans, and 360 000 Indo-Chinese by 1980, when Congress for the first time enacted comprehensive refugee legislation.

The sharp rise in immigration after 1965, the shift of the sources from Europe to Latin America and Asia, and the growing sense that the Government was not in control of these flows (because of the crisis nature of refugee influxes and the widespread disregard of the southwestern border with Mexico) created pressure for new legislation. This was duly enacted in 1986 (a law that dealt primarily with stemming the entry of undocumented workers from Mexico) and in 1990; these further amendments to the immigration law, oddly, increased the total legal limits, but introduced a slightly broadened focus on the economic skills and potential of immigrants, while preserving the overriding commitment to family reunion.

IMMIGRATION AND THE FORMATION OF STATES

Both Australia and the USA began life as settler societies founded as colonial outposts of European powers. This constitutes an apparently strong convergence of the two cases, but important distinctions need to be drawn (Parkin 1977).

One of the few serious attempts to understand settler societies in a comparative framework is Louis Hartz's *The Founding of New Societies* (1964), where Richard Rosecrance argues that Australia was established by a radical fragment of British society and that this produced a radical culture in its new setting. As he puts it, the British who came to Australia between 1800 and 1860 were 'largely a homogeneous group of city folk of humble economic and social origins' (1964, p. 280). Australia, he goes on, was not touched by the aristocracy, hardly by the middle class. It was and is a labouring country (p. 282). Useful as the notion of a cultural fragment is, it is susceptible to exaggeration. Rather than being the 'city folk' Rosecrance describes, large numbers of the first settlers were from the countryside. The Irish were almost entirely rural in origin, as were many of the Scots and the English. The convicts were for the most part urban, to be sure, but this was not true of the Irish. While it might appear that the early settlers were extremely homogeneous, this overlooks the significant differences that separated the various elements within the Anglo-Celtic peoples. Many of the settlers—Irish, Highland Scots and Welsh—did not speak English. Nor were all the early settlers of humble origins. If the majority were poor or worse, there were also large landowners and members of the substantial middle class. New South Wales, Victoria and Tasmania all developed rural upper-class squirearchies. Australian radicalism emerged not out of the convict society, but out of the gold rush of the 1850s. Many of the diggers had paid their own fares to Australia, indicating a certain attainment of social station. In addition, a good part of the leadership of the Chartist movement in Victoria in the mid-nineteenth century was middle class in origin. Irish lawyers who immigrated were also central to political developments in the early days of the colony.

The immigrants who came to American shores during the founding period before 1787 were more diverse than those going to Australia, the New England colonies being the closest approximation to the Australian model. Dutch, French and German settlers contributed to the early ethnic mix and, after the revolution, immigration further diluted the dominance of the Anglo-Irish. It has been estimated that in 1790, of the 80 per cent of the total population that was White, only about 63 per cent were of English, Scottish or Irish origins (Archdeacon 1983, p. 25). America contained many more persons of bourgeois status than were to be found in Australia. Apart from the slaves, who were not thought of as part of society, most of those able to reach America did so on their own resources, which prohibited immigration for the destitute. One exception to this generalization was the convicts who were transported from England to North America; some 50 000 arrived before the American Revolution (Archdeacon 1983, pp. 1–26). Proportionately, of course, convicts had a much smaller effect on American life than did their larger numbers in a less populated Australia.

American culture emerged as individualistic, competitive and market oriented. There is a strong commitment to equality, but this is in terms of the rights of citizenship rather than material or social status (Tocqueville 1969; Potter 1954). The settler origins of the two countries had decisive effects on their subsequent character and development. British influence was more pervasive in Australia, leading to a variety of consequences of a political and cultural nature, and the sorts of British settlers who went there contributed to the emergence among the common people of a class-based conception of society. The United States, on the other hand, was less thoroughly a British settlement, was more bourgeois in social composition, and exhibited a strong tendency towards the acceptance of an ideology of individualist liberalism.

FRONTIER SOCIETIES

The early settlers in both countries were impressed with the vastness of the continents on which they had landed and though it took some years of exploration before the real scale could be appreciated, it seems reasonable that a sense of almost infinite space would have been engendered. Encompassing roughly the same area, the two countries have nevertheless developed in sharply different ways.

Whatever the difficulties and hazards, the American settlers pushed forward in ever larger numbers until the whole continent was conquered, settled, and, eventually, brought into full membership in the collectivity. The existence of the frontier in America provided both symbolic support for the idea that immigration was necessary to populate the continent and for the notion that it could serve as a safety valve against social tensions in the crowded eastern urban centres. It seems to have contributed to the acceptance, albeit occasionally reluctantly, of massive immigration in certain periods.

In Australia the outback, or bush, was far more forbidding and presented a less hospitable environment for settlement, even though the Aboriginal population put up much less resistance to the European invaders than did those in North America. Australia is today one of the most highly urbanized countries in the world with fully 80 per cent of its population living along the Boomerang Coast stretching from Adelaide to Brisbane. Huge expanses of the interior, the north, and the west are largely uninhabited and show few signs of significant change in this regard. The frontier as a boundless territory open for settlement, exploitation, and adventure was, then, both more real in the American context and more short-lived. The vastness of Australia made it, in its earliest days, not a land of unparalleled opportunities, but a prison on a continental scale as escape into the bush meant almost certain death (Hughes 1987). Even today, Australians do not so much occupy their land as surround it, tenaciously clinging to the ribbon of civilization established along the coasts. Australia is perhaps the last frontier society in the advanced world, but its frontier actually provides scant opportunities for anything other than mineral exploitation and challenging recreational exploration.

Ironically, although few Australians have been willing or able to make a go of it in the bush, and a negligible number of immigrants in recent years have settled outside the metropolitan areas, public discussions on immigration continue to raise the idea that Australia is an empty land waiting to be filled. This is also, apparently, a widely held view abroad. The persistent strength of this view makes it seem likely that the emptiness of the continent made immigration more palatable to Australians than it would otherwise have been.

If we turn from conceptions of space to the effect of frontier life on social values, we find contrasting patterns in the two countries. Rosecrance argues that the frontier was not an egalitarian force in Australia, as it was in the USA: 'while the American frontier was on balance an egalitarian force, the Australian frontier tended to foster conflict and social cleavage in Australian society. The antagonism of squatter and swagman, pastoralist and farmer is a striking characteristic of Australian history during the nineteenth century, and it prevails in diminished force even today' (Rosecrance 1964, p. 286).

This is a bold and sweeping generalization that bears close examination. Rosecrance embraces Frederick Jackson Turner's thesis that the availability of immense tracts of free land, the social and economic opportunities afforded in the wilderness, and the absence of established systems of social control promoted a kind of crude egalitarianism and individualism along the American frontier (Turner 1963, 1962; Billington 1959). In Australia, on the other hand, he argues that the harshness of the bush, the leading role of the squatters, and the economic necessity of cumulating large landholdings to make grazing profitable effectively prevented the creation of a significant class of small farmers and led to the proletarianization of the rural population. He observes, nonetheless, that the attempt to create a 'squattocracy' failed.

Recent research on the American West has tended to dispute the traditional view that it was a rough-hewn society of equals. There is the fact that women were systematically excluded from the status of equals, as recent feminist historiography has reported. Moreover, social mores and landownership systems were far less egalitarian than is commonly supposed. In the case of Australia it is important to be clear where the frontier was. In Victoria and South Australia a fledgling upper class did take root in the countryside. In north Queensland, though, which may better lay claim to being the frontier, the sugar plantation system was broken up and the ultimate character of social life there was markedly egalitarian.

If the Australian frontier encouraged the creation of a hierarchically stratified society, it also promoted working-class solidarity. This, in turn, facilitated the emergence of a strong workers' movement, as we shall see. Whatever the verdict on the impact of the frontier on Australian values, the gold rush of the 1850s, which coincided with the end of transportation, was definitely an equalizing phenomenon. By the late nineteenth century there were strong cultural values of mateship, a fair go, and a levelling impulse to identify with losers and to resent anyone who exhibited socially superior attitudes. The frontier in America, whatever its contribution to democratic values, had debilitating effects on the development of working-class institutions. Moreover, the gold rushes in the United States failed to leave a legacy of solidarity among ordinary working people.

UNFREE LABOUR: SLAVERY AND THE CONVICT SYSTEM

Both Australia and the United States had systems of unfree labour during their founding years, but these were divergent in character and consequences. The introduction of the American slave system had a number of disastrous impacts on American life. The slave-owning élite was, of course, finally defeated in 1865, but the remnants of that class and the social attitudes it spawned poisoned politics in the former confederacy for a century, until the civil rights movement of the early 1960s.

Australia was established as a penal colony, but the paradoxical outcome of these convict beginnings was to strengthen the egalitarian aspects of the developing society. The key difference in the two cases is that while the American slaves, once they were freed, continued to constitute a separate and disadvantaged class, the convicts, in contrast, were absorbed into the general population and vanished with hardly a trace. Certainly no semi-permanent, socially disadvantaged lower class descended from transportees ever developed, despite the best efforts of early Exclusivists to establish clear lines of social demarcation. The American slaves were torn from non-western African cultures at a different stage of technological development than the Europeans who settled America. They were then forcibly excluded from educational, social, and economic advancement. Even after emancipation the installation of the Jim Crow system of segregation in the south and the institutionalization of systematic discrimination elsewhere ensured that they would remain behind the social level of the general society (Woodward 1966). They also bore visible badges of their inferior status in the pigment of their skin.

The convicts were in a much more favourable situation. Slavery was formally outlawed throughout the Empire in 1833. The convicts, wretched as they were and harsh as their lot was, were not slaves. They could not be bought or sold, their servitude was temporary and for a fixed period, their children were born free, and once they received their ticket of leave they were often given a plot of land and allowed to merge into the free population. Being from the same race and ethnic group as the free settlers facilitated this assimilation. Convicts who were assigned to the custody of free Australians as labourers may have constituted the functional equivalent of a slave class in economic terms, but they had rights and were able to lodge complaints with the judiciary for ill-treatment, an avenue that was used with some regularity.

In sum, while both countries had early experience of unfree labour, the convict system in Australia contributed to the development of values of social solidarity and a heightened sense of class consciousness among the working class. In the USA slavery and the political and economic conflicts it engendered were among the most important factors inhibiting the success of class-based political movements. Among the primary consequences of the centrality of the transportation system to the early settlement of Australia was that it involved the authority of the state in the direct organization and administration of immigration. The slave system produced no such precedent, run as it was through private enterprise. This difference has been maintained throughout the histories of the two countries as the public authorities in Australia have been much more interventionist with respect to immigration than have those in the United States.

DEMOCRATIZATION AND WORKING-CLASS POLITICS

The divergent experiences of settlement and early labour systems contributed to labour movements of widely disparate strength. These, in turn, played dissimilar roles in the forging of the immigration policies of the two states. Both countries were born democratic, but universal manhood and female suffrage were achieved sooner in Australia than in the USA, though the federal character of both countries makes generalization difficult. Levies had to be paid in order to vote (poll taxes) in some states of the American south long after World War II, and formal obstacles to the exercise of the ballot by Blacks were not eliminated until the passage of the 1965 *Voting Rights Act*, a piece of legislation that cannot yet be dispensed with (see DeSipio and de la Garza, ch. 12 in this book). The extension of suffrage in Australia was accompanied by the rapid development of a workers' movement which culminated in a trade union system that encompassed a greater share of the labour force than in most western countries, and in a labour party, eventually known as the Australian Labor Party (ALP), that set the world pace for attracting votes and obtaining power. The history of the American labour movement could not be more different; business resistance to unionization, government repression of labour or socialist parties, race and ethnic hostilities, and an unreceptive political culture effectively prevented the development of a serious working-class movement in America.

Stronger trade unions in the USA might have been able to resist the massive immigration that occurred during the late nineteenth and early twentieth centuries. This, in turn, would have tightened the American labour market and enhanced workers' bargaining power. There were, of course, numerous outbreaks of violence against the importation of immigrant strikebreakers (as in the Pennsylvania coalfields), but these never amounted to a concerted campaign and they ultimately failed even to retard the pace of immigration. Moreover, the hostilities unleashed in these confrontations between indigenous and immigrant workers compounded the divisions in an American working class already cleaved by racial antagonisms and further diminished effective political organization (Mink 1986).

Australian labour opposed Chinese migration in the nineteenth century, an opposition that fed directly into the White Australia Policy (Jupp 1991, pp. 41–53). Afterwards, labour consistently advocated immigration control (as the natural companion to protectionism) and criticized the programme of assisted passages. However ill-conceived these policies may appear by contemporary standards, there can be little doubt that the barriers to immigration supported by the labour movement contributed to the favourable employment and wage conditions that set Australia apart from most other western countries in the late nineteenth and early twentieth centuries.

CULTURE AND NATIONALISM

The distinctive way in which nationalism developed in the two countries is central to an understanding of the experience of immigration. National identity affects attitudes with regard to the sorts of people that are acceptable as immigrants, the capacity of the society to absorb newcomers, and, especially, what is expected of immigrant groups in terms of adaptation to their new home. In both countries, national identity had to be created in opposition to the existing and traditional ties to the countries from which settlers came.

The best evidence that American nationalism crystallized at an earlier stage of development and more fully than that of Australia is that there is no debate in the USA today about whether an American identity does or should exist, while such discussion is common in Australia. As a new nation, membership in the United States was not based primarily on kinship ties or ethnic origins, but involved a simpler, essentially voluntarist test: adherence to the principles of American self-government (Schuck and Smith 1985, p. 1). Over time America's self-image as a shining beacon of democracy and opportunity, an image embraced by many people around the world, became a kind of overweening justification for a generous immigration intake policy. Although nationalist fervour and feelings of racial superiority were also the source of anti-immigrant agitation and discriminatory immigration laws, it seems clear that the struggle for America's soul was won by the forces advocating an inclusive nationalism.

Australian nationalist impulses developed later, were less robust, and more readily subordinated to British interests. For example, the Australian identification with Great Britain lasted much longer than that of the USA. The Australian colonies did not throw off British rule as did revolutionary America. Federation was achieved only in 1901 within the context of continued subordination to the Crown, and it advanced nationalist identity only modestly. Immigrants from a wider variety of nations populated North America from the earliest days of European settlement, producing a social heterogeneity in the seventeenth century that was not seen in Australia until well after World War II. There, the long dominance of the Anglo-Irish, the decimation of the Aboriginal population, the decline of immigration between 1860 and 1945, and the White Australia Policy all conspired to make Australia exceptionally homogeneous until the mid-twentieth century.

If we are concerned with Australians' approach to immigration, though, it is not necessarily a distinctively Australian identity that is relevant. The first settlers certainly did not think of themselves as Australians. The Whites who first settled Australia did have a strong national identification, namely with the British Isles, and this entailed a well-developed sense of cultural and political superiority to the non-British races. These attitudes, in conjunction with labour union protectionism, were reflected in the White Australia Policy, which was a mechanism for ensuring continued Anglo-Irish dominance.

The problematic character of a distinctively Australian as opposed to British national identity is perhaps more relevant to receptivity to multiculturalism than it was to earlier reactions to immigration. It is only in the last several decades, as immigration to Australia has brought into the country persons from non-European backgrounds, that a fresh round of controversy has erupted over what it means to be Australian, complete with official pronouncements (see, for example, The Report of the Committee to Advise on Australia's Immigration Policies, 1988, pp. 4–5). It is ironic that it is in relatively homogeneous Australia that the claims of ethnic groups for cultural differentiation through multiculturalism have made greater official inroads than similar claims in pluralistic America (S. Castles et al. 1989; see also the chapters by Castles and DeSipio and de la Garza in this book). The ambiguous status of national identity is the most obvious explanation.

THE POLITICAL ECONOMY OF IMMIGRATION

Both Australia and the United States are liberal, democratic regimes with federal constitutions. The most basic difference in political structure is that Australia has a parliamentary system with a government based on more or less disciplined political parties, while the United States has a presidential system of separated powers and parties that neither govern nor behave like political parties elsewhere. The impact of these divergent political institutions on immigration policy and politics is treated at length in Freeman and Betts (ch. 5 in this book). Here we will concentrate on two broader issues of political economy: the internal institutional links between labour and capital, and the external position of the countries in global and regional trading systems and military alliances.

On the first point the two countries could hardly be less alike. Australia was a world leader in the emergence of a highly organized and activist labour movement. Early victories for the eight-hour day and a living wage, the establishment of the world's first labour governments in Queensland in 1899 and in the new federation in 1904, and the highly institutionalized role of the national trade union federation (ACTU) in the centralized collective bargaining system make Australia appear closer to the corporatist societal model than the USA, which sits at the far pole as a more or less pure pluralist society with weak and withering trade unions and no national bargaining structures at all. The interactions between the influence and cohesion of labour movements and immigration are complex. On the one hand, immigration flows affected the influence of organized labour. The perennial scarcity of labour in Australia, compared to its relative abundance in the United States, was certainly a prime factor in the differential success of labour in the two settings, and immigration controls helped to maintain scarcity in Australia and reduce it in the United States.

On the other hand, comparison of the Australian and American cases suggests three general consequences for immigration that follow from labour strength. (1) Organized labour's ability to affect immigration policy, especially the rate, size, and skill components of new entries, is positively related to overall labour strength. (2) At given levels of immigration, a strong labour movement is better able to control and reduce the adverse consequences of increased labour supply. In other words, one cannot simply assume that influxes of labour of proportional magnitude going to two different countries will have the same effect on wages and working conditions. Hypotheses must be couched in the light of the institutional context of the countries involved. (3) Strong trade unions and working-class parties are able to provide workers with legitimate focuses for nativist fears and impulses, thereby controlling and channelling them in the process. There is evidence, for example, that there has been less anarchic and spontaneous nativist activity in Australia than in the USA over the years.

Sharp contrast exists between the role of the United States as a global power in the Atlantic and Pacific, economically and geo-politically, and

Australia's position as a vast but economically small, dependent state, located on the semi-periphery, highly vulnerable to changes in world commodity prices and trading behaviour, and still formally involved in the remnants of a colonial relationship. Both situations impose constraints on the management of immigration. Ironically, it is the larger power that has encountered the greatest difficulty in controlling its borders.

The extensive commitments and responsibilities of the United States as the leader of the Western Alliance and global capitalist order tend to reduce its immigration policy options. External autonomy is joined, in this instance at least, to constrained policymaking at home. The history of American immigration policy, and here it is best to restrict discussion to the 45 years after World War II, is filled with instances of foreign policy and global leadership questions intruding into immigration decisions and leading to choices that may not have been optimal from a purely national perspective. This is most glaring in the case of refugee policy, where advancing the struggle between East and West often became the sole criterion by which a country's citizens were or were not deemed to be in danger of persecution. The astonishing laxity with which successive American governments have viewed the porousness of the country's border with Mexico must also be interpreted as much as an attempt to assure regional stability as to satisfy labour market demands at home. It is also, of course, a recognition that the geographical propinquity of two highly unequal economies makes secure borders beyond the reach of even a superpower.

The American political system, however, has not been very efficient in turning immigration policy to military, diplomatic, or foreign economic objectives. The Congress has controlled the immigration issue and it has been consistently susceptible to interest groups, ethnic lobbies, and other provincial concerns. The result has been that immigration politics in the United States have been a scene of structural conflict between the executive and legislative branches (see Freeman and Betts in this book).

Precisely because it was small and relatively insignificant on the global stage, Australia was able to maintain a racialist control policy until relatively recently. Defended militarily by Britain and then the United States, Australia's geographical isolation was its real defence until World War II. It could ignore its location in the Asian Pacific region because its economic, political, and cultural ties were with Europe and North America. White Australia was something of an embarrassment, but it caused few serious consequences. Recent evidence suggests that this ability to do as it pleases with immigration is diminishing with the progressive integration of the Australian economy into the Asian region. With Britain's entry into the European Community and the emergence of Asian capitalism, Australia has had to rethink its position. One reason that is often advanced as a justification not only for a non-discriminatory immigration policy, but also for a multiculturalism at home, is that it is an essential component of good trading relations with rising Asian economic giants (Garnaut 1989). How far these changes of attitude have gone to relax Australian policy is hard to say; in their public utterances officials imply that they have little choice given the sensibilities of their Asian neighbours.

CONCLUSIONS

Perhaps the most striking difference between our two cases is that the role of the state in immigration matters has been far more longstanding, extensive, and decisive in Australia than in the United States. The policymaking machinery and institutional structures in the two countries are markedly divergent. The centralized parliamentary system of Australia contrasts sharply with the decentralized, fragmented American presidential system of separated powers. The theme of centralization versus fragmentation may be carried over to the social structures as well. Capital–labour relations are much more highly organized in Australia than in the USA, as are the interest groups that speak for immigrants in the political process. Finally, although both countries have been fundamentally shaped by immigration from their earliest days as outposts of European settlement, Australia has always been more homogeneous ethnically than the United States.

Whatever the compelling differences between the two countries, their immigration experience in the last few decades has been increasingly shared. A chief aspect of this common fate is a decided shift in policy away from the discriminatory practices of the past to a new commitment to universalism and non-discrimination. Partly because of these policy reforms both countries have overseen a change in the source countries of immigration away from Europe and towards the Third World, especially Asia. Both countries have persevered in the development of programmes of mass immigration through the 1970s and 1980s, despite their increasingly straitened economic circumstances and their isolated positions as havens for the world's immigrants and refugees.

These historical and contemporary circumstances set the context in which Australian and American immigration policy choices in the 1990s will be made. They suggest several issues that are appropriate for the comparative analysis of the two cases, analysis that will be carried out in the following chapters.

Which of the two countries will be better able to develop policies to manage immigration effectively? This is a matter both of handling the increasing pressures for entry and 'controlling the borders' and in realizing the potential benefits of immigration in the national interest. On the one hand, our initial review indicates that Australia has the better designed policymaking structure to regulate and control immigration, and is in a much more favourable geo-political situation as far as immigration is concerned. On the other hand, public scrutiny and interest in immigration policy decisions are more intense in Australia and may constrain the flexibility of its policymakers more than their counterparts in the USA.

What will be the economic and social consequences of immigration for the two societies? In particular, what will be its impact on social cohesion and national identity? In which society is anti-immigrant sentiment more likely to find political expression? From the viewpoint of those persons who go to Australia and the United States to live, which society will be more hospitable and accessible? Which will devise the settlement policies and provide the environment to make the transition from migrant to citizen easier? Finally, what can the policymaking élites of the two countries learn from the experiences, both successful and unsuccessful, of the other?

PART I

CONTROL OF IMMIGRATION: POLICY AND POLITICS

2

PROBLEMS OF IMMIGRATION CONTROL IN LIBERAL DEMOCRACIES

THE AUSTRALIAN EXPERIENCE

Robert Birrell

The question of immigration control will be familiar to all who are attentive to recent immigration movements. Even the nations of western Europe, most of whom have disavowed any interest in attracting migrants, have recently found themselves the recipients of substantial migrant flows. Many of these have been asylum seekers. Their numbers grew from about 17 000 in 1983 to 350 000 in 1989 (Swedish Ministry of Labour 1990, p. 3).

Western European nations have found it difficult to exclude asylum seekers once inside their frontiers, however thin some cases may be. The elaborate and time-consuming legal machinery almost all of them have in place to process these claims, and the legal protections available to claimants, make exclusion very difficult, even though, after processing, only about 20 per cent of asylum seekers actually acquire legal status as refugees (Swedish Ministry of Labour 1990, p. 3).

Australia too, has experienced an upsurge of such claims. By 30 April 1991 the Department of Immigration, Local Government and Ethnic Affairs (DILGEA) had accumulated a backlog of over 28 000 persons seeking grant of residence status in Australia, mostly on grounds of marriage to an Australian resident and on humanitarian/compassionate grounds. A further rapidly growing backlog of asylum cases had accumulated under the Government's new Refugee Status Review Committee (see Freeman and Betts, ch. 5 in this book).

This chapter explores the Australian Government's efforts to control these onshore migration applications. This has proved to be a difficult task, in large part because of the role the Australian courts have played in opening up avenues for onshore claims. In 1989 the Government introduced a new legislatively based system of migration regulations designed to contract some of these avenues and to limit future court influence on migration selection policy. This effort was only partially successful. The following analysis of this initiative indicates how intensely contested and problematic immigration control now is in Australia.

THE WILL TO CONTROL

Has the Australian Government achieved a satisfactory degree of control over immigration? The public rhetoric on the issue is fulsome. In 1978 when the Liberal–Country Party Government enumerated a set of nine principles guiding immigration policy, the very first was: 'It is fundamental to national sovereignty that the Australian Government should determine who will be admitted to Australia. No person other than an Australian citizen, or a constituent member of the community, has a basic right to enter Australia' (M. MacKellar, Ministerial Statement 7 June 1978). This principle has been reaffirmed many times. For DILGEA officials this reaffirmation is often phrased within the context of their administrative role. Faced with many more applicants than can be accommodated they tend to see their function in control terms. As the Deputy Secretary of DILGEA recently put it, 'All states have the sovereign right to determine who may enter and remain within their territory . . . Immigration rules are essentially about control of the borders; about filtering those who would seek to enter' (Gibbons 1990, p. 1).

Yet despite these statements astute observers sometimes question whether they are taken seriously. Since the Government has been recruiting migrants at a rate higher than any other western nation (except Israel), there is cause to wonder whether it is concerned about parallel growth in the numbers who evade the offshore selection system by coming here as visitors, students and so on, and then seek to gain permanent residence. As to those illegally in Australia, until recently the Australian Government has not shown much interest in apprehending and deporting illegal migrants.

To sceptics this may be linked to the benefits employers gain from the competition illegals offer in certain labour markets. The comparative evidence indicates that governments seem fairly relaxed about this competition as long as the illegals involved do not add to the social welfare burden (Freeman 1986, p. 60).

Despite these qualifications there is no doubt that the Australian Government, or at least sections of it, has taken control seriously. The paradox is that DILGEA officials and ministers have made the running on the issue. This seems paradoxical because since its post–World War II formation as a separate Department of Immigration (Ethnic Affairs was added late in 1975), its officials have been required to justify the merits of immigration to the Australian people. Why then quibble about onshore migration applications or illegal movements?

The answer lies in the Government's concerns to maintain the legitimacy of its overall migration programme. Over the years the Government, and DILGEA in particular, has gone to great lengths to assure the public that its elaborate overseas selection system is crafted to deliver the greatest benefit to Australia. This effort is diminished to the extent that it is circumvented by the onshore change of status avenue and by illegals who are widely perceived as queue jumpers unlikely to have been selected if they had applied offshore. Illegals are seen to make a mockery of the selection system, and they threaten to undermine public acceptance of an active immigration programme.

Then there is the delicate subject of the make-up of the national community. Immigration is always going to be an emotional issue in a nation with a developed sense of ethnocentrism, as is the case in Australia. Immigration involves inviting new members into the community. It must be handled carefully if Australians are to feel they are partners in the choice of these members. Those who evade the overseas selection system tend to be regarded as interlopers, as unwanted guests. The tumultuous debate set off by Professor Geoffrey Blainey in 1984, when he asserted that changes in immigration selection policies were, unbeknown to most Australians, remaking their society's ethnic make up, was a sharp reminder to the Government that it had to be seen to be in control of migration selection.

The functions of recruiting, excluding and controlling migration movement are intermeshed. Because of this DILGEA has inevitably had to take on the control role within the Australian Government. It has become a thankless but important task in a context where other government departments, such as education and tourism, have been keen to diminish restrictions on migration movements. This background helps explain the paradox that DILGEA is simultaneously an advocate of immigration and of more effective methods of controlling immigration movements.

BACKGROUND TO AUSTRALIA'S CONTROL PROBLEMS

During the 1950s and 1960s control was not a major issue for Australian immigration authorities. The 1958 *Migration Act* embodied a long tradition of ministerial and thus administrative discretion in the implementation of government policy. The details of selection criteria were not specified in the Act. The Government changed its policy at will, often without informing the public. Immigration officers could enforce these changes with little interference from those affected.

This situation began to change in the 1970s with increased political pressure for ministerial intervention on behalf of individual applicants for change of status, and with changes in administrative law. As to the former, Australia's ethnic communities were becoming more active in local politics. Some of their members had a vital interest in the Government's selection system, particularly the rules on family reunion. One of the reasons was that by the mid-1970s this was almost the only avenue of entry to Australia following the Labor Government's tightening of the rules on independent entry. The result was intense pressure on the Government, and especially the Minister for Immigration, to use his discretionary powers to intercede on behalf of applicants. By the mid-1970s thousands of such requests were being received annually. Thus the administrative discretion enjoyed by immigration officials was contributing to a massive administrative load. In the 12-month period from March 1977 to March 1978, 15 500 ministerial representations were received, 60 per cent of which required the minister's signature (Hawkins 1989, p. 122).

Meanwhile pressures for clearer administrative guidelines open to public scrutiny and administrative accountability were coming from another source. This was from the movement for citizen empowerment relative to the state and its bureaucratic agencies. All branches of the Australian Government were subject to these pressures during the 1970s. The most important legislative outcome as far as immigration was concerned was the passage of the *Administrative Decisions (Judicial Review) Act* of 1977. This codified and strengthened pre-existing administrative case law. It gave all those affected by administrative decisions, including non-residents, legal access to the Federal Court if they wished to make a case that a decision had been improperly reached within the policy and regulatory guidelines under which the decision maker was operating.

The Act laid down the range of criteria which had to be met before a decision could be considered free from objection. These included that the 'rules of natural justice' had not been breached, that all the proper procedures required by law had been followed, and that the person making the decision had properly exercised his or her power. In the latter case the Act specified that this condition would be violated where a decision maker 'Took an irrelevant consideration into account in the exercise of a power' or 'failed to take a relevant consideration into account' (Section 6iii).

These political and administrative pressures prompted the Fraser Government to review its administration of the migration programme. In 1980 the Government for the first time incorporated a component of immigration policy into legislation. This took the form of an amendment to the 1958 *Migration Act*, subsequently known as Section 6A. This amendment specified which onshore change of status applications could be approved. Its intent was to limit access to this mode of entry, and in the process reduce the administrative burden on the department. As the minister at the time said, 'The only way in which this abuse of the discretionary powers of the Migration Act can be overcome is to limit the type of cases for which change of status may be approved' (Macphee, House of Reps, Hansard 27 Nov. 1980, p. 151).

Only those who were spouses, children and aged parents, temporary workers, refugees or those with 'strong compassionate or humanitarian grounds' could be considered. Applicants in the latter three categories had to have valid entry permits, that is, they could not apply if illegally in Australia. The Government wanted to limit the motive for illegal entry 'by removing its principal incentive—the prospect of entering as a visitor and subsequently gaining the right of permanent residence here' (Macphee, House of Reps, Hansard 27 Nov. 1980, p. 151). The context was concern about the growing numbers of illegals. The Government had instituted an amnesty in June 1980, and was anxious to forestall another build up in numbers.

As to the provision for 'compassionate' and 'humanitarian' cases, the officers drafting the provision thought it would rarely be used and strictly enforced (Arthur 1991; p. 2). That the courts would subsequently redefine these terms so as to open up avenues for permanent entry was not anticipated.

IMMIGRATION CONTROL IN THE 1980s

The US courts have played a significant role in broadening the rights of non-citizens to apply for permanent residency even though 'illegally' in the country (see Bean and Fix, ch. 3, Miller, ch. 4 in this book). This would be expected given the US reputation for judicial interventionism and the constitutional backing provided to citizens aggrieved by alleged state encroachment on their rights.

What most will find surprising is that in Australia, where the courts have historically not played such an activist role and where the constitution does not incorporate any parallel Bill of Rights, the evidence is that the courts have recently had more impact on immigration administration than has been the case in the USA. The point will be illustrated via DILGEA's attempts to control onshore claims for permanent residence on compassionate–humanitarian and marriage grounds.

The Australian Experience with Onshore Asylum Claims

DILGEA's first efforts to give legislative effect to policy via the 1980 6A Amendment proved ineffective. The letter of this legislation was never implemented. Onshore change of status claims by illegals continued to be processed where they were based on refugee or compassionate–humanitarian grounds. This seems to have been a political decision. The Government was reluctant to face criticism from ethnic and human rights interest groups. The only 6A restrictions implemented with regard to illegals concerned those applying on employment grounds.

The courts too played a role in the extension of these rights to illegals. In 1985, when for a brief period the policy stance on 6A was hardened, an appeal to the Federal Court led to a rebuff to DILGEA. In Tang, the court held that illegals were entitled to make an application for permanent residence. It noted that, 'what Parliament had given as a discretion could not be transformed into an absolute rule by administrative fiat' (Joint Standing Committee on Migrant Regulations 1990, p. 37). This view was consistent with that argued by the Human Rights Commission's 1985 review of immigration legislation. While noting that in practice DILGEA did process refugee and humanitarian–compassionate applications from illegals, the commission argued that they had a moral right to apply and that the legislation should be reformed to reflect this 'right'. The commission drew on the International Covenant on Civil and Political Rights (of which Australia was a signatory) which stated that 'all individuals within a state are to have their rights recognized without distinction of any kind' (Human Rights Commission 1985, p. 12).

In effect all persons in Australia (regardless of the legal basis of their stay) were given standing by the courts to have their claim reviewed. As well, the courts amplified the criteria used to make judgements on these claims. Judges tended to reflect the prevailing changes in Australian élite attitudes towards immigration issues in which the would-be migrant was seen as a victim of Australians' alleged prejudices and DILGEA's bureaucratic insensitivity. Indeed some on the Bench reviewing immigration cases, including Justice Einfeld, were leaders in speaking out on behalf of minority rights.

Reflecting these pressures, DILGEA was required to elaborate its grant of residence status rules. By 1988 DILGEA officers deciding onshore claims faced a broad and discretionary set of guidelines. The humanitarian category was defined as including individuals 'who, because of membership of a particular group/class or because of beliefs held, (have) been or would be singled out for severely disadvantageous treatment by the state in the applicant's country of origin or last permanent residence'. The policy guidelines indicated that this 'disadvantageous treatment' could include 'discrimination against family, friends or other people closely identified with the applicant', plus circumstances of 'war, revolution and inter-communal violence' in the country of origin (DILGEA, Instruction Manual, Grant of Residence Status 1988, no. 10).

The courts also influenced the interpretation of these rules. This can be illustrated through court determinations on how officers should decide whether an applicant faced 'disadvantageous' or 'discriminatory' treatment on return home. In Dahlan's case (decided Dec. 1989), which involved an Indonesian journalist who had been critical of the Indonesian Government and feared reprisals, DILGEA had ruled that he faced no greater difficulties than other journalists in Indonesia. The court decided that it was an error to employ the standards of the home country, rather than Australian standards (Arthur 1991, p. 5; *Folklore*, vol. 2, no. 1, p. 4).

A further significant elaboration of this viewpoint was given in the case of *Chan Yee Kim* v. *The Minister of Immigration and Ethnic Affairs*. This concerned a claim for change of status on refugee grounds, initially considered and rejected in 1983. The High Court of Australia finally decided in favour of Chan in 1989. (The case is reported in *The Commonwealth Law Reports*, vol. 169, part 3 and henceforth will be cited as Chan.) It has profound implications for subsequent asylum claims made on refugee or humanitarian grounds. All such cases will have to take into account the Dahlan and Chan judgements (subject to changes in the law).

Chan's claim for refugee status arose when he was just 17 in 1968. He was a member of the Red Guards, but belonged to a faction which lost out in his locality. He was subsequently 'exiled' to another location and, though free to move about within that area, was not permitted to return to his home village. His attempts to 'escape' led to detention of several months, after which he managed to flee to Hong Kong in 1974, from where he subsequently illegally entered Australia in 1980 as a stowaway (Chan 1989, pp. 418–19).

Chan claimed that these restrictions on his movements amounted to persecution on the basis of his 'membership of a particular social group or political opinion' and thus was within the meaning of the 1951 UN Convention on refugees as amended by the 1967 Protocol. He was not able to prove that he personally held political views contrary to the Chinese regime at the time. Rather, he relied on the fact that his father had been a member of the Kuomintang, and that this led to his 'persecution' by the Chinese authorities.

The High Court set itself the task of deciding whether DILGEA was incorrect in determining that Chan's experience did not amount to a 'well founded fear of persecution within the meaning of the Convention and Protocol' (Chan 1989, p. 423). It agreed that the question of persecution should relate to the current situation and not that at the time Chan fled from China. However, none of the five High Court judges reporting on the case made any serious attempt to evaluate what Chan's position was likely to be should he have returned in 1989. Rather they relied on the situation in the early 1970s when the alleged persecution took place. They based their judgement on two separate questions. One was, what constituted 'persecution', and the other, under what circumstances was fear of persecution 'well founded'.

In defining persecution Judge McHugh declared that it is not a 'necessary element of "persecution" that the individual should be the victim of a series of acts. A single act of oppression may suffice'. Moreover this act need not be that of 'loss of life or liberty'. Disregard of human dignity would be sufficient (Chan 1989, p. 430).

This is a remarkably generous conclusion. In the context of Communist Chinese society, students and workers, let alone those who lose out in factional struggles, are routinely assigned to particular locations and punished if they refuse to remain there. A definition as broad as this potentially encompasses a wide cross-section of Chinese society. Of course unless a political, racial or religious element is involved such assignment would not be relevant to refugee status. But in Communist China politics is linked to all aspects of life. True, as Judge Gaudron stated, 'It is not reasonable by the standards of civilized nations to categorize exile and detention for reasons of political opinion as discrimination "to a limited degree" [and therefore] not constituting persecution', as had occurred in Chan's case (Chan 1989, p. 416). By the standards of 'civilized nations', though, much of what is required of residents in China would be seen as 'discriminatory' in these terms. As with Dahlan's case this significantly liberalized the interpretation of asylum claims.

As to the meaning of 'well founded fear' of persecution, the five judges were able to select from diverse international case law and academic commentary on the subject. In some jurisdictions (notably Britain) the dominant view was that a claimant had to show that objective judgement of the situation would support the view that persecution as defined above would occur. It was not enough that the claimant was personally fearful. In others, notably the USA, the emphasis was more on the subjective state of mind of the claimant.

The Australian judges chose the liberal, subjective way of assessing 'persecution'. Judge McHugh concluded that, 'As the US Supreme Court points out in Cardoza–Fonesca, an applicant for refugee status may have a well founded fear of persecution even though there is only a 10 per cent chance that he will be shot or tortured or otherwise persecuted. Obviously, a far fetched possibility of persecution must be excluded. But if there is a real chance that the applicant will be persecuted, his or her fear should be characterized as "well founded" for the purpose of the Convention and Protocol' (Chan 1989, p. 430). Judge Mason likewise indicated that 'if an applicant establishes that there is a real chance of persecution then his fear, assuming that he has such a fear, is well founded, notwithstanding that there is less than a 50 per cent chance of persecution occurring' (Chan 1989, p. 389).

This liberal criterion will make it difficult for Australian decision makers to reject the claims of anyone asserting fear of persecution. Moreover the claimant does not have to have personally suffered such persecution. It is enough that he or she belongs to a social category, even a small proportion of whom have been so afflicted. As indicated, Chan's main claim to refugee status was that he belonged to a family with a Kuomintang background, which he asserted was the basis of his persecution. Judge Dawson concluded, 'such treatment as was suffered by the appellant was because his family was perceived to be anti-revolutionary and because the appellant was perceived to be of the same persuasion'. Dawson goes on to emphasize that, 'It would have been sufficient to constitute a Convention reason that the appellant was a member of a particular social group, namely, his family, irrespective of his personal political opinions' (Chan 1989, p. 369).

The net result of these High Court opinions is that they open the way for a whole class of appellants such as about 40 000 Peoples' Republic of China (PRC) students in Australia in 1991, to claim membership of a social category—Chinese students—some of whose members had been persecuted at the Tiananmen Square affair. Though their political views would cross the spectrum, and most could claim no personal involvement in the student movement, all could claim to be fearful of persecution (as the court has defined it) if required to return to the PRC.

Change of Status on Spouse–De Facto Grounds

This issue became a difficult one for the Australian Government during the 1980s because there was a sharp increase in such claims, and because some were accompanied by sensationalist media reporting of alleged 'rackets' involving illegal payments to bogus marriage partners. In 1988–89, 7437 permanent residence visas were granted on marriage grounds.

Most of these visas were issued to persons entering Australia as visitors. In recent times nearly half of these had overstayed their visas, and therefore were illegally here at the time of their change of status application (NPC 1990, p. 13). Discussions with DILGEA case officers assessing marriage claims indicated that they believed a significant proportion of these 'marriages' were contrived for migration purposes.

Yet despite this only some five per cent of the marriage–de facto cases were rejected in the late 1980s, and in most of these one of the parties admitted there was fraud involved, or asserted it afterwards in revenge for being duped. The reasons for this low rejection rate are diverse. One is that the staff responsible for assessing marriage claims had very little investigatory backup should they suspect a bogus claim. By 1989 in Sydney, where the majority of applications were received, staff did not even have the time to interview applicants.

But it is probably more fundamental that, in the period since the passage of the 1977 *Administrative Decisions (Judicial Review) Act*, and the establishment of an Immigration Review Panel in 1982, a pervasive 'administrative culture' had developed among case officers. It was believed that the administrative law system was loaded in favour of the applicant, and that it was both futile and potentially threatening to one's career to reject a case. Rejection implied the possibility of appeal to a review panel or, more remotely, a re-examination of the case in the Federal Court where all the officer's actions would be critically assessed. The saying, 'Before administrative law reform Prohibited Non-Citizens were afraid of immigration officers. Now, immigration officers are afraid of PNCs', was no joke.

Critics of DILGEA's administrative discretion often suggest that it was used to prejudice the applicant's case. This once may have been the case, but in the recent environment officers have had to apply policy, then think of all the discretionary circumstances that might militate against a negative decision.

The courts have also ruled so as to weaken DILGEA's capacity to reject applications. A recent Federal Court case (decided 8 May 1990) illustrates the point. This concerned a Malaysian, Mr Dhillon, who had married an Australian citizen in Malaysia in November 1987. He came to Australia on a migrant visa in May 1988, but following his arrival Mrs Dhillon and some of her friends made a statutory declaration that the marriage was a 'marriage of convenience' on his part to gain resident status here.

DILGEA then detained Mr Dhillon. However a few days later, following discussion with her husband, Mrs Dhillon retracted her statutory declaration, claiming that she and her husband intended to resume the marriage. Despite this, the case officer decided the marriage had 'been contrived for the purpose of enabling [Dhillon] to obtain a visa to migrate to Australia' and therefore refused him grant of residence status.

The Federal Court decided in favour of Dhillon on the grounds that though one of the parties may have entered the marriage with a view to immigration what matters is whether the parties had a mutual commitment to life as husband and wife. Since DILGEA did not take this issue properly into account (according to the court) the decision was not taken in accord with the principles of 'natural justice'.

Prior to this case it was DILGEA policy to deny change of status to a spouse–de facto applicant where one of the parties to the relationship indicated that they had been 'duped'. Such duplicity was regarded as relevant to whether the relationship was genuine and continuing. Dhillon's case challenges this policy. It now appears that a marriage–de facto claim can only be rejected where both parties to the marriage were involved in the contrivance. This sharply reduces DILGEA's capacity to police marriages contrived for immigration purposes.

The Australian Government's Response

The circumstances described above prompted the Australian Government (at the urging of DILGEA officers and the minister, Senator Ray) to initiate radical changes in migration legislation. In 1989 the Government incorporated the entire body of its migration policies in legislative form. The goal was to give precise legal definition to policy so as to remove politics from the decision-making process and to minimize opportunities for the courts and appeal tribunals to reinterpret the rules. By so doing the Government moved to a US style of immigration administration. DILGEA officers were well aware that it was the legislative precision of the US rules on eligibility (covering the preference and quota system), which explained the limited influence of the courts on US immigration criteria, at least relative to Australia.

Though this meant giving up administration autonomy it was a price most DILGEA officers were prepared to pay. Hostility towards the courts' 'interference' pervaded the DILGEA bureaucracy. Many judges reciprocated, sometimes via openly critical comments on DILGEA's agenda.

The key features of the June 1989 *Migration Legislation Amendment Act* and the policy regulations legislated later in 1989 were as follows. (1) The Act almost entirely removed the minister from the decision-making process (once policy was in place). It therefore blocked what had been a major avenue of political influence for those aggrieved by a DILGEA decision. (2) The regulations were drafted so as to remove all doubt concerning the appropriate decision open to an officer. They specified all the factors relevant to a decision and the criteria applicable in making a judgement. By law, the decision maker had to follow these criteria (as did the review authority and the courts). As DILGEA's legal branch described the outcome, 'A person seeking an entry permit will be required to satisfy these criteria. If these criteria are not satisfied the delegate *cannot*, as a matter of law, grant an entry permit. This will not be an inflexible application of policy, but mere compliance with the law (as established in the regulations) . . . This is contrasted with the current situation where the delegate finds that the applicant does not satisfy the requirements of the policy and must then decide whether there are any matters outside the contemplation of policy which justify a favourable decision' (*Folklore* October 1989, vol. 1, no. 2, p. 8). (3) Illegals were not given standing within the administration of the Act. They were not allowed to apply for an entry permit except on humanitarian or refugee grounds, or if they were an aged parent or dependent relative who would have received a visa if he or she had applied overseas. Nor were they to have access to the Review Tribunal or the minister to plead their case. Furthermore, they were to be subject to mandatory deportation after a 28-day 'period of grace'.

Finally, in specifying the regulations accompanying the Act late in 1989, the Government introduced a number of policy initiatives affecting change of status claims. These caused great controversy, partly because of their toughness, but also because in presenting the legislation to Parliament in April 1989 Senator Ray had declared that it would be policy neutral. His words were, 'In drawing up these Regulations I intend to reflect only current policy, which in turn reflects the Government's public response to the CAAIP Report' (Ray 1990, p. 3).

The most important of these changes were the following. (1) Visitors arriving in Australia after December 1989 were not permitted to apply for change of status on marriage or de facto grounds while in Australia. Even if legally in Australia and married to an Australian citizen, the regulations required that the applicant move offshore before proceeding further with the application. (2) The compassionate category for Grant of Residence Status was truncated to a purely family category covering aged dependent relatives and a few other minor categories of relatives, all of whom had to be sponsored by an Australian resident. (3) Applicants claiming change of status on humanitarian grounds faced far more restrictive barriers. The event triggering the claim, such as a war or natural disaster, had to have occurred after the applicant reached Australia, and it had to be gazetted by the minister.

The Political Response

The *Migration Legislation Amendment Act* came into force on 19 December 1989. This was a sensitive time politically since it preceded a federal election to be held in March 1990. The Act was a product of an unusual set of circumstances in which DILGEA's longstanding administrative interests found support in a resourceful minister, Senator Ray, prepared to use his influence to win Cabinet over to the administrator's viewpoint.

The Government, though, had other constituencies to accommodate, notably those whose perspective was that of the migrant 'client'. The time was propitious for their intervention because of the impending election. Their leaders were alarmed at the implications of the new regulations and immediately pressed for changes. Their objective was to swing the pendulum back to the circumstances of the 1970s where ministerial discretion favoured the applicant (e.g. see the submissions by R. Merkel and the National Immigration Forum, Joint Select Committee on Migrant Regulations, Submissions to the Committee 1990, vol. 2).

The public discussion of the new regulations was dominated by these viewpoints. In a remarkable show of unanimity Australia's major welfare, humanitarian and ethnic organizations spoke as one on the issue. For example, in Victoria, Bishop Hollingworth of the influential Anglican Brotherhood of St Laurence joined with social welfare, civil liberties and ethnic leaders (including Walter Lippmann of the Victorian Ethnic Communities' Council) in an open letter to Mr Hawke condemning the regulations. They concluded as follows: 'We ask you, as Prime Minister to take urgent steps to review and assess the effects that could flow from the rigidity of the Regulations which in their present form would undoubtedly undermine the credibility of the Government's social justice policy' (*Welcare* April 1990). Representatives from the Jewish and Lebanese communities were particularly concerned about the changed humanitarian rules since these threatened to arrest the flow of peoples such as Soviet Jews, who would be unlikely to satisfy the new criteria.

As the media depicted it, the debate was between a cruel, heartless immigration bureaucracy and all those with compassion for the downtrodden migrant and his or her Australian sponsors. This was a dangerous situation for the Government, since it stood to lose far more votes from ethnic communities aggrieved by the new rules than it did from the majority of Australians who would have supported the Government's stance but for whom the issue was marginal relative to issues of taxation, employment, and so on. The situation was exacerbated by the administrative tangle DILGEA got itself into through having to rush the implementation of the immensely complex and difficult to comprehend system of new regulations.

The Labor Government's Response in 1990

The Labor Government's response was muted prior to the March election. The only concessions were a series of delays to the regulations concerning illegals in Australia as of 19 December 1989. DILGEA, though, had come under severe attack for the 'harshness' of its new regulations and its administrative shortcomings. This had forced the Government on to the defensive, and prompted the Prime Minister to promise that the regulations would be reviewed after the election.

In the aftermath of the election, with DILGEA weakened by the criticism it had received and the loss of Senator Ray (who had moved to a new portfolio), the Prime Minister, Mr Hawke, struck. He replaced the previous head of DILGEA, Ron Brown, with a member of the Prime Minister's Department, Chris Conybeare (who had served in Mr Hawke's office). A few days later his deputy, Tony Harris, resigned his position. Mr Hawke also appointed Gerry Hand as minister. Hand's record of sensitivity to community and humanitarian concerns (while Minister for Aboriginal Affairs) seemed to confirm a new policy thrust for DILGEA.

These events were the subject of intense media speculation. All such commentary emphasized the role of the ethnic communities, in what many interpreted as a 'coup' by the Prime Minister to ensure that ethnic concerns were taken account of. As one journalist put it, 'Mr Hand has been appointed, in part, to sell the Government's immigration policies to the ethnic communities and stitch up their support for the Labor Party' (*Australian* 21–22 April 1990).

The full story of these events has yet to be written. What matters in this context, though, is not which version, if any, is correct, but the widespread currency of the ethnic 'coup' theory. The expectation had been created that Senator Ray's tough line on immigration control was about to be dismantled. In the ethnic press Mr Hand's arrival was regarded as a precursor to a new and more accommodating policy towards ethnic interests. For example, *Il Globo* declared that 'Mr Hand has no option than to resist the anti-immigration lobby, [and] re-establish the respect and confidence destroyed in recent years of the public with regard to processes and representatives of the immigration bureaucracy' (*Il Globo* 23 April 1990).

Largely because of these expectations and the accompanying publicity, DILGEA's new management team were engulfed by a media backlash before they could even begin to settle down to their alleged task. Through the 1980s there had been periodic upsurges in public interest in the immigration issue driven by worries about the 'ethnic challenge' to Anglo–Celtic cultural and political dominance in Australia. This debate was unleashed again in May and June 1990, triggered off by the 'coup' and by a remarkable denunciation of Mr Hawke's immigration policies by Senator Walsh (formerly Minister for Finance). He declared that immigration policy was being driven by ethnic lobbying rather than by rational evaluation of the case for more migrants, 'because some feared a political backlash from "ethnic leaders" ' (*Australian Financial Review* 8 May 1990).

While the debate sparked off by Walsh's remarks soon subsided it left a residue of caution within the Government regarding any obvious dismantling of the regulations. To have done so would have confirmed Senator Walsh's case. Senator Walsh represented the voice of economic rationalism. By early 1990 the very success of Senator Ray's opponents in building a coalition of welfare, humanitarian and ethnic interests hostile to the new regulations hardened the belief among the economic rationalists that the Government was about to fall prey to yet another 'soft' welfare-oriented interest group. While business interests still favoured high migration, this interest was by now clearly separate from issues of control and selection. The Government had to worry about criticism from this quarter (increasingly evident within Liberal–National Party ranks), as well as from nationalists agitated about the political and cultural challenge of the ethnic movement.

Immigration Control Under New Management

The reference point in discussion here will be the original objectives of the 1989 amendments to the Act. As indicated, these were to remove the incentive for illegal migration by curbing opportunities for change of status once here as a visitor, student and so on, and to ensure that the regulations determining selection were sufficiently precise to limit the scope for court reviews and to remove political pressures for discretionary decisions.

The new minister, Mr Hand, signalled his priorities in a 9 May 1990 ministerial statement. He reaffirmed the Government's control objectives, including 'minimising abuse of the system by illegal entrants'. But he balanced this by promising 'to respond sensitively and with compassion when individual cases arise that require special consideration' (Hansard, House of Reps 9 May 1990, p. 137).

Reference to 'sensitivity' and 'compassion' set the bureaucratic alarm bells ringing. These fears, though, have proved exaggerated. There has been no wholesale return to discretion, whether at the officer or ministerial level. It is already safe to conclude that two of the central reforms of the 1989 Act both survive and appear to be operating as the Government intended. The first is the removal of the minister from the decision-making process as it affects individual cases, and the second is the tight specification in legislation of the rules governing visa and entry permits.

As regards the policy changes written into the 1989 Act, the picture changes. These were an essential part of the strategy to diminish the incentive to visit Australia in the hope of subsequently winning permanent residence. These changes have been significantly watered down.

The Treatment of Illegals

Despite the tough talk since the last (and 'final') amnesty in 1980 the arrangements for those illegally in Australia as of 19 December 1989 amount to a de facto amnesty. These people were repeatedly advised towards the end of 1989 (through the media) that they must come forward by 19 December if they were to avoid the automatic deportation rules to come into effect at that date. Since then there have been a succession of extensions. Mr Hand continued this pattern during 1990, finally (it seems) bringing the process to an end in October 1990 with the announcement that pre-December 1989 illegals had until December 1993 to apply for change of status. This is an extraordinarily long time. Though the main route to permanent residence is a marriage or de facto relationship with an Australian (supposed to be in place as of 15 October 1990), it is hard to see those who have not found a spouse by this time being deported. This 'soft' amnesty has also been extended to those who became illegal between 19 December 1989 and October 1990. They too could apply for change of status under the old rules by 31 October.

Persons illegally in Australia can also apply under the 1989 regulations for asylum on humanitarian or refugee grounds. Thus, there remain large windows of opportunity for illegals to regularize their status.

Persons becoming illegal after October 1990 can still apply for change of status via marriage, but to do so they must apply within 28 days of becoming illegal, and must not have been refused another visa, for example an extension of their visitor's visa on an earlier occasion. As the law now stands, all other illegals will have to leave Australia and apply offshore if they wish to claim permanent residence on the basis of marriage to an Australian resident. Also, illegals can no longer appeal their case to the Immigration Review Tribunal.

The Government has, however, rejected the main recommendation of the Joint Standing Committee on Migration Regulations (JSCMR) set up in May 1990. It was given broad terms of reference to consider changes to the *Migration Act.* It began with a review of the illegal issue, and in September 1990 produced its first report entitled *Illegal Entrants in Australia: Balancing Control and Compassion.* Its central recommendation was that those illegally in Australia for five or more years, who apply by October 1990, should be entitled to stay permanently if they can show they were 'absorbed' into the Australian community.

It is significant that only four of the 10 active members of the committee supported this recommendation. The Liberal–National Party members opposed it, as did Labor Senator Jim Kiernan. The dissenters vigorously opposed any further concessions on the grounds that this would undermine the Government's control objectives.

Spouse–De Facto Rules

The 1989 regulation preventing visitors from applying in Australia on marriage–de facto grounds was a significant attempt to reduce this category. It has not survived the Government's review of the 1989 regulations. The Government followed the recommendations of the National Population Council and the Parliamentary Joint Standing Committee on Migrant Regulations for a return to the pre-1989 arrangements. In January 1991 Mr Hand announced that visitors legally in Australia will be able to apply onshore.

However, the rules on the bona fides of these marriages have been strengthened. Henceforth visitors and temporary entrants (students, etc.), who apply onshore will be granted a conditional two-year visa (similar to that provided for under the US *Immigration Marriage Fraud Amendments Act* of 1989). At the end of this two-year period they must demonstrate that the relationship is 'genuine and ongoing'. It remains to be seen whether this measure will be any more effective than has been the case in the USA, given the problems of assessing 'genuineness' and community sensitiveness about any 'field investigation'.

Asylum Categories

The 1989 amendments implied a sharp curtailment of onshore claims based on humanitarian grounds. They did not, however, survive Mr Hand's review and were repealed in June 1990. As indicated, these 1989 amendments had been vigorously contested by ethnic and humanitarian advocates. The resulting tussle during 1990 between these advocates and those concerned about any new widening of the regulations covering the humanitarian category indicates the current relative strength of the two camps.

The new regulations were announced early in 1991. They largely reflected DILGEA worries. The proposals to gazette human rights incidents and to limit claims to events occurring after the applicant's arrival in Australia were dropped. But the new regulations were carefully crafted to bypass the case law generated since the passage of the 6A1e legislation. There was no longer any reference to claims based on 'strong compassionate or humanitarian grounds'. Instead, those seeking residence as humanitarian claimants henceforth had to show that their 'particular circumstances and personal characteristics provide them with a sound basis for expecting a significant threat to personal security on return as a result of targetted action by persons in the country of return' (Ministerial Press Statement 1991, no. 15).

Cases such as the post-Tiananmen Square PRC students would in most instances be excluded by this ruling. It remains to be seen whether the courts will resist this interpretation. The Government, though, made its intent quite clear. Henceforth, the claimant must show a personalized and significant threat to himself or herself on return home. Belonging to a 'class' of persons who might be threatened would not be sufficient.

The situation of refugee asylum claimants has not been affected by the above rulings. The definition of a refugee remains that of the UN Convention and 1967 Protocol. Since currently all asylum claimants are evaluated on both refugee and humanitarian criteria we need to ask why the Government did not also introduce new rules on refugees in order to evade the courts' liberal interpretations of past claims.

The answer is that it was not prepared to take the international and domestic flak likely to arise from tampering with the UN definition. This indicates something of the difficulties a nation such as Australia, eager to maintain a good image on human rights, faces in tightening up on refugee asylum claims.

As regards compassionate claimants the Government has stuck to its tough 1989 line that only those with close family relationships to Australian residents will be considered under this category.

CONCLUSIONS

The experience described indicates a mixed bag. The Australian Government has not been able to sustain as tough a line on immigration control as DILGEA officers wanted. This reflects the political strength of the ethnic communities in Australia and the sympathy of the intelligentsia towards the ethnic and humanitarian cause (including in the courts). Nevertheless, though many of the control measures legislated in 1989 were annulled or watered down, the regulation of residence claims has overall been tightened.

Some would argue that this situation is only temporary. Australia is being pressed to enter the global marketplace and encourage international movement for educational, tourist and business purposes, and (so it is argued), attempts to limit subsequent permanent residence claims are likely to founder.

We do not think this is the case. Rather, there is likely to be continued struggle between control advocates and their antagonists. The Government will always have an interest in control if only to legitimate its larger migration programme. In addition we appear to be witnessing a breakdown of 'bipartisanism' on the issue.

Economic rationalists, particularly within the ranks of conservative politicians, now tend to link immigration control to their economic policy agenda. The Hawke Government's concern to placate its ethnic–humanitarian constituency was regarded as part of a larger unwillingness to take the 'hard' decisions to wean Australians away from welfare 'dependency', industry protection and other institutions allegedly inhibiting industrial efficiency.

The earlier reference to the unwillingness of conservative members of the JSCMR to endorse a softer line on illegals and the intense public debate provoked by the Hawke Government's plan to 'review' the 1989 Migrant Regulations following the 1990 federal election illustrate these developments. While further conflict over these issues is certain the outcome is not.

3

THE SIGNIFICANCE OF RECENT IMMIGRATION POLICY REFORMS IN THE UNITED STATES

Frank D. Bean and Michael Fix

Immigration is a difficult issue for Americans to confront. The people of the United States often define themselves as a 'nation of immigrants,' yet many citizens see immigration as a threat to their culture, their jobs and occasionally even their national security (Schuck 1990; Fuchs 1990a; Tucker, Keely and Wrigley 1990). Given this ambivalence, it is not surprising that the nation has only rarely adopted major changes in its immigration laws during the twentieth century. Restrictionist legislation in the form of national origin quotas was enacted in 1924 and more liberal, expansionist measures eliminating such quotas and instituting family reunification criteria as bases for admission were passed in 1965 (Fuchs 1990a; Reimers 1985). In abolishing race and ethnic origin as grounds for admission, the 1965 legislation reflected the domestic policy emphases of the era on civil rights as well as the foreign policy goal of establishing good relations with Asian countries that had recently achieved political independence (Cafferty et al. 1983).

The legislation, however, had unanticipated consequences for immigration patterns, which began to change during the 1970s. One of the major shifts was towards increasing numbers of new entrants. In the 1970s, 4.3 million immigrants came. By the end of the 1980s immigration had reached levels nearly as high as those in the early part of the twentieth century (Bean, Vernez and Keely 1989). Over 6.3 million immigrants were granted legal permanent residence during the decade, including 66 000 aliens legalized in 1988 and 492 000 in 1989 under the provisions of the 1986 *Immigration Reform and Control Act* (US Immigration and Naturalization Service 1990). According to the estimates of the US Bureau of the Census, supplementing this number were 100 000 to 300 000 undocumented immigrants per year (Passel 1986). If one conservatively assumes that all the legalizing aliens entered the country during the 1980s, the total level of immigration during the decade varied somewhere between about 6.7 and 8.7 million persons, a range whose midpoint exceed the levels of all previous decades except the 1900s, when 8.3 million immigrants were admitted (US Immigration and Naturalization Service 1990).

Besides changing its volume, immigration also changed its composition during the 1970s and 1980s (Fix and Passel 1990). New arrivals less frequently came from Canada and European countries. More often they originated in Asian and Spanish-speaking nations. In the 1960s, for example, only about one in two immigrants came from Asian or Hispanic countries, whereas in the 1980s over four in five did (US Immigration and Naturalization Service 1990). Immigration from Mexico, which even in the 1960s constituted the largest flow from any single source country, increased from about one in seven immigrants in that era to almost one in five during the 1980s. Conversely, European and Canadian entrants declined from about one in two to about one in seven (US Immigration and Naturalization Service 1990).

Another major shift was that illegal immigration began to increase. In 1964 the United States and Mexico terminated the Bracero Programme for temporary agricultural workers. But with reliance on this source of labour relatively well institutionalized in the American Southwest, undocumented migration, rather than ceasing, steadily rose as population growth in Mexico generated surplus labour and as the demand for such workers steadily increased in the United States (Bean, Schmandt and Weintraub 1989). Visa-overstayers, or persons who entered the country legally and then stayed beyond the expiration dates of their visas, also increased (Bean, Edmonston and Passel 1990). Although the difficulty in gauging precisely the magnitude of stocks and flows of illegal migrants to the United States has always invited exaggerations about the size and growth of the illegal population, even the most cautious and careful assessments agreed that the numbers increased during the 1970s (Passel 1986). In consequence the Select Commission on Immigration and Refugee Policy concluded in 1981 in its final report that 'one issue has emerged as most pressing—that of undocumented/illegal immigration' (US Select Commission on Immigration and Refugee Policy 1981, p. 35).

The rising numbers, changed composition, and increased illegality of immigrants generated a national debate about whether the country should change its immigration policy. Doubts about the country's ability to absorb substantial numbers of immigrants developed. Although the economy grew appreciably during much of the 1980s, real wages remained at a stagnant level after the early 1970s (Levy 1987). Concerns emerged that national immigration policy promoted new arrivals too numerous and too poorly skilled to best serve the needs of the country in an era of increased global competitiveness (Borjas 1990; Chiswick 1990). It was against this backdrop that Congress passed the *Immigration Reform and Control Act* (IRCA) in 1986 and the *Immigration Act* of 1990.

Given the infrequency with which the United States reforms its immigration, it is appropriate to ask whether these pieces of legislation represent major policy changes, as some observers have argued (Schuck 1990), or agglomerations of patchwork provisions born of political compromises that reduce their chance of effectiveness? Will these laws prove to be major shifts in US immigration policy that will lead to substantial shifts in the kind and degree of immigration as occurred after the national origin quotas were adopted in 1924 and after family reunification criteria were passed in 1965? Are IRCA and the 1990 Act accomplishing the main purposes for which they were enacted? Are the political concerns that created the impetus for changing national immigration policy in the late 1980s reflected in the outcomes of the legislation?

This chapter seeks to address these questions by examining the major provisions of these laws, together with the principal reasons for their passage and the extent to which they appear to be working to achieve their objectives. In a broader vein, we strive to ascertain whether US immigration policy is entering a new era of restrictiveness or whether it is increasingly expansionist in outcome (Bean, Vernez and Keely 1989). If restrictionism versus expansionism describe the ideological poles of the current debate over immigration policy during the 1980s (Schuck 1990), it is important to examine both pieces of legislation in terms of whether they are increasing or decreasing immigration to the country. While viewing these laws in terms of the extent to which restrictionist and expansionist movements affected their passage and content necessarily and inevitably oversimplifies a more complex political reality, such an examination is useful because of the important historical role such orientations have played in shaping US immigration policy (Higham 1963). It also helps to show the part such orientations played in generating the recent impetus for immigration reform in the United States and in affecting the political compromises that made passage of the legislation possible.

THE *IMMIGRATION REFORM AND CONTROL ACT* OF 1986

The IRCA, which was passed in 1986, consisted of six major sets of provisions. These included: (1) employer sanctions (designed to remove the 'magnet' for undocumented immigration by making it illegal for employers to hire workers lacking appropriate documents); (2) legalization (making it possible for illegal aliens residing continuously in the country since 1 January 1982 to legalize their status); (3) the special agricultural workers (SAWs) programme (designed to allow agricultural workers in perishable crops who had been employed for 90 days in the years immediately preceding IRCA's passage to apply for permanent resident alien status); (4) state legalization impact assistance grants (SLIAG) (which authorized $1 billion per year for four years beginning in 1988 to reimburse state governments for the costs of public assistance, health and educational services for the newly legalized population); (5) a systematic alien verification for entitlements (SAVE) programme (requiring all states to verify that non-citizens were eligible for welfare benefits); and (6) increased enforcement (focusing mainly on increased border patrol, inspections, and other enforcement activities).

Although the legalization and SLIAG provisions were inclusionary in nature and resulted in 3.1 million illegals applying for legal status (Gonzalez-Baker 1990), IRCA's major purpose was to curtail illegal immigration into the United States. The main instrument set up to accomplish this objective was employer sanctions. Because of fears that employer compliance might lead to increased discrimination against 'foreign looking' US minorities, the employer sanctions section of IRCA also included anti-discrimination provisions that extended the protections of US Civil Rights law to prohibit discrimination on the basis of citizenship status. IRCA thus, in effect, enjoined employers to walk a tightrope between not hiring certain kinds of workers while not discriminating against others.

Assessments of whether IRCA has achieved its main purpose of curbing undocumented migration must ascertain whether the stock and flow of illegal entrants to the country has been reduced subsequent to the enactment of the law and, if so, whether the reduction has been achieved without paying a price of increased discrimination on the part of employers against legal minorities. A number of different sources of data help to shed light on the former question (Bean, Edmonston and Passel 1990). One relevant kind of evidence comes from apprehension statistics, which are periodic tallies of the number of times persons entering the country illegally are apprehended by the US Border Patrol or by other Immigration and Naturalization Service (INS) enforcement personnel.

Evidence About Undocumented Flows

Several recent studies have used time series methods to analyse such data as an indicator of illegal migration into the United States across the southern border. One group of studies, conducted by researchers working at the Urban Institute (Bean et al. 1990; Espenshade, White, and Bean 1991; White, Bean and Espenshade 1990), has modelled the number of successful border crossers as a function of the size of the Mexican population likely to migrate, the propensity to migrate, and the likelihood of capture. The propensity to migrate is modelled with economic factors, seasonal factors, and factors related to IRCA. The likelihood of capture is indicated by INS effort in terms of border patrol enforcement hours and border patrol resources (budget). Similar approaches have been adopted by Espenshade (1990) and by Crane and his associates (1990).

Such analyses of apprehensions data involve certain problems (see Passel, Bean and Edmonston 1990). Despite these, several consistent findings emerge from the above research studies. First and foremost, a clear reduction in the flow of undocumented immigrants across the US–Mexico border appears to have occurred in the post-IRCA period. Furthermore, this reduction took place in the presence of increased INS effort, indicated by more linewatch hours and upgraded equipment—factors that would increase apprehensions, not decrease them. The research also suggests that a significant portion of the drop in apprehensions can be attributed to the legalization of large numbers of Mexicans in the general legalization and SAW programmes. Second, the studies are broadly consistent in finding that about one-third to one-half of the reduction can be attributed to IRCA. Bean et al. (1990) also attempted to partition the decline into components due to removal of the SAWs from the illegal labour migration stream and due to other IRCA effects, which would include any deterrent effect of employer sanctions. They found that about half of the decrease in apprehensions was attributable to SAW legalizations and about half to other IRCA effects. In other words, about one-fifth to one-fourth of the decline of apprehensions between late 1986 and 1989 was due to IRCA effects other than SAW legalization.

Other research addresses the effect of IRCA on the magnitude of immigration across the US–Mexico border based on other kinds of evidence. One recent study (Bustamante 1990) reported the results of a data collection project that has been following the number and kind of undocumented persons crossing the border at one of its highest traffic points—at Canyon Zapata just outside Tijuana, Mexico, about 20 miles south of San Diego, California. Bustamante's data show a clear decline in the post-IRCA period, with the numbers of crossers in late 1988 falling significantly below the corresponding figures for 1986. Other Mexican data is reported by Wayne Cornelius (1989; 1990), who draws upon 946 interviews conducted in 1988–89 in three communities in the Mexican states of Jalisco, Michoacan, and Zacatecas—states that have traditionally sent migrants to the United States. About 83 per cent of the surveyed undocumented immigrants and potential immigrants thought that IRCA had made getting a job in the United States harder. Furthermore, about 20 per cent of potential immigrants (those who were thinking of going to the United States) gave an IRCA-related reason for not making the trip.

Other research relevant to the question of whether IRCA has had deterrent effects on flows is equivocal. Donato, Durand and Massey (1991) found that IRCA might have lowered the probability of first-time undocumented migration to the United States from communities in Mexico, but they note that other factors could also explain this result. Crane et al. (1990) attempted to find evidence of a decline in the stock and flow of undocumented workers resulting from employer sanctions by examining the change over time in wages of dishwashers and car washers in cities with significant undocumented populations and those without. They concluded that they could find little evidence of an IRCA-related effect on undocumented workers in these occupations.

Evidence About Illegal Stocks

Other studies present evidence that is more relevant to stock than flow assessments. Woodrow and Passel (1990) examined 1980 Census data and a series of CPS (Current Population Survey) data sources from the 1980s (including the June 1988 CPS) in order to estimate the size of the illegal population included in these data sources and its change over time. They found that the undocumented population of the United States declined after IRCA to the point where the total number in 1988 may have been smaller than the number in the country in 1980 (estimated by Passel [1986] to be in the range of 2.5 to 3.5 million). Although they did not find evidence for a decrease in the overall net flow of illegal migrants, their results indicated the possibility of a decline in the flow of undocumented immigrants from Mexico (thus supporting the evidence reported above from apprehensions data regarding flows across the US–Mexico border). In still another study, Warren (1990) developed estimates of visa overstayers in the United States, based on data for two years before the passage of IRCA and two years after IRCA. His research represents the first successful attempt to quantify the number of visa overstayers, an important, but largely unstudied component of illegal migration to the United States. When examined in terms of the number of overstayers per nonimmigrant entry, Warren's data show a decline in the rate of overstays.

In sum, the evidence from all of these research studies is generally consistent in indicating that IRCA brought about a reduction in illegal immigration to the United States during the two years after the legislation was passed. After that, the research suggests that undocumented immigration is again on the rise. To what extent can the reduction that occurred be attributed explicitly to the deterrent effects of employer sanctions? While the legalization programmes accounted for a substantial part of the reduction, they did not account for all of it, suggesting that sanctions might explain the residual (Bean, Passel, Edmonston 1990). However, the fact that the implementation of sanctions occurred gradually over a three-year period, with the INS fully enforcing compliance only in 1989, the third year after the law was passed, suggests otherwise that sanctions may not have accounted for the decline. The greatest reductions took place in the first and second years of the legislation, not during the third year, when sanctions were most strongly enforced. Thus, the decreased flows may have owed less to the deterrent effects of sanctions than to generalized patterns of anxiety and rumour, especially in Mexico, about what the effects of the law might be. Once it was learned that the legislation was not going to lead to draconian outcomes (such as undocumenteds being thrown in jail), the process of undocumented labour migration resumed unabated.

Evidence About Discrimination

If sanctions seem to have had little (lasting) effect on illegal immigration, is it also the case that IRCA seems to have led to little increase in discrimination? In response to fears that sanctions might cause widespread discrimination, the legislation provided for expedited congressional review and possible repeal after three years if the General Accounting Office (GAO) found evidence of widespread discrimination in its third-year evaluation (Fix 1991). This in fact was the conclusion the GAO reached when it issued its report (US General Accounting Office 1990). The evidence that formed the basis for the conclusion that sanctions led to increased discrimination in hiring against ethnic minorities derived primarily from the two studies conducted by the GAO in 1988 and 1989. The studies relied on the self-reported retrospective answers of employers, a significant share of whom revealed that since 1986 they had introduced discriminatory practices on the basis of their understanding of the 1986 immigration law. Specifically, five per cent of respondents reported that, as a result of IRCA, they began a practice of not hiring persons because of their foreign appearance or accent. Eight per cent reported that as a result of IRCA they applied the law's employment verification system only to foreign-looking and sounding persons. Fourteen per cent responded that they began a practice to (1) hire only persons born in the United States or (2) not hire persons with temporary work eligibility because of IRCA (US General Accounting Office 1990). These results were supported by an Urban Institute audit of employers which revealed that Hispanic testers were three times as likely to encounter unfavourable treatment when applying for jobs as were closely matched Anglo auditors (Cross et al. 1990).

Unlike data on sanctions' impact on flows, the basic findings of the GAO have been severely criticized by some scholars and politicians who claim the results carry little weight because no pre-IRCA baseline of discriminatory behaviour exists. As a consequence, it is argued, insufficient evidence exists on which to base a judgement that employer sanctions caused additional discrimination (Teitelbaum 1990). While this argument has merit, it approaches the whole question by assuming initially that discrimination did not increase as a result of sanctions and then seeking evidence to invalidate this assumption. Hispanic minorities, however, perceive the matter in altogether different terms. Hispanics placed the burden of proof on demonstrating that discrimination did not increase. Their approach assumes initially that discrimination increased as a result of IRCA and then seeks evidence that it in fact did not. That there might be some merit in the minorities' initial assumption is evident in the fact that the drafters of IRCA wrote anti-discrimination measures into the law. In any case, for those minority observers approaching the matter from this perspective, the findings of the GAO studies and the Urban Institute hiring audit that discrimination existed (and might have increased as a result of IRCA) provided scant reason for them to question the validity of their initial assumption that discrimination increased as a result of the legislation.

In short, the results of the GAO studies conducted in 1988 and 1989 cross-validate each other. Together with the supporting evidence provided by the Urban Institute hiring audit and the numerous studies of sanctions-related discrimination conducted by other public and private agencies, these results imply that some new discrimination can be tied to IRCA. The fact that the findings of several studies conducted by several different institutions converge around the same result increases confidence in the GAO survey results. Given the vital interests at stake—that is, the right to work and all that flows from it—policymakers may need some affirmative evidence indicating that sanctions are not linked to increased discrimination before they dismiss the results of the GAO study and others.

Put simply, then, it appears that over the first few years of implementation, employer sanctions appear to have had a limited effect in curbing illegal immigration, but they seem likely to have led to some measure of increased discrimination against foreign-looking native minorities. To this point (nearly five years after IRCA was passed), employer sanctions do not appear to have been enforced very effectively (Fix and Hill 1990). Even with uneven levels of enforcement, the danger of increased discrimination appears to have been realized. Recently rumours have emerged that the INS is planning to enforce sanctions more vigorously. If this in fact takes place, it remains to be seen whether the flow of undocumented migrants will be reduced as a result, and also whether any reductions will be accompanied by further increases in discrimination.

THE *IMMIGRATION ACT* OF 1990

The *Immigration Act* of 1990, with the revised *Clean Air Act* and the budget bill, was one of three major legislative packages to pass at the close of the 101st Congress. The most visible features of the legislation that bear on admissions and exclusions include: a cap on legal immigration, increased overall admissions, emphasis on skilled versus unskilled workers, diversity visas, increased family-based immigration, and reduced illegal population.

Cap on Immigration

The bill places a cap on overall immigration to the United States for the first time since the laws of 1921 and 1924. The cap is set at 700 000 for fiscal years 1992–94 and at 675 000 thereafter. However, the cap is 'pierceable' and can be exceeded as early as 1993 (Interpreter Releases 1990). The pierceable cap reflects a political compromise between those interested in restricting immigration and those interested in protecting family reunification. The final version of the law allows an unlimited number of visas for immediate relatives of US citizens (now about 220 000 per year), while at the same time setting a floor of 226 000 visas for other family-based immigration. The overall cap would be exceeded if immediate family admissions were to rise significantly while other family-based admissions reached 226 000. This scenario could occur, for example, if a large number of persons legalizing under IRCA decided to naturalize as soon as they were eligible to do so, and then brought in their parents and other immediate relatives. Finally, entrants admitted as refugees (approximately 131 000 for 1991) are not counted against the cap, nor are those legalizing under IRCA. A second major provision in the bill increases overall admissions. Immigrant admissions can increase from their current level of 492 000 per year to 700 000 during fiscal years 1992 through 1994, and to 675 000 for fiscal years 1995 and later.

Employment-Based Admissions

The number of visas reserved for workers under the new law will increase significantly from its current level of 58 000 per year to 140 000. This number is somewhat misleading, however, and is almost always incompletely reported because the 140 000 figure includes both workers and their families. In fact, if past ratios hold, workers themselves will constitute only about 40 per cent of the total. As a result, the new law will increase the number of new workers by only about 34 000 per year. However, the legislation will change the skill mix of employment-based admissions significantly. The bill reflects a strong bias in favour of professionals and skilled workers as opposed to unskilled workers. Visas for the unskilled category will decline by almost half from current levels and are capped at 10 000 in the new law. The law also authorizes 10 000 visas a year for investors who would employ 10 or more persons and invest more than $1 million. Of these visas, 3000 are set aside for investors in targeted areas with high unemployment; for these investors, the minimum outlay required is $500 000.

Diversity

The *Immigration Act* of 1990 also establishes diversity visas to 'seed' immigration from countries that have sent comparatively few immigrants to the United States in recent years. During fiscal years 1992–94, at least 40 per cent of the diversity visas will be dedicated to Irish applicants—many of whom are expected to be illegal aliens currently working in the United States. Eligibility for one of these 'transitional' visas requires only that the applicant have a firm offer of employment from a US employer. Beginning in fiscal 1995, applicants for diversity visas must have a high school diploma or two years training. Again, national origin will be critical as the 55 000 diversity visas will be made available, using a complicated formula, to countries that have sent comparatively few immigrants.

Family-Based Immigration

The family provisions of the Act are driven by a congressional interest in promoting the nuclear family, by an interest in eventually diversifying the immigrant stream, and by a less-publicized interest in reducing the size of the nation's illegal population. Significantly, the increased number of workers authorized by the bill did not come at the expense of family-based admissions. Family-based admissions, themselves, will be up almost 20 per cent for the first three years under the *Immigration Act* of 1990 and 10 per cent thereafter. A new category of family admissions under the Act is the provision of 55 000 visas per year for three years that go to immediate family members of those legalizing under IRCA's so-called amnesty programmes.

Several changes in the family parts of the new law are particularly significant. Family admissions are 'capped' under the new law at 520 000 for fiscal years 1992–94 and at 480 000 from 1995 on. These caps represent an increase from the current levels of about 435 000 per year for family-based admissions. However, Congress set a floor of 226 000 annual admissions under the preference system. This provision would mean that a sharp rise in admissions of immediate relatives of US citizens would not crowd out entrants under the preference system and could allow family-based admissions to rise above the cap. Permanent residents from countries with long backlogs for visas will now be able to bring in more immediate family members than before. This increase will be achieved by allowing admissions from these countries to exceed the seven per cent per-country of all visas (about 25 000) cap that applies to all family and employment-based admissions. In the short run (i.e., fiscal years 1992 through 1994), this provision will slow efforts to diversify the immigrant stream. Some diversification may occur after backlogs from these sending countries are reduced. The new law also retains a comparatively large number of visas for brothers and sisters of US citizens. This class of visas has been an important vehicle for Asian immigration and can also be seen as slowing efforts to diversify the immigrant stream.

Reducing the Size of the Undocumented Population

Another major feature of the law concerns the undocumented population. First, the bill bars the deportation of, and grants work authorization to, all spouses and children of the 2.5–2.8 million persons who will eventually legalize under IRCA, if the spouses and children were in the United States before 5 May 1988. The numbers in this category could fall in the 350 000 to 500 000 range (Interpreter Releases 1990). Second, as we note above, the bill provides 55 000 visas per year for three years to immediate relatives of persons legalizing under IRCA. Many of these relatives live in the United States, but presumably some of them live abroad.

The bill also offers the temporary protected status of 'safe haven' for a minimum of 18 months for the roughly 350 000 to 500 000 Salvadorans living in the United States. Most of these persons were not eligible for legalization and remain undocumented. Under the safe haven provision, Salvadorans continuously present in the United States since 19 September 1990 must register with the INS between 1 January 1991 and 30 June 1991. Those deemed eligible will have to re-register every six months in order to remain authorized to work in the United States. Finally, the law legalizes at least 16 000 Irish per year for three years under the transitional diversity programme sketched above. Altogether, then, these programmes have the power of changing the legal status and work eligibility of over 1 million persons. In terms of sheer numbers, the legalization and safe haven provisions obviously swamp the 34 000 new skilled workers admitted to the country annually under the bill.

The Overall Thrust of the 1990 Act

On balance, as the above discussion of the major features of the *Immigration Act* of 1990 makes clear, the legislation will have the effect of expanding the amount of immigration coming into the country. Despite this, two of the bill's major features were born of ideas about limits and thus are consistent with restrictionist orientations. One is the cap on overall immigration. Even though this cap can be 'pierced' under certain circumstances, the greatest achievement of the Act for many observers is that a ceiling on immigration has been written into law. The second is the emphasis on skilled immigrants. To a considerable extent this feature of the law grew out of the idea that family reunification criteria had been resulting in more immigrants with lower and lower skills, thus making it harder to strengthen the country's economy in a time of greater global competitiveness (e.g., Borjas 1990; Chiswick 1990). Apart from the extent to which this in fact might be true (see, for example, Bach and Meissner 1990), those who thought this was the case found it politically impossible to reduce family reunification immigration. The fall-back position was to push for increasing the proportion of immigration explicitly based on skills. The result again is the simultaneous presence of, as well as a tension between, both restrictionist and expansionist elements in the law.

THE SIGNIFICANCE OF THE 1986 AND 1990 LAWS

As the years of experience with IRCA continue to accumulate, the evidence seems to mount that the legislation has thus far not been successful in stopping, or even in substantially reducing, the flow of undocumented immigration to the United States. The legalization programmes, on the other hand, can without exaggeration be characterized as very successful (Gonzalez-Baker 1990). The 1990 Act is too recent to have generated experience comparable to that of IRCA, but in many respects its effects can be more easily discerned in the laws' provisions themselves than was the case with the 1986 law. Whereas IRCA relies upon indirect means to try to affect clandestine flows, the 1990 Act stipulates how many and what kinds of persons can legally obtain permanent residence visas. In this sense, its consequences are written into law and it is possible to see what its effects will be on future legal flows. So even at this early date after the passage of the *Immigration Act* of 1990, we can discern its consequences for the amount of legal immigration to the United States, just as we now have enough experience to infer the effects of IRCA on illegal immigration.

Restrictionist tendencies were important in the development of both pieces of legislation. Whereas IRCA was largely an effort to curtail illegal immigration (Bean, Vernez and Keely 1989), the 1990 Act was in considerable measure an attempt to place (under certain circumstances) a cap on the volume of legal immigration and to decrease the fraction of immigration not based on skills criteria. In a certain sense, the impetus behind both reflected a growing concern that national immigration policy in the 1980s was generating new arrivals too numerous and too poorly skilled to best serve the needs of the country in an era of increased global economic competitiveness (Borjas 1990; Chiswick 1990). Although many issues were part of the policy debates leading up to the legislative changes, the driving force behind the policy shifts involved perceptions about the consequences of immigration for the country, including the usually unstated worry that increasing numbers of undocumented and Third World immigrants might be hard for the country to absorb.

Given these concerns, it is somewhat ironic that the changes in immigration policy brought about by the legislation seem likely to foster immigration levels during the 1990s that will surpass those of the 1980s. As noted above, the *Immigration Act* of 1990 leaves virtually intact the family unification provisions of previous law while providing for both increased immigration on the part of persons meeting certain skill criteria and the legalization of sizeable numbers of family members of persons previously legalizing under IRCA. Supplementing family reunification and skills-based entrants will be flows of undocumented migrants that also appear likely to be at least as high as those of the 1980s. Five years after Congress passed IRCA, the evidence indicates that, while the law initially exerted a slight dampening effect on undocumented flows, illegal immigration may now be approaching the high levels characteristic of the years immediately preceding IRCA's enactment (Bean, Passel and Edmonston 1990; Donato, Durand and Massey 1991). Also, undocumented migration among Mexican women and children and Central Americans appears to have increased to even higher levels than those preceding the passage of the legalization (Bean, Espenshade, White and Dymoski 1990).

The conclusion that emerges from these considerations is that the immigration reforms of 1986 and 1990 are expansionist in their effects. Certainly they have not been very disturbing of the status quo up to this point. What started out for many observers as efforts to place restrictions on US illegal and legal immigration ended up as uneasy compromises between restrictionist and expansionist factions (or in some cases between restrictionists and civil libertarians who, less worried about restricting immigration than about how restrictions would be implemented, balked at such proposals as secure verification of employment eligibility for civil libertarian reasons, even though such measures might have reduced some of any increased discrimination resulting from employer sanctions). But in the short run, at least, the compromises appear to have handicapped the effectiveness of restrictionist measures more than they have expansionist ones, with the result that the overall thrust of the policy changes seems to be slightly expansionist in effect, if not in intent.

With efforts now mounting to repeal the employer sanctions provisions of IRCA, the balance of forces behind the political compromises reached in both IRCA and the 1990 Act may find themselves again put to the test. Few US residents believe in open borders; public opinion polls have consistently revealed that popular opinion favours decreasing the number of immigrants who are admitted to the country (Simon 1987). Peter Schuck, a self-professed expansionist when it comes to immigration, notes what he perceives to be an emerging political consensus favouring some growth in immigration levels along with increased use of labour-oriented criteria in determining admissions. He contends that this liberalization of immigration policy is implicitly 'coupled with a demand for stepped up enforcement against illegal aliens' (Schuck 1990, p. 111). His observations are consistent with the Select Commission for Immigration and Refugee Policy's (SCIRP) vision that US immigration policy should be one of 'closing the back door while keeping the front door open' (Fuchs 1990b).

In this view, an essential goal of immigration policy is to create a symbol and perception of commitment to controlling membership within the society. Schuck (1990) writes,

> Americans' demand for limits, I believe, springs from a deeper anxiety ... The master theme of immigration politics is the fear that we are losing control of our way of life. We seek to relieve this anxiety by focusing on things, like immigration, we think we can control. Virtually all participants in the long debates about the 1986 reforms managed to agree on one slogan, continually recited as if it were an incantation: 'We must regain control of our borders.' This slogan was intended to conjure up a memory of a past golden age when we actually exercised control, an age that of course never existed. It also exalted a compelling ideal according to which the nation deliberately chooses whom it wants, excludes those whom it does not want, and sanctions those who violate its rules. The Border Patrol's recent growth testifies to the ideal's evocative force.
>
> Expansionists should not dismiss this popular demand for border enforcement as a macho fantasy about decisive government, impregnable territory, and firm control. Individuals, families and tribes define and defend their turf, not just nations. They may believe, with Frost, that good fences make good neighbours, but Michael Walzer stresses a more potent motive: the same fence that keeps most people out is necessary to enable those within to think of themselves as co-venturers and to flourish as a community. Immigration threatens Americans' sense of control by seeming to jeopardize three fundamental values: national autonomy, economic security, and the 'social contract' that secures the welfare state. Because each of these concerns has some basis in fact, public demands for tougher laws limiting who can enter, work, and claim welfare benefits seem plausible. Past reforms have not succeeded in allaying the public's anxiety.

At the time of IRCA's enactment it remained unclear whether the law would usher in a new restrictive phase in American immigration policy (Bean, Vernez and Keely 1989). Now, in the wake of the enactment of the *Immigration Act* of 1990, which increased overall legal admissions by at least 40 per cent, it seems clear that it did not. Hence IRCA and the 1990 Act may reflect a consensus—at least among law-makers—that tolerates increased admissions as long as the perception of control remains in place. The central control mechanism in IRCA, the employer sanctions, appears to be more symbolic than real in its effects. The chief control mechanism in the 1990 Act, the cap on legal admissions, is also more symbolic than real because the ceiling is 'pierceable' and because overall the Act increases immigration. Thus, both pieces of legislation give the appearance of control while evidently not changing illegal immigration very much (in the case of IRCA) nor holding the line on legal immigration (in the case of the *Immigration Act* of 1990). Thus, the volume and pattern of immigration in the 1990s seems likely to replicate and probably exceed that of the 1980s.

4

NEVER ENDING STORY
THE US DEBATE OVER ILLEGAL IMMIGRATION

Mark J. Miller

Illegal immigration is a relatively new issue in most western democracies, but it has a longer history in the United States. Now largely forgotten, there was a mass deportation of primarily Mexican nationals during the 1930s. In 1954 'Operation Wetback' returned almost one million presumably illegal residents to Mexico at the height of the Bracero Programme, a temporary foreign worker recruitment scheme that brought over five million Mexican nationals to the USA between 1942 and 1964 (Kiser and Kiser 1979, pp. 33–66). In the mid-1970s, public and governmental concern over illegal migration led to the creation of a series of governmental study groups and the Select Commission on Immigration and Refugee Policy (SCIRP) which recommended measures aimed at curbing illegal entry and residency. In Australia, public and governmental concern over illegal migration also mounted during the late 1970s and, by 1982, a series of steps were announced aimed at reducing the alien population residing and/or working illegally in Australia. Subsequently, further steps to curb illegal immigration and employment were announced in 1985 and 1990 (for more details see Birrell, ch. 2 in this book).

A major reason behind recent efforts in the USA and Australia to curb illegal migration is preservation of legal immigration systems based on the rule of law. By definition, illegal migration involves violation of laws, rules and regulations applicable to non-citizens. The Australian and American legal immigration systems differ considerably for historical reasons elucidated elsewhere in this book. Their illegal migration problems and issues also differ widely. Estimates of the illegally resident alien population in the USA ran into the millions, even after the legalizations authorized by the 1986 *Immigration Reform and Control Act* (IRCA). Australian estimates of the illegally resident alien population—about 90 000—dwarf in raw comparison, but less so when taken as a proportion of total population. The greater estimated magnitude of illegal immigration to the USA as compared to Australia undoubtedly has much to do with the contiguity of the former to Mexico and its proximity to the Caribbean and Latin America as contrasted with the geographical isolation of Australia. The insularity and remoteness of Australia testifies to the continuing significance of geographical variables even in the age of the global village.

Understanding how and why Australia and the US have responded to the illegal migration challenge is important for at least three reasons. First, immigration is a significant public policy issue in each society. Understanding immigration is increasingly central to the two societies and to politics in general. Second, in a period of post–cold war restructuring of international politics, both Australia and the US are engaged in a re-examination of strategic and alliance relationships. The high politics of immigration and its link to trade issues in particular renders an accurate understanding of immigration policy issues increasingly central to bilateral relations. On the plane of multilateral engagements, Australia and the US are actors in a plethora of international organizations concerned with international migration issues. Mutual understanding is essential to co-ordination and co-operation between the two within these international organizations. It goes without saying that the effectiveness of international organization responses to the global immigration question will be fraught with consequences for both Australia and the US in the future.

The endeavour here, then, is to elucidate the US response to the shared challenge posed by illegal migration, primarily through analysis of the 1980s debate over IRCA. The debate originated in the 1970s and continues today. Immensely complex, the issue of illegal immigration has been the subject of numerous books, theses and articles, relatively few of which have been of a comparative nature (for Australian legalization procedures, see Birrell, ch. 2 in this book).

THE SCIRP RECOMMENDATIONS

Three issues have dominated the debate over illegal migration: the wisdom of enacting laws which penalize employers who hire aliens not entitled to work (employer sanctions); the appropriateness of offering legal status to illegally resident aliens (legalization); and the desirability of expanded temporary foreign worker recruitment. Border enforcement also has been a key concern and the question of the need for a counterfeit-proof identity document has figured in the debate over employer sanctions. By the late 1970s the US and Australia, along with the United Kingdom and Ireland, differed from the continental European democracies in that they had not enacted laws punishing illegal employment of aliens. Many European democracies had long had such laws, but the growing concern over illegal migration and employment had led to enactment or reinforcement of employer sanctions virtually throughout western Europe (Miller 1987). Canada too had adopted employer sanctions in the 1970s (Robinson 1985, p. 484). In Canada and western Europe, enforcement of employer sanctions was generally weak but not entirely ineffective. Significantly, the UK had opposed a European Community draft directive that called for imposition of employer sanctions. The British did not feel that illegal migration and illegal alien employment were severe enough to warrant the imposition of employer sanctions. Moreover, British citizens, like Australians and Americans, did not possess national identity documents as did most continental Europeans. Therefore, internal controls at places of employment were deemed impractical.

It is frequently alleged that the idea of imposing employer sanctions in the US was (or is) a 1970s European import. Nothing could be further from the truth. Relatively few persons are aware of the history of the employer sanctions concept. It probably did originate on the continent. Employer sanctions were on the books in Weimar Germany and were enacted but apparently never enforced under the Cartel de Gauches Government in inter-war France (Miller 1987, p. 26). It was the Mexican Government, though, that introduced the concept into US immigration policy discussions during the Bracero Programme period (Kiser and Kiser 1979, pp. 89, 99). The Mexican Government was concerned by large-scale illegal recruitment and employment of Mexican nationals outside the procedures stipulated in the Mexican–US labour agreement that authorized bracero employment, particularly in the state of Texas. The Mexican Government saw imposition of employer sanctions as a way to ensure US employer compliance with the terms of the bilateral labour agreement.

Employer sanctions were nearly promulgated in the 1952 *Immigration and Nationality Act* (INA). However, according to one source, a Texas legislator who later would become president, Lyndon Baines Johnson, was able to rewrite the employer sanctions provision of the INA in such a way as to preclude its use against employers of aliens not entitled to work in the US. Thus was created the so-called Texas Proviso of the INA which expressly prohibited punishment of employers who hired aliens ineligible to work in the US. In the UK a law against harbouring aliens is sometimes used to prosecute employers of illegally resident aliens. While some British officials refer to this as a kind of employer sanction, such usage is imprecise. In the US the Texas Proviso forbade similar punishment of employers for harbouring aliens.

By 1972 the liberal Democratic Congressman from New Jersey, Peter Rodino, had introduced legislation calling for enactment of employer sanctions (Eig and Vialet 1985, p. 28). Public concern over illegal migration from Mexico and the Caribbean mounted in the 1970s, in part due to estimates which placed the illegally resident alien population at over 10 million, although the scientific basis of the estimate was questionable (see Bean and Fix, ch. 3 in this book).

Meanwhile, bracero recruitment had been unilaterally terminated by the US Government in 1964. Mexico officially regretted this decision, and powerful agricultural and employer interest groups that had long succeeded in staving off discontinuation of bracero recruitment, which originally had been justified on wartime manpower shortage grounds, lobbied with renewed vigour for a return to Mexican foreign worker recruitment in the 1970s. Their voice was echoed by a number of influential scholars who saw in temporary foreign worker admissions a way to replace illegal foreign workers with legally-admitted foreign workers. A massive temporary foreign worker policy, however, was anathema to organized labour, many church-affiliated organizations and many minority organizations.

The latter tended to favour an amnesty or legalization opportunity for illegally resident aliens. The legalization option was also supported by many who saw it as the only way to right the legacy of de facto toleration of illegal migration and employment by the Federal Government. Still others argued for the option as the only practical step open to the Government short of a disruptive campaign of deportation similar to Operation Wetback which, in the changed political climate of the mid to late 1970s, was inconceivable. The many opponents of legalization saw it as undermining respect for the law and as rewarding law-breakers. Others felt it would encourage even greater illegal entry.

Faced with a barrage of legislative proposals and mounting controversy, the Carter Administration backed the creation of SCIRP. Only once before had a national commission been established to study immigration, the Dillingham Commission whose studies and recommendations paved the way to adoption of the restrictive quota acts of 1920 and 1924. SCIRP consisted of cabinet members, congress members, senators and selected private citizens. It was led by the well-known Catholic priest and university president, the Reverend Theodore Hesburgh. SCIRP's mandate was broad but essentially it was to study and make recommendations concerning illegal migration on the one hand and the legal immigration system on the other. It conducted nation-wide hearings and, after two years of study and deliberation, it reported. Fatefully, these recommendations were communicated to a new president, Ronald Reagan. Concerning illegal migration, SCIRP recommended adoption of employer sanctions, but it did not endorse a national identity card concept. It also supported legalization and 'streamlining,' which is more expeditious administration, of US temporary foreign worker policy, while opposing a massive increase in temporary foreign worker admissions (SCIRP 1981).

THE LEGISLATIVE IMPASSE OF 1981–86

In the autumn of 1981 extensive hearings were held by the US Senate Subcommittee on Immigration and Refugee Policy on various aspects of contemplated legislative initiatives to combat illegal migration. Senator Alan Simpson of Wyoming, who had been a congressional member of SCIRP and who served as chairman of the US Senate Subcommittee, assumed the leading role in a bipartisan effort to introduce and pass legislation reflecting the SCIRP recommendations in the US Senate. Former SCIRP member Romano Mazzoli of Kentucky led a similar effort in the House. Congressman Peter Rodino also continued to play a key leadership role on the contemplated immigration legislation. By 1982 a number of bills pertaining to immigration reform had been introduced in both the House and the Senate, including bills by Senator Simpson and Congressman Mazzoli which expressly sought to translate SCIRP recommendations pertaining to illegal migration into law. The Simpson and Mazzoli bills differed in detail, in some respects significantly so, but both included provisions for employer sanctions and legalization (Eig and Vialet 1985, pp. 32–4). The Senate bill passed by an overwhelming margin in August 1982. It enjoyed bipartisan support partly because it reflected SCIRP recommendations. The bill was also skilfully managed by Senator Simpson.

The relative ease of passage of the immigration reform legislation in the Senate contrasted sharply with its fate in the House, where opposition crystallized to the three major provisions—employer sanctions, legalization and maintenance of small-scale temporary foreign worker recruitment.

As immigration reform stalled in the House, a situation attributable in part to the lukewarm or ambivalent stance of the Reagan administration towards the SCIRP compromise, the momentum and consensus created by SCIRP dissipated. The House of Representatives never took action on immigration reform in 1982. The Mazzoli bill was virtually amended to death. Consequently, when the 98th Congress convened in 1983, immigration reform bills were reintroduced to both houses. The Senate again quickly and overwhelmingly approved legislation, only somewhat modified from that passed in 1982. The House again moved slowly, in part because several major committees considered highly diverse immigration reform-related bills. When the House finally took action in June 1984, the immigration legislation passed by a narrow margin of 216 to 211. A House–Senate conference, however, was unable to resolve differences between the bills adopted by the two chambers, so the legislation expired at the end of the session. When the 99th Congress convened in 1985 the legislation was again introduced to the House and the Senate, but the 1981 to 1984 legislative impasse had demonstrated that the political opposition to SCIRP-inspired immigration reform was so powerful that legislation would only be passed if concessions were made.

Opposition to the employer sanctions provision was led by Hispanic and liberal Congress members. A large number of interest groups generally to the left of the political spectrum or identified with Hispanics, such as the American Civil Liberties Union and the Mexican–American Legal Defense Fund, strongly opposed employer sanctions on the grounds that they would lead to additional discrimination, especially in employment, against Hispanics. A number of employer associations objected to employer sanctions on the grounds that the paperwork involved could be burdensome and that employers should not be involved in immigration law enforcement. Still other individuals and groups opposed employer sanctions on the grounds of administrative infeasibility. A 1982 General Accounting Office (GAO) study concluded that employer sanctions in other countries had not been an effective deterrent to illegal migration. This conclusion was revised in a subsequent GAO report.

Employer sanctions proved to be a particularly divisive issue for Democrats. By the summer of 1984 all three major Democratic candidates for the Presidency announced their opposition to the Simpson–Mazzoli bills on the grounds that the legislation was potentially discriminatory. Even within the normally heavily Democratic Mexican–American voting bloc, however, there was considerable support for immigration reforms. All in all, Hispanics were about evenly divided on employer sanctions. Among Democrats and US voters generally, there was broad support for enactment of employer sanctions.

Opponents of employer sanctions played a key role in stalling House action on immigration reform. To a limited degree, opponents of employer sanctions became objective allies of other antagonists of the SCIRP compromise, most notably the advocates of expanded temporary foreign worker recruitment. Growers of labour-intensive agricultural products, such as fruits and vegetables, concentrated in the Southwestern states and in Florida, have traditionally exerted a great deal of influence upon US temporary foreign worker policy (Kiser and Kiser 1979, pp. 97–120). Associations of growers have been able to mobilize political support that favours agricultural interests in general. Growers associations carry extraordinary political clout as well because they are able to raise large amounts of money available for donations to political campaigns. Despite relatively recent reforms of electoral financing in the US, interest groups are still able to exert political influence through such contributions. Individual growers and grower associations poured money into the campaign war chests of Congressmen from both the major parties who supported expansion of US temporary foreign worker recruitment.

As major economic beneficiaries of a status quo in which illegal migration supplied an abundance of cheap, pliable workers, growers were alarmed about the possible consequences of employer sanctions and legalization. Grower representatives warned of crops rotting in the fields for want of workers to pick them. They claimed an adequate supply of American workers could not be attracted to stoop labour jobs. The spectre of immigration-reform-related adjustment problems extended to prices of land. If the supply of illegal labour were cut off, land prices in labour intensive agricultural areas would plummet. Hence, growers had a major stake in blocking immigration reform based on the SCIRP consensus. In addition to lobbying Congress members, engaging in a public relations campaign against immigration reform that did not accommodate their interests, and contributing to the election campaigns of a good many Congress members, grower interests were also able to colonize key posts in the Reagan Administration, particularly within the Department of Agriculture. A number of Reagan administration officials were growers themselves or closely linked to grower associations. Even supporters of immigration reform increasingly agreed that special measures should be considered to ease the transition for growers dependent on illegal aliens.

After a while the ability of grower interests to block immigration reform made a political compromise with them appear necessary. In June 1984 the House of Representatives voted in favour of an amendment offered by Congressman Leon Panetta of California which provided for the large-scale admission of foreign workers for perishable commodities in Western US agriculture. To supporters of the SCIRP approach, the Panetta amendment represented the victory of narrow economic interests over the national interest and effectively doomed immigration reform as envisaged by SCIRP.

In autumn 1984 a Texas congressional election involving a challenger opposed to legalization attracted national attention. The foe of legalization narrowly lost his bid. But legalization emerged as a political issue in several regions and the perceived political backlash against legalization affected the immigration bills considered by the 99th Congress. Indeed, in introducing legislation co-sponsored by Congressman Mazzoli in 1985, Congressman Rodino specifically warned against a political backlash, which he feared would eventually erode public support for immigration.

Opponents of legalization argued that the measure would only serve to reward law-breakers and encourage additional illegal migration. These objections struck a responsive chord in public opinion. Consequently, when Congressman Rodino introduced his legislation, the cut-off date for eligibility for legalization was set at 1 January 1982—a date which many Congress members believed to be too generous. The original cut-off date proposed in the Simpson bill reintroduced into the Senate in 1985 had been 1 January 1980, but this date became a victim of the legislative impasse over immigration reform. As political opposition to legalization mounted, it became increasingly difficult for supporters of the generous SCIRP legalization programme to advance the eligibility date. The legislative impasse had the effect of rendering the legalization provision increasingly less generous as each year went by. Conservative backers of immigration reform resisted updating the eligibility for legalization date on political as well as administrative grounds. It was widely felt that the programme should not be open to illegal aliens who arrived after 1 January 1982 so as not to reward those individuals who came to the United States with the specific hope of obtaining legal status.

Political opposition to legalization, enactment of employer sanctions and restrictions on recruitment of temporary foreign labour were not the only factors impeding immigration reform, but they were the major concerns. By October 1986 it appeared that attempts to reform US immigration had failed. Only a last-minute compromise on the issue of temporary foreign workers, the so-called Schumer proposal, enabled passage of the legislation. The major innovation of the amendment by Representative Charles Schumer of New York was a provision enabling aliens illegally employed in perishable agriculture to adjust to legal status under special industry-specific rules. The House eventually voted in favour of legalization by the narrowest of margins, and on 6 November 1986 the legislation was signed into law.

MAJOR PROVISIONS OF THE *IMMIGRATION REFORM AND CONTROL ACT* OF 1986

The new law offered legalization to illegally resident aliens who could prove residency before 1 January 1982. If an eligible alien applied and received preliminary approval of the application, work authorization was granted and the alien was not to be deported. Once the application was approved, the alien was granted temporary resident status which, if maintained for 18 months, made the newly legalized person eligible to apply for permanent resident status. As of the 19th month, the successful applicant had one year in which to apply for adjustment to permanent resident status. If the person failed to apply, he or she could lose temporary status, at least in principle. Other conditions which successful applicants had to meet included continuous residency, admissibility as an immigrant, and certain minimal English language skills and knowledge of civics requirements.

Two major groups of illegal aliens benefited from special legalization procedures: Cuban or Haitian nationals who entered before 1 January 1982, and aliens who worked for at least 90 days in seasonal agriculture between 1 May 1985 and 1 May 1986. Of the two special cases, the special agricultural worker (SAW) legalization procedures merits the most attention as controversies over the effects of immigration reform upon seasonal agricultural labour have been intense.

The legalization period for alien agricultural workers was longer than for Cubans and Haitians. It ran from 1 June 1987 through to 30 November 1988. The first 350 000 successful SAW applicants who could prove that they worked at least 90 days in each of the 12-month periods ending on 1 May 1984, 1985 and 1986, benefited from quasi-automatic adjustment to resident alien status by as early as December 1989. Other successful SAW applicants, but who do not number among the 350 000 eligible for adjustment of status on 1 December 1989, became eligible to adjust their status as of 1 December 1990.

Apart from completing a different form and enjoying a longer legalization eligibility period, special agricultural workers had fewer restrictions placed upon them than did aliens legalizing in the major programme. For example, SAWs could travel abroad and commute to work from abroad. They also could apply for adjustment of status from outside the United States. SAWs did not need to remain employed in the agricultural sector. Another special provision in IRCA allowed for so-called replenishment agricultural workers to be admitted over the period 1990 to 1993 in case of a shortage of workers.

Legalization applicants could apply directly to the Immigration and Naturalization Service (INS) or to federally recognized 'qualified designated entities'. An example of a qualified designated entity was the Migration and Refugee Service of the United States Catholic Conference and its diocesan affiliates. A qualified designated entity was authorized to advise an alien on preparation of an application, but all final decisions regarding legalization were made by INS. Applicants were charged a fee of $185 per person or $420 per family. In addition to completing the required forms and paying the fees, applicants had to pass a medical exam, submit evidence of continuous residency since before 1 January 1982 (in the case of non-agricultural workers) and give proof of financial responsibility. Most of the newly legalized aliens were ineligible for state and federal assistance.

As of 6 November 1986 it became unlawful for employers to knowingly hire, recruit or refer for fee any alien who is ineligible to work in the United States. Under IRCA's so-called grandfather clause, however, aliens employed before this date are unaffected by the new law and they may continue to be employed. The new law applies to all employers.

Since 6 November 1986 new employees must attest in writing that they are entitled to work and employers must verify that they have examined documents listed in a new form (called I–9) which establishes a new employee's identity and employment eligibility. This requirement extends to all new employees, not only to immigrants. The employer then is obligated to retain the form for three years after the hiring or for one year after an individual's employment ends, whichever is later. An employer must complete the form within three business days of hiring.

As of 1 June 1987 a year-long first citation period began following a six-month public information period. During the first citation period, employers were not fined for their first violation, although they could be fined for subsequent violations. This first violation grace period ended on 1 June 1988, and thereafter a civil fine of $250 to $2000 per illegally employed alien could be levied for first offences. Second offence fines are $2000 to $5000 per illegal alien and subsequently $3000 to $10 000 per illegal alien. Criminal penalties of up to six months' imprisonment await those employers convicted for 'pattern and practice' violations in addition to fines of $3000 per illegal alien employee detected. Employers who fail to maintain I–9 forms may be fined $100–$1000 per job applicant, even if the applicants are US citizens.

There are some exceptions to these general employer sanctions provisions. Until 1 September 1987 employers were still able to hire aliens who had applied for legalization or who intended to do so. Employer sanctions became effective in the seasonal agricultural services industry only after the end of the legalization application period on 30 November 1988.

Other important IRCA provisions include a prohibition against employment discrimination on the basis of national origin and citizenship status. This prohibition pertains to citizens and to resident aliens, the newly legalized, and refugees and asylees who intend to become US citizens. A special office was created in the Justice Department to investigate and prosecute employers who discriminate. Employers may be forced to rehire aggrieved individuals with back pay and to pay civil fines of up to $2000 for each individual who suffers discrimination. The new law also bolsters the INS's enforcement capabilities and provides for a Systematic Alien Verification for Entitlements which is designed to prevent public assistance disbursements to ineligible alien claimants. Under this new plan, state agencies may check with the INS computer records for eligibility. If an alien's name cannot be verified, the alien is entitled to try to prove his or her eligibility. Benefits cannot be ended during the period given to the non-citizen to establish his or her case.

IMPLEMENTATION OF IRCA: MIXED RESULTS

A move in Congress to extend the legalization period was defeated. Almost two million aliens applied for legal status under the major programme. About 95 per cent of those applicants were approved and are now either temporary residents of the US or permanent resident aliens. It was feared that the rather complex administrative requirements, which included an obligation to attend an English language class, would significantly reduce the number of aliens who applied, and were approved, and who also then went on to become permanent resident aliens. It now seems though that most approved applicants will become permanent resident aliens.

This may not be the case for many applicants to the second major legalization programme—the programme available to alien farm workers. About 1.3 million aliens applied to the SAW programme, however the approval rate in this programme was much lower. Indeed, in the spring of 1991 the US Government was preparing to notify several hundred thousand applicants of the reasons why their applications were refused. Many are suspected to have made fraudulent applications. These aliens will have an opportunity to rebut the INS finding; it may be that many of them will succeed in refuting the Government. A court decision in the Southern District required INS to reconsider tens of thousands of denied SAW applications. The courts have intervened despite the language of IRCA which sought to limit judicial review of the legalization decision. Hence, it is unclear how many of the SAW applicants will eventually become permanent resident aliens. Much will depend on the outcomes of adjudication that could last years. Nonetheless, it is safe to assume that the IRCA legalization programmes will result in about three million aliens becoming permanent resident aliens. Already in Fiscal Year 1989, INS reported over one million admissions of permanent resident aliens. Over 300 000 of those were aliens who legalized under IRCA.

Another reason why it is difficult to supply definitive information on the results of legalization more than two years after the end of the SAW application period is that legalization is still going on for children and spouses of aliens who applied for and were approved for legalization under IRCA provisions, most importantly those of the major programme. IRCA did not include a derivative legalization provision for family members of applicants who also were illegally present in the US but who could not or did not apply for legalization. For some time district commissioners of the INS were empowered to exercise their judgement to grant a kind of temporary, protected legal status to family members out of humanitarian considerations. The *Immigration Act* of 1990 included a 'family fairness' provision which authorized the systematic legalization of spouses and children of legalized aliens. No one knew how many additional aliens would qualify. The low estimate was about 250 000 (Tabraham and Rosenberg 1990, p. 1). Moreover, the 1990 Act authorized a legalization-like policy for certain nationals, primarily from El Salvador.

As for employer sanctions, by September 1989 about 3500 violations for knowingly hiring unauthorized aliens had been detected and notices of intent to fine communicated. Additionally, about 36 000 violations for non-compliance with the paperwork requirements were detected. Total fines assessed were about $17 million and since the coming into force of employer sanctions (September 1987 to September 1989) about 77 000 inspections to verify compliance with the law had been made (GAO 1990, p. 5).

In March 1990 the GAO concluded that a widespread pattern of employment discrimination had resulted from the implementation of sanctions. While this result had been feared, and the GAO finding was hotly contested, the finding set into motion a provision of IRCA which required Congress to review employer sanctions and perhaps eliminate them. The Task Force on IRCA-Related Discrimination was therefore created to study the implementation of sanctions. It reported to Congress in autumn 1990.

The Task Force recommended that the process of employment verification be simplified. Essentially, the idea was to reduce the 17 documents to two; one for aliens and one for citizens and to make them counterfeit-proof (Task Force on IRCA-Related Discrimination 1990, pp. 43–50). The Task Force further recommended that the mechanisms for enforcing anti-discrimination provisions be strengthened, primarily by giving the Office of Special Counsel for Immigration-Related Unfair Employment Practices more enforcement personnel. Third, the Task Force recommended a greater emphasis on education about the 1986 law as many employers who appeared to discriminate simply did not understand the rules. Specifically, some employers fired illegal alien workers who had been hired before November 1986, and some employers did not insist that all new employees fill out the employment verification document. In some cases Caucasians were not asked to supply a document but, 'foreign-looking' new employees were.

Some argue that IRCA was a total failure; others argue that it was a great success. Both assessments seem problematical. IRCA made a difference for the several millon aliens who legalized, and sanctions have deterred others. It is clear that too few personnel are committed to enforcing employer sanctions. The Task Force recommended that the Department of Labour inspectors take a more active role in enforcement. The results of sanctions have disappointed many, but perhaps there was an exaggerated belief in their capacity to reduce illegal immigration and employment. Sanctions often were seen as a one-shot panacea rather than just one part of a long-term, comprehensive effort to curb illegal migration.

Some opponents of IRCA are saying, 'I told you so'. In the early 1990s few remember their role in weakening sanctions by opposing a requirement for a counterfeit-proof employment document. Such a document would have made the employer verification system less subject to fraud and it also would have reduced sanctions-related discrimination.

The disappointing results of IRCA nonetheless clearly were a factor behind the passage of the *Immigration Act* of 1990 and the commencement of the Free Trade Agreement (FTA) talks with Mexico. One of the principal arguments made in support of FTA is that it would promote economic exchanges and economic growth in Mexico that in the long run will reduce the outflow of Mexicans northward.

Employer sanctions, therefore, survived a renewed political challenge in the summer of 1990. By the summer of 1991 another congressional effort to eliminate them was under preparation. Hence, adoption of IRCA by no means ended the debate over sanctions. Nor had the debate over legalization ended. With the likelihood that another commission mandated by IRCA would be recommending expansion of legal temporary foreign worker recruitment when it reported, the US debate over what to do about illegal migration appeared to have progressed little over the decades.

THE *IMMIGRATION ACT* OF 1990: END OF AN ERA IN US IMMIGRATION LAW AND POLICY?

President Bush's decision to sign into law a measure that would increase legal permanent immigration to the US by 35 per cent was clearly linked to the policy conundrum over what to do about illegal immigration, even though the Act itself was mainly concerned with legal immigration. Arguably, signature of the Act brought to closure a quarter-century-long cycle in US immigration law and policy. The onset of the period was defined by the unilateral US decision in 1964 to terminate recruitment of Mexican temporary workers and the adoption in 1965 of amendments to the *Immigration and Nationality Act* which eliminated national origins quotas in legal permanent immigration. Both of these initiatives reflected Lyndon Johnson's Great Society ideals, namely ending discrimination, injustice and poverty. However, the 1965 amendments to the INA for the first time subjected the western hemisphere to the quantitative and qualitative limitations of US immigration laws (Vialet 1980, pp. 23–6). By 1968 Mexican nationals as well as nationals from other western hemispheric states were subject to a hemispheric cap of 120 000 immigration visas per year within what eventually would become a truly global immigration policy. However, unlike immigration from the eastern hemisphere, western hemisphere immigration was not restricted by a 20 000 per country limit. Not until 1976 would western hemispheric immigration be restricted to a maximum of 20 000 visas per year per country, distributed on a first-come, first-serve preference system.

In several respects the 1990 reform appeared incompatible with that of 1965. It is in this sense that a discernible period or cycle in US immigration law came to an end. The IRCA and the 1990 Act were complementary, particularly in that the 1990 law increased the availability of immigration visas to spouses and children of aliens who legalized in 1987 and 1988. As well, both laws meshed generosity with a desire to control and regulate international migration.

For three consecutive years the 1990 law authorizes 55 000 visas for spouses and children of aliens who legalized under the provisions of the IRCA of 1986. IRCA's legalization policy was sharply criticized for failing to provide derivative legal status to immediate family members of applicants for legalization (Sanger 1986, pp. 295–301). However, there was already an enormous backlog of applications from many legally resident aliens for family unification. The adjustment of several hundred thousand legalized aliens to resident alien status will increase demand for visas by those resident aliens who want to bring in their family members from abroad. The additional visas over three years should alleviate the expected backlog.

More significantly, though, the 1990 law signalled a break with the past in that it recognized the significance of international migration in the web of transnational politics and a more interdependent world economy. Here the contrast with the rationale behind the 1965 amendments was stark. Whereas apprehension over rapidly growing populations in nearby Latin America played an important role in the adoption of the 1965 amendments (Vialet 1980, pp. 28–30), the 1990 law was heralded as vindicating the view that increased immigration would promote economic prosperity (Pear 1990). The expanded quotas for highly skilled aliens, in particular, were seen as enabling the United States to compete more effectively in global highly skilled labour markets, and the overall increase in immigration would spur economic growth.

Adoption of the 1990 law clearly reflected the ascendancy of economists who advocate a *laissez-faire* approach to immigration and the clout of the pro-immigration lobbies. The conjunction of the new wind of classical liberalism influencing thinking about international migration policies and the search for a definition of the United States' role in the emerging new world order makes one sense that the past approach to US immigration policy may be eclipsed, although a new approach has not yet been fully articulated (see Bach, ch. 9 and Bean and Fix, ch. 3 in this book).

The recent signing of a free trade agreement with Canada and the announcement in the autumn of 1990 that the Bush Administration hoped to conclude a free trade agreement with Mexico is particularly noteworthy. The IRCA of 1986 authorized the creation of a Commission for the Study of International Migration and Cooperative Economic Development. This commission reported its findings and recommendations in July 1990 (Commission for the Study of International Migration and Cooperative Economic Development 1990). It reached the unsurprising conclusion that the search for economic opportunity was the primary motivation for most unauthorized immigration to the United States and that economic development and the availability of more and better jobs in nearby developing countries such as Mexico was the only way to diminish migratory pressures over time. This was hardly ground-breaking analysis, as a succession of previous governmental task forces and SCIRP had arrived at much the same conclusion. But much has changed since 1980.

The legalization policy and employer sanctions of the 1986 law have only diminished illegal alien residency and employment at best in the face of steadily growing external and internal factors which augment the volume and intractability of the illegal migration phenomenon. More significantly, the international order long dominated by the cold war between the United States and the USSR has collapsed. The progress towards a single European market within an expanded European Community, combined with apprehensions over the future of international trade, access to international markets for American goods, and American economic competitiveness has given a powerful impetus to the creation of a North American free trade area. In the early 1980s, supporters of a North American free trade zone appeared visionary but totally out of touch with political reality.

The Mexican Government would like to see labour included in a free trade agreement with the United States, but the United States has resisted inclusion of labour. A freedom of movement provision similar to Article 48 of the Treaty of Rome would prove to be a 'poison pill' that would weaken, if not kill, US support for a free trade agreement with Mexico. Article 48 allows free movement of labour and portability of industrial and social rights. If applied in North America it would stimulate mass transfers from poor Mexico to rich USA and Canada, thus causing resistance in Canada and the USA. Hence, the US appears to be wagering that the long-term benefits of a free trade agreement should promote job creation in Mexico and a gradual reduction in wage differentials between Mexico and the United States which eventually will reduce migratory pressures.

Immigration control, of course, is only one of several concerns that underlie the initiation of talks with Mexico (Stevenson 1990). The implications of the Bush Administration's diplomatic initiative have yet to be fully grasped in the United States; a battle over the wisdom of signing a free trade agreement is looming on the horizon. By no means should the creation of the US–Mexico free trade zone, which may also include Canada, be regard as a *fait accompli*. However, both the signing of the 1990 law reforming permanent legal immigration and the recent free trade agreement initiatives reveal the outline of a novel approach to regulation of international migration which better recognizes the link between international migration and international relations.

As late as 1986 the US delegation to the OECD's conference on the future of migration sought to decouple North–South issues from a discussion of convergence in immigration problems and issues faced by all industrial democracies. The foreign policy of the Reagan years precluded serious discussion of many pressing issues. Perhaps the 1990 immigration law and the initiation of free trade agreement negotiations with Mexico signal a more pragmatic and reasonable approach to complex issues of interdependency than witnessed in the Reagan years.

During the 1980s about 6.3 million persons were granted permanent residency in the United States. In the first decade of this century, 8.8 million immigrants were admitted. But the average annual number of immigrants admitted from 1980 to 1989 was 2.7 immigrants per thousand US residents as compared to 10.4 per thousand from 1900 to 1910. Thus, the annual immigration rate was about four times higher during the 1900 to 1910 period (1989 Statistical Yearbook of the Immigration and Naturalization Service 1990). Immigration is once again recasting the ethnic, racial and cultural composition of the United States, and the 1990 legislation would suggest that this process will accelerate. The capacity of the United States to absorb and integrate immigrants has thus far not shown serious signs of weakening, although most Americans clearly want to reduce immigration, particularly illegal migration.

Immigration issues loom as key foreign and domestic policy concerns in the 1990s in the United States no less than elsewhere. Yet one suspects that by its history and traditions the US is better equipped to meet the challenge of regulating international migration than many other states. Such modest optimism, however, is muted by awareness of the long history of nativist reaction to immigration to the US. As immigration reshapes the US into an increasingly multicultural society, a broader debate may ensue on the wisdom of high levels of immigration, on political and cultural grounds in addition to economic grounds. From a historical and comparative viewpoint, the 1990 law was, above all, remarkable for the narrowness of the criteria pertinent to the debate over its wisdom, which were chiefly economic, even though foreign policy concerns also appeared to facilitate its adoption.

5

THE POLITICS OF INTERESTS AND IMMIGRATION POLICYMAKING IN AUSTRALIA AND THE UNITED STATES

Gary P. Freeman and Katharine Betts

The politics of immigration are shaped by the ways in which issues are defined and options delineated, by the institutions and actors who formally make policy decisions, and the pressures that are brought to bear on them. This chapter seeks to assess the relative contribution of each of these factors to immigration policy outcomes.

AUSTRALIA

Australian-born people who are now aged 50 or more grew up in a society that was not characterized by mass immigration and where the non-English-speaking foreigner was a rarity. While the phrase 'country of immigrants' is used to describe Australia, it does not strike the same chords there as in the United States; the early history of homogeneity means that Australia has not been used to taking pride in being 'a universal nation'. Attempts to define immigration as part of a new multicultural identity for Australia are not generally well received.

Post-war immigration was first presented as a question of defence and of labour for reconstruction, and it enjoyed bipartisan political support throughout the high migration years of the 1950s aand 1960s. In the early 1970s a Labor Government led by Gough Whitlam cut the intake sharply, but with the return of the conservatives in 1975 the programme began to grow again. When a Federal Labor government was elected under Bob Hawke in 1983, the number of immigrants contracted briefly, but after 1984 the intake continued to grow, reaching net figures higher than those of the long recruitment drive in the 1950s and 1960s. However, though bipartisanship had been re-established, conditions in the 1980s were unlike those of the earlier immigration boom and, with continuing unemployment, there was a stronger need to make a case for immigration.

The old economic justification was now used more forcefully, with advocates claiming that more migrants would increase national wealth and decrease unemployment. This argument could have helped to allay some fears, were it not for the fact that it was soon joined by a new way of defining the intake, a way that had no immediate appeal to people anxious about jobs and housing in tougher economic circumstances. In this new explanation, immigration was to be a means, not of meeting Australians' own needs for defence or economic growth, but of expressing humanitarian, internationalist and anti-racist values and, in so doing, meeting other people's needs.

This new definition of the immigration programme can, for convenience, be called 'altruistic'. It was not deliberately fostered by the politicians and officials responsible for immigration; they held to the economic rationale. Rather it was promoted by lobby groups arguing the case for refugees, initially from Indo-China, and by migrant interest groups pressing for extended family reunion. It was strongly articulated for the first time in the late 1970s, but its roots go back to the 1950s and it appeals to a social constituency among the local Australian intelligentsia broader than that of ethnic leaders and refugee activists alone. By the late 1980s the intake, in per capita terms, was two or three times larger than either the US or Canadian intake (Young 1989), and opinion polls showed that it was increasingly unpopular. But bipartisanship among political élites, reinforced by intellectuals' enthusiasm for the altruistic definition, helped insulate growth policies from serious criticism.

Why should the new altruistic definition of immigration have met with widespread support, active and tacit, among the intelligentsia? The altruistic definition appealed to strongly held values acquired by many intellectuals during their formative years. Internationalism, anti-racism, and anti-colonialism—all burning issues on the campuses in the 1950s and 1960s—were readily transferred to the immigration programme in the 1970s (Betts 1988, pp. 81–3, 102, 112–13).

A broader explanation for the altruistic definition's attraction for tertiary educated people should take account of their social location. Many of the Australian intellectuals who are now influential in academia and public life are first-generation tertiary educated. Commitment to cosmopolitan values has helped to mark these new professionals as a distinctive group that has rejected not only the identity associated with their working and lower-middle-class backgrounds, which they saw as boring, parochial, and suburban, but also the traditional values of the British-oriented establishment, which was tainted by British colonialism, racist immigration policies, and the Vietnam War. Cosmopolitanism was congruent with the altruistic definition of immigration, and became more so as immigration was increasingly coupled with multicultural settlement policies.

The themes of immigration for altruistic reasons or immigration for economic growth are central to the way in which the topic is currently debated, but the domestic and foreign policy framework is also relevant in Australia. From the beginning of European settlement Australians have been worried about defence, especially defence against the populous Asian countries to the north: the original thinking about immigration (and fertility), encapsulated in the nineteenth-century slogan 'populate or perish', was necessarily set in a foreign policy framework. During the late 1950s and 1960s, reformers claiming that the White Australia Policy was an 'international stigma' tried hard to make rather different connections between foreign policy and immigration (see Immigration Reform Group 1962, p. viii; Palfreeman 1975, p. 353); good relations with neighbours, as well as basic morality, demanded not large numbers of patriotic Australians to guard the coast, but a race-blind immigration programme.

With the Indo-Chinese refugee crisis, and the independent arrival of some refugee boats in northern Australia, the emphasis shifted from stigma and symbolism back to harder realities, and a new formulation of the old defence argument acquired some currency. This held that Australians must share their continent by way of a generous migration policy, and show that they were doing so, because of the defence risks they faced and because sharing and altruism could work as an effective defence strategy. Morality could serve as a form of defence, disarming hostility by correct behaviour, but, if Australians were 'selfish', others would come and force them to share their country anyway (Zubrzycki 1978, p. 2). This new version of the defence argument, like the old version, rests on shaky empirical grounds (Betts 1988: pp. 20–2), but, unlike the old version, with its imagery of Asian hordes and the need to repel them with brute force, it works well with the anti-racist, internationalist definition of immigration.

In the 1980s Asian immigration was re-interpreted again: it should be encouraged, not to forestall any putative defence threat, but to help strengthen trading ties with the fast-growing economies to the north. For some commentators the argument for Asian immigration now rested, not on a moral obligation to share with the poor, but on an economic need to try to forge stronger links with the rich. In the words of the Garnaut Report, 'Migration has a pivotal role to play in helping Australia to get maximum benefit from the growth of East Asia' (1989, p. 300). The argument that Australia needs a close relationship with Asia is well established with the 'economic rationalists', a loose coalition of politicians, bureaucrats, academics and private sector economists influential on both sides of Parliament House. They are committed to free trade, deregulated markets, and a residual social welfare system.

The robustness of the altruistic definition presents a problem for élites trying to re-establish an economic focus for the programme. If they succeed they will lose a key set of justifications for immigration which work well with the new professional middle class and ethnic community leaders. If they do not succeed they face a growing legitimation problem with the economic rationalists and with the general public, whose dissatisfaction with immigration has increased in the face of both rising numbers and the strength of altruistic rhetoric. The economic definition at least takes the people's anxieties seriously; the language of altruism dismisses them as nothing but irritating symptoms of incurable racist and parochial tendencies. Élites responsible for the programme also need the economic justification to shore up arguments that immigration is pulling its weight in restructuring the economy, and thus convince the economic rationalists that it is worth supporting.

THE INSTITUTIONAL CONTEXT

Immigration to Australia is governed by federal law. For most of the post-war period the relevant piece of legislation has been the *Migration Act* of 1958, a lightly revised version of the *Immigration Restriction Act* of 1901, which assigned considerable discretion over admissions to the Minister for Immigration. This discretion gave Cabinet and the Department of Immigration the capacity to take steps to vary the size of the intake, and the nature of the selection procedures, without necessarily having to submit these changes to Parliament. This discretion has been used, as for example in modifying the White Australia Policy in 1966, to change policy without exciting public discussion or protest.

For most of the time the main players have been the Minister, Cabinet, and, apart from a brief interlude in 1974 and 1975, the Immigration Department itself, now the Department of Immigration, Local Government and Ethnic Affairs (DILGEA). The Department has been a key source of migration policy for almost all of the post-war period. The principle of ministerial discretion might seem to give the political incumbent paramount influence but, in fact, relatively frequent ministerial changes militate against this. For example, there have been 13 different Ministers for Immigration between 1973 and 1991: three under Whitlam, three under Fraser, and six under Hawke.

Apart from New Zealanders, who have virtually automatic right of entry, the current programme is divided into three streams: family, economic and humanitarian migration, which includes refugees. All three streams are administered by DILGEA. Until recently, the humanitarian stream was made up of two categories: refugees and the Special Humanitarian Program (SHP) for refugees who did not meet the specific criteria provided by the Geneva Convention. It acquired a third category in April 1991, the Special Assistance category, which will facilitate entry for Soviet Jews and other groups who do not meet the stricter guidelines applied to the new humanitarian programmes (see Hartcher 1991; and Birrell, ch. 2 in this book).

Since 1981 the basic policy making structure of Cabinet, Minister for Immigration, and Department of Immigration, has been modified by the growing role of the courts, particularly the Federal Court. This has provided a means of appeal for Australian residents disappointed in their attempts to sponsor family members overseas, but its main influence has been on people who are already in Australia either on temporary visas, or illegally, and who wish to apply for change of status to permanent resident, a procedure called grant-of-resident status. Like the onshore asylum seekers this category of onshore would-be migrants was once tiny but has grown rapidly.

Birrell describes the way in which the Department's attempts to cope with growing numbers of onshore applicants met with reversals in the Federal Court (see ch. 2). In consequence, the Government decided on a more thorough review of the 1958 Act, and the *Migration Legislation Amendment Act* was passed in June 1989. The key change that the new Act introduced was that selection procedures, including the procedures governing grant-of-resident status, were set out in explicit, legal regulations, almost eliminating the old principle of ministerial discretion. A new, two-tier system of review of immigration decisions was also introduced, the first tier being the Migration Internal Review Office, an autonomous organization within the Department, and the second the Immigration Review Tribunal, which is a statutory body independent of the Department (Review 90 1990, pp. 63–4, 21).

Whether the new Act and the end of ministerial discretion will return control of policy to the traditional institutions remains to be seen. Dr Andrew Theophanous, Chair of the Joint Standing Parliamentary Committee on the new immigration regulations, is keen to restore as much ministerial discretion as possible (Theophanous 1991). This reflects anxiety on the part of some ethnic leaders that lack of discretion for the Minister means lack of influence for lobbyists. One journalist reports that when Gerry Hand succeeded Robert Ray as Minister in 1990, he received a letter from Hawke saying, 'Do not hesitate to replace the regulations so that there may be more discretion' (Hartcher 1991).

Moreover, discretion is a part of the new Special Assistance Category introduced in 1991, and the Minister retains discretion over onshore applications for temporary residence on humanitarian grounds. In contrast, the Immigration Review Tribunal creates an important new agency with a capacity to affect policy that is outside the ambit of the Minister and the Department. The Joint Standing Parliamentary Committee may also become more influential. Not only has the legality of individual decisions come under closer scrutiny, the law itself is being more closely monitored. The outcome of the changes of the 1980s will depend partly on the way in which the new institutional structure develops and partly on the strength of the interest groups that are concerned with immigration.

POLITICAL PRESSURES

The interest groups arguing for a larger migrant intake are divided into two camps mobilized around either economic growth or altruism. The family reunion lobby and refugee activists use the language of duty, moral obligation, philanthropy and multiculturalism, though they may add the claim that 'altruism' has economic benefits. In contrast, the politicians and bureaucrats more directly responsible for running the programme prefer to speak of GDP, skills in demand, economies of scale and job creation.

The 'altruistic' coalition has a relatively broad social base among the Australian intelligentsia, but the 'economic' coalition also has a range of supporters, numerically not as large, but potentially influential. Its origins lie within the earlier post-war growth lobby, active since the 1950s. This lobby consisted of business interests oriented towards the domestic market, especially in investing and speculating in land, housing and other forms of urban development, and some employers looking for cheaper labour, skilled or unskilled (see Birrell and Birrell 1978 and 1987). It is still active today through bodies such as the Housing Industry Association, but the new focus on 'economic rationalism' and the need to enhance Australian exports has added different overtones to these old pressures. The old growth-of-the-domestic-market lobby was uninterested in exports, but it can accommodate the new arguments by emphasizing skilled immigration, and the economic coalition now strongly favours skilled migrants and people with capital to invest.

The concept of a 'balanced' programme, where it is argued that an increase in family reunion migrants or refugees must be complemented by an increase in skilled migrants, or vice versa, underpins a growing intake and means that both camps can be satisfied. The two sets of interests provide the pressures that result in substantial numbers of new migrants and they help to explain why growth policies are unopposed by the major parties. Though the ethnic rights lobby and the refugee activists have stronger ties with the Labor Party and the traditional growth-of-the-domestic-market lobby has been closer to the Liberal–National parties, these two interest groups bear on Government and Opposition alike. Both sides of the House are affected by the economic rationalists with their 'closer links with Asia' argument. Though political bipartisanship is becoming rather more fragile, the immediate background to today's political bipartisanship can be understood in these terms (see Betts 1988, pp. 120–40, 168–75).

The June 1988 FitzGerald Report on immigration policy recommended that immigration should be increased and given a tighter economic focus, that extended family reunion migrants should not be given special privileges, but should compete for places on the same basis as independents, that selection criteria should emphasize English language skills and that, in an attempt to increase public acceptance of immigration, multiculturalism might be abandoned. The report offended ethnic leaders, and the Federation of Ethnic Communities' Councils (FECCA) organized a conference in July 1988 to respond to it. They then established the 'National Immigration Forum' to monitor policy.

The Hawke Government distanced itself from many of the FitzGerald Report's recommendations. The Opposition, in contrast, welcomed them. Its leader, John Howard, endorsed the recommendations on multiculturalism by talking of the need to think in terms of 'one Australia', and he also asserted the right of the Australian people to alter selection criteria as they wished in order to preserve social cohesion. In the debate that followed Howard was seen both as an opponent of existing ethnic interests and as a politician who wished to impose some kind of unspecified limit on the Asian component of the intake (Birrell and Betts 1988). His contribution to the debate, and the storm of protests about racism that it provoked, increased ethnic sensitivities about discrimination, and in December 1988 Howard was hissed and heckled when he addressed the FECCA national congress (*Age* 2 Dec. 1988, p. 3).

The FitzGerald recommendations on family reunion, English, and multiculturalism were not adopted by the Hawke Government, and Howard lost the leadership of his party and the Opposition. The then Minister for Immigration, Senator Robert Ray, favoured FitzGerald's recommendations on extended family reunion, but could not convince the Caucus Immigration Committee. After 22 committee meetings Andrew Theophanous, as chairman of the committee, was invited to put his case to Cabinet. He convinced Cabinet that the family stream should be kept separate from the economic stream, that 50 per cent of the places should be reserved for family reunion, and that extended family applicants should not be assessed for English language skills (Theophanous 1991).

The FitzGerald Report had constituted one attempt to reassert the economic definition of the programme, the 1989 Act was another. Together with some immigration lawyers, ethnic leaders claimed that the regulations under the Act had been drawn up in secret and without consultation, and that they were harsh, insensitive and discriminatory (*Age* 2 February 1990; *Age* 16 March 1990, p. 13). The then Minister, Senator Ray, and his departmental head, Ron Brown, were widely criticized for their part in their genesis. After the federal election in March 1990, Ray moved to the Defence portfolio and Brown was forced to resign; the request for his resignation was brought to him, apparently quite unexpectedly, by Mike Codd, the Secretary of the Department of Prime Minister and Cabinet. In the words of one journalist he was 'king hit' in a 'move of clinical precision' (Sheridan 1990; Hartcher 1991). Brown's departure was widely interpreted as a response to ethnic pressure groups working through the Office of Multicultural Affairs (OMA) and the Department of Prime Minister and Cabinet.

Whether the 'ethnic coup' within DILGEA and the change of Minister and departmental head are sufficient to lead to the ascendency of the altruistic definition within the Department itself is an open question. Certainly the Department has been under strong pressure both from growing numbers of onshore applicants, often backed by the courts, and the creation of the new 'special assistance category' suggests that the altruistic camp has scored a victory. It is also true that many politicians feel they are under heavy pressure from ethnic lobbyists (see O'Reilly 1988, p. 68, and 1990, p. 34; Jenkins 1990, p. 17; Hartcher 1991).

THE UNITED STATES

Americans are much more likely than Australians to think of themselves as an immigrant people in whose history immigration has played a glorious part. Few motifs resonate more deeply in the collective psyche than the idea of the United States as a land of opportunity for the poor and oppressed of the world (Handlin 1951). Remaining true to this commitment is one of the principal justifications for having a generous immigration policy. Continuing immigration is one means to validate America's existence. Indeed, in the USA the burden of proof is always on those who argue against mass immigration, as the nation's identity seems to make continuing large intakes a self-evidently desirable policy.

Americans are uncomfortable with justifying immigration in strictly economic terms. Although there is an ambiguous consensus that immigration has contributed significantly to the expansion of American wealth, support for immigration typically wanes during recessions and immigration policy is poorly designed to serve economic goals. Policy is formulated by the Congress, an institution ill-equipped to direct economic policy and poorly motivated to use immigration towards that end. Moreover, the numbers to be admitted annually in various categories, with the exception of refugees, are spelled out in laws that remain on the books for years and are cumbersome to amend. The executive cannot, like the Australian cabinet, change immigration ceilings annually. Nor can it assume that the legislature will approve its recommendations.

If immigration has not been notably integrated into national economic policymaking, it has been tightly linked to the labour needs of American agriculture, as we shall show. The success of growers in protecting their access to migrant farm workers suggests that when a well-organized economic interest is strongly affected by immigration, it can bend policy to its ends. At the level of national policy, however, the economic consequences of immigration are too small to generate support for any particular set of economically oriented changes in the law (see chs 6 and 7 in this book).

The Civil Rights Movement has arguably been more important than economic issues (see DeSipio and de la Garza, ch. 12 in this book). It is no accident that the 1965 amendments to American immigration law removing the national origins quota system, and hence discrimination on account of ethnicity and race, came at the same time as the passage of landmark civil rights and voting rights acts. Once having confronted the inadmissibility of racial distinctions in the treatment of citizens, it was a small step to the argument that they were inadmissible in the treatment of immigrants as well (Bach 1990, p. 142; Fuchs 1990b, p. 254).

Policy towards prospective immigrants and refugees has been deeply affected by the more general expansion of the language of rights in American politics in the last three decades. An activist legal profession and judiciary have vigorously advocated the rights of all sorts of claimants against official decisions. Advocacy groups, committed to an immigration policy based on the pursuit of the same ideals of humanitarianism and social justice that animate many Australian supporters of mass immigration, have filed numerous lawsuits on behalf of recent immigrants, legal or not, and have generally succeeded in defining immigration policy controversies as matters of constitutional interpretation rather than political choices (Hollifield forthcoming).

Those who make American immigration policy have traditionally paid little heed to its international ramifications. The only significant exception is that refugee policy, over which the executive has considerable authority, has been subordinate to national security objectives, at times being little more than an adjunct to the fight against communism. As the international stature of the USA has grown, and as the world economy has become more interdependent, domestic factors may be losing their hegemony. In 1982 the Council on Foreign Relations, an influential private body, established a study group on the interaction between foreign policy objectives and immigration policy (Teitelbaum 1985). A recent review of the same subject concludes that unilateralism in immigration decisionmaking has begun to change since the early 1960s (Tucker 1990, p. 2), in part in response to direct attempts by the Mexican government to influence immigration policy reform (Glazer 1990).

THE INSTITUTIONAL CONTEXT

Congressional dominance has given immigration policy a patchwork character rooted in the negotiation and compromise of legislative decisionmaking. Given the highly decentralized structure of the Congress, effective authority has been lodged in the immigration subcommittees of the House and Senate judiciary committees. The Judiciary subcommittees enjoy jurisdiction over immigration, rather than those of the labour or foreign relations committees, because the immigration bureaucracy is housed in the Justice Department.

But the Justice Department does not enjoy a monopoly over immigration matters. Within the executive branch, six separate agencies exercise legal authority over some aspect of immigration policy. This administrative balkanization contrasts sharply with the centralized bureaucracy that oversees Australian policy. The chief agency responsible for implementation of immigration law in the US is the Immigration and Naturalization Service (INS). The INS grew out of the Bureau of Immigration which was established by the *Immigration Act* of 1891 and was originally located in the Treasury. Its present location in the Justice Department underscores its law enforcement orientation (Morris 1985). Its lowly status is indicated by the fact that the Commissioner of Immigration who heads the INS is not a Cabinet officer and does not even report directly to the Attorney-General. The INS is chronically understaffed and underfunded, its record-keeping and computer facilities outdated.

A long pattern of incompetence and confusion over its objectives has eroded congressional confidence in the agency. Some critics complain that the Department has emphasized law enforcement to the detriment of delivery of services. As it stands, the agency does neither task very well. The Border Patrol is located in the INS and its plight is perhaps symptomatic of the larger problem. With a tiny budget and staff, it is given the responsibility to control illegal entry along thousands of kilometres of unfenced borders and numerous points of entry by air and sea. Attempts at strict control of the border have often met with swift public outcries, despite apparent public concern over undocumented aliens.

The courts have increasingly hampered enforcement efforts. Since 1968 INS activities have been subjected to more extensive scrutiny under the Fourth Amendment prohibition against arbitrary searches and seizures (Morris 1985, p. 116). The courts have held, for example, that agents who restrain an individual with physical force have made a 'seizure' and brought the Fourth Amendment into play. In 1973 they ruled that roving vehicular searches were unreasonable, but in 1975 upheld brief vehicular stops based on reasonable suspicion. Since 1977 the courts have held that a person must be considered 'detained', and hence reasonable suspicion is required, even if he or she is free to walk away. Warrants are necessary to raid workplaces. All these decisions have made the work of the agency more difficult, especially in the interior. With certain episodic and limited exceptions, there is little support in the USA either among the public or the politicians for the strict enforcement of the immigration laws, at least not in particular instances. The shabby condition of the INS is the more or less predictable outcome of this ambivalence (Harwood 1986).

The predominant motif of contemporary immigration policymaking has been the struggle between the executive (in the form of the President and the State Department) and legislative branches of Government. Presidents have been concerned that the laws being enacted by Congress were detrimental to US foreign policy interests. Presidents have been, in this sense, more liberal in their immigration outlook, pushing for a more generous and internationalist policy. They have fought discriminatory aspects of selection criteria likely to offend foreign leaders. The executive has been responsible for closely linking refugee policy, over which it has had much more influence, to foreign policy objectives, as noted above.

Presidential vetoes have not altered the basic contours of US immigration law, but an obscure administrative tool, the parole power, has. A minor provision in the *McCarran–Walter Act* of 1952 gave the Attorney-General discretionary authority to parole any alien into the United States in an emergency or if it was 'deemed strictly in the public interest'. This provision passed the Congress only because it was thought to serve cold war interests in individual cases, but it has emerged as a central measure of immigration policy used repeatedly by presidents to usurp control of policy from Congress. Successive presidents turned the parole power into a makeshift refugee policy before a formal programme was finally adopted in 1980. The first refugees to benefit *en masse* from the procedure were Hungarians in the late 1950s. The practice became so institutionalized that, on the signing of the 1965 *Immigration Act*, which introduced controls over western hemisphere immigration for the first time, President Johnson announced that he would use the parole power to admit anyone from Cuba who sought admission (Zolberg 1990a, p. 111). Parole was also the means by which the vast majority of Vietnamese refugees entered the United States (Zolberg 1990a, p. 112). Altogether over one million refugees have benefited from this unilateral procedure. The Congress tacitly sanctioned its use by voting for funds to support refugees admitted by parole (Reimers 1985, p. 245).

POLITICAL PRESSURES

Congress ultimately makes immigration policy, but it receives a great deal of advice, solicited and not, along the way. The road to the 1921 and 1924 national origins quota bills was paved in part by the work of a commission set up by Congress in 1906. It met for three years and issued a 42-volume report highly critical of the qualities of recent immigrants. In the run-up to the passage of the 1986 *Immigration Reform and Control Act* (IRCA), a Select Commission on Immigration and Refugee Policy (SCIRP) was established by President Carter (Select Commission on Immigration and Refugee Policy, US Immigration Policy and the National Interest 1981). The IRCA itself called for the creation of an additional commission to explore the relationship between the economic development of the sending countries and undocumented migration to the USA. SCIRP helped shape the response to undocumented workers, serving as a forum for the drive for an amnesty programme (Zolberg 1990b, p. 322). It is too early to know if the recommendations of the commission on economic development will have any impact on Congress (Unauthorized Migration: An Economic Development Response 1990).

Although policy is strongly related to domestic political considerations, it has not responded in any direct way to tides of public opinion or electoral expression. One student of immigration politics in the nineteenth century discusses the 'paradox' that though there was strong protest against immigration from the early 1830s to the Civil War in 1860, not one piece of legislation to restrict immigration ever came to a vote in Congress (Calavita 1984, p. ix). Polls today consistently show that the public does not favour larger numbers of immigrants, even while expressing general support for immigration. Yet Congress substantially increased the annual intake in 1990. Immigration has not been a major electoral issue nationally. This predisposes Congress to respond to organized interests rather than the public.

Political parties have not been important as organizers of the electorate or as formulators of distinctive positions on immigration. This is not because, as in certain western countries (including Australia), the leadership of the parties has taken an explicit decision to exclude conflict over immigration from the political agenda, but because of the non-programmatic character of parties in the USA. It is a measure of the consensus on immigration that Republicans and Democrats agree on the desirability of large numbers, and immigration reforms are often the result of cross-party alliances.

Immigration politics is more strongly affected by the activities of highly organized interest groups than by the parties. We will consider three major types: economic, ethnic, and issue or ideological groups.

Employers have at times actively recruited workers abroad and they have lobbied Congress for favourable legislation. The National Chamber of Commerce opposed early versions of Simpson–Mazzoli in the

1980s because they included employer sanctions, but came around to supporting IRCA in 1986 because it was the best bill that could be passed (Zolberg 1990b, p. 327). Employers' associations were influential players in the drive for the 1990 amendments to the immigration law, amendments that markedly increased the numbers of legal immigrants, gave added emphasis to the skills category, and created a business immigrant slot (for details see Bean and Fix, ch. 3 in this book). Robert Bach argues that the dominant coalition currently favouring expansive immigration policies is an odd mixture of organized business and its political spokespersons and liberals who support immigration out of humanitarian commitments and more mundane ethnic interest group politics (ch. 9).

Agribusiness has long played a crucial role in immigration policy. IRCA contained special provisions for farm workers as a consequence of intense lobbying by growers' representatives. The so-called SAWS provision, the temporary worker programme for agricultural workers, the arrangement for 'replenishment workers' in case of a shortage of agricultural workers, and the prohibition of INS searches of the fields without a warrant or the owner's consent are discussed in detail by Miller (ch. 4). Growers were well organized and funded and played a significant role in changing the initial provisions of Simpson–Mazzoli (for a detailed overview, see Zolberg 1990b, pp. 324–5; Bean et al. 1989, p. 30).

Organized labour has been less successful, though not without clout. When the 1965 immigration reform enshrined family reunification as the predominant criterion for admission, rejecting the alternative of labour qualifications, it was generally seen as a victory for the trade unions. Moreover, labour won in its effort to exclude immigrants coming to work if there were sufficient citizen residents already available to fill the position. Hence, the Office of Labor Certification in the Labor Department must certify that no qualified American workers are available before individuals can obtain work visas. When the Bracero Programme was abolished in 1965 it was the realization of a long-standing labour objective (on this general subject, see Briggs 1984).

The most important ethnic interest groups actively concerned about immigration are Mexican Americans and Cubans—Asians having not yet organized effectively. Mexican Americans, and Hispanics generally, had no visible national organizations until the Ford Foundation subsidized the creation of the Mexican American Legal Defense and Education Fund (MALDEF), which has become the leading Hispanic civil rights organization (Chavez 1990, p. 15). Other important groups include the League of United Latin American Citizens (LULAC), the National Association of Latino Elected and Appointed Officials (NALEO), the American GI Forum, and the National Council of La Raza.

Mexican Americans are divided over the immigration issue in part because the community is split between native Americans and immigrants (de la Garza 1985). In 1960, 85 per cent of the Mexican-origin population was US-born. In 1990 over half were either immigrants or the children of immigrants (Chavez 1990, p. 16). A disparity exists between leaders and rank and file over immigration, but surveys show that various positions on immigration policy evoke about half positive and half negative responses from the general Mexican American community.

Mexican American élites ended up strongly opposing IRCA primarily because they feared that employer sanctions might heighten discrimination against all Hispanics, regardless of their legal status. Mexican American leaders also opposed the procedures used in the amnesty programme. As MALDEF put it, it was 'a disguise for a whole new series of raids into the undocumented community' (quoted in de la Garza 1985, p. 104). The Mexican American Congressional Caucus was deeply opposed to Simpson–Mazzoli and it is an interesting question why these elected leaders took such pro-immigration views in the face of indifference or opposition from their Mexican American electorates (see the survey results reported in de la Garza 1985, 1982; Miller et al. 1984; and in Reimers 1985, pp. 236–7). The extent to which the treatment of undocumented aliens from Mexico had become a civil rights issue may be part of the answer.

Black American interest groups are critical of immigration policies because they have been coalition partners with Hispanics. The position of Blacks on immigration matters has changed dramatically in the last 30 years. From about 1860 to 1960, Blacks were opposed to immigration, seeing it as directly threatening Black employment and resenting what they perceived as the preferential treatment and more rapid economic success of immigrants (Fuchs 1990a). This antagonistic stance was more or less completely reversed in the 1960s for the Black leadership class; ordinary Blacks (and Hispanics as well) remained either hostile or indifferent towards immigration. Nonetheless, 'national black leaders expressed sympathy with refugees, made no effort to restrict lawful immigration, and by 1984 actually gave strong support to Mexican–American groups in opposing legislation to curtail illegal immigration' (Fuchs 1990a, p. 296).

Philosophically predisposed to defend refugees and immigrants, Black political leaders found much more concrete reasons to do so in their growing efforts to establish a coalition with national Mexican American leaders. Immigration was the principal issue that threatened to divide these two minority groups. The big test came in the late 1970s with the battle over employer sanctions. The Black caucus voted unanimously with the Mexican American members of the House on every critical vote on the Simpson-Mazzoli immigration bill in 1984 (Fuchs

1990a, p. 303). Another indication of how important opposition to sanctions and support for amnesty was for Blacks who hoped to obtain the support of Mexican Americans is the way in which presidential candidate Jesse Jackson sought to position himself as an advocate of illegal Mexican aliens and an opponent of sanctions.

This alliance was broken in 1986 when IRCA was passed. At that time, the Mexican American members themselves were divided and ten Black members voted for the bill. Fuchs argues that this split did not really damage the Black–Mexican American alliance (p. 305). More recent events, however, may have done so. When the General Accounting Office reported in 1989 that there was evidence that employers were discriminating against all Hispanic job-seekers as a result of IRCA, Hispanic organizations renewed their calls for repeal of employer sanctions. When the Civil Rights Leadership Conference did not join this call, Hispanic groups threatened to withdraw. Black-Hispanic tension has also been heightened by conflicts over representation in congressional and local election districts. Greater Hispanic representation through redistricting may come at the expense of the number of Black elected officials. At the root of these tensions is the fact that Hispanics are rapidly overtaking Blacks as the largest minority group in the country. Furthermore, as the proportion of all Hispanics who are of recent immigrant origin grows, immigration policy, and the treatment of undocumented aliens, moves to the top of the Hispanic political agenda and, at the same time, sharpens the conflicts of interests between Hispanics and Blacks (Chavez 1990).

The actual power of ethnic lobbies is difficult to establish. They were unable to prevent the imposition of employer sanctions, but they were able to persuade Congress to enact a broad legalization programme for undocumented workers as a quid pro quo. Reimers concludes that since the 1960s the various ethnic and other pro-immigrant advocacy groups have eclipsed the patriotic and veterans groups that had supported restriction in the past (1985, p. 245). Their pressure can be seen as an important cause of the policy liberalizations that have been such a marked characteristic of reform since 1965, though they operate in a generally liberalized climate of national and international opinion about race and human rights that would have pushed policy in the same direction in any case.

Although issue groups are found on both sides of immigration debates, perhaps the most important is the Federation for American Immigration Reform (FAIR) which not only lobbies Congress, but has commissioned national polls of opinion on immigration matters and undertaken other research. Environmental groups lack the high profile in the American immigration debate that they have achieved in Australia. Environmentalism is a liberal issue and liberals find it uncomfortable to oppose immigration or to support efforts to keep poor

Mexican peasants from seeking economic opportunity in the United States. Economic assistance to Mexico and population planning are the preferred alternatives to immigration for these groups, but their influence is slight.

CONCLUSIONS

Immigration plays a less central role in the national myth of Australia than it does in the United States, but it is nonetheless a more salient political issue in modern Australia. This is true even though Australian political élites have tried to reduce conflict over immigration through an interparty consensus. No such consensus has been engineered in the USA, but arguments over immigration policy have not been very intense.

Immigration generates conflict between the same sorts of interests in both countries, but their relative weight varies considerably. The labour unions have been more influential in Australia than in the USA, especially during earlier periods of the countries' histories. It is inconceivable that the Australian Council of Trade Unions would tolerate widespread illegal entry into the country of the kind that has occurred in the USA for decades. Though their voice has been muted on the migration question during the post-war period, Australian trade unions have in the past served as a focal point for people worried about the effects of a large intake. However, defence anxieties, a healthy labour market, and the Labor Party's bipartisan approach to the programme blunted union criticism during the 1950s and 1960s. Since the late 1970s a growing desire to be seen to be concerned with migrant welfare has given unions an added reason for silence.

With respect to business groups, the greatest distinction between these cases is that agricultural employers are exceptionally powerful in the USA, fairly dictating policy on temporary farm workers. No business group in Australia has demonstrated equivalent clout. Nonetheless, employer groups in both countries who benefit from population growth have been at the forefront of immigration advocacy.

The ethnic lobby in Australia is more centralized and more closely linked with the government than is the case in the USA (indeed, it is largely publicly funded). FECCA provides an organizational focus for Australian ethnic activists that does not exist in the USA. Moreover, ethnic influence in Australia appears to be primarily located among the 'old immigrants' from southern and eastern Europe, while in the USA the most active and important ethnic interest groups are run by Mexican Americans and Cubans as the more established immigrant groups from Europe have largely receded from the scene. Ethnic attempts to influence immigration law are probably seen as more legitimate in the traditionally pluralistic and interest-group-driven American political system. Also, members of the US Congress are more accessible to the lobbies than are the persons responsible for Australian policy. Representatives of immigrants in the US, though, must compete for attention with traditional minorities, especially Blacks, and this split is a major consideration within the Hispanic community, which is a native minority and, increasingly, an immigrant minority as well.

The general public is unhappy about immigration in both Australia and the United States, though in both countries this discontent is unfocused and relatively unorganized. There are, however, a number of reasons for suggesting that feelings run higher in Australia. The Australian intake is larger in per capita terms. It is also a more active programme; Australian officials still talk of immigration 'targets', the Americans of 'ceilings'. Size and activity make the intake more visible and this visibility is accompanied by a stronger effort to justify immigration as a positive economic benefit. Though the public is sceptical about the economic definition, they are more receptive to it than to arguments couched in altruistic terms (see polls discussed in Betts 1988, ch. 5). Economic justifications of immigration also play well in the USA, though they are simply a part of the generally positive view of immigrant contributions to the American experience.

PART II

IMMIGRATION AND THE ECONOMY

6

MACROECONOMIC CONSEQUENCES OF INTERNATIONAL MIGRATION

William Foster and Glenn Withers

Very real differences exist between Australia and the United States in their approaches to economic research on immigration and in issues studied. In Australia there is an established tradition of analysing the economic consequences of international migration at the macroeconomic level. The Australian literature is replete with examinations of the relationship between migration movements and national aggregates such as gross domestic product, investment, balance of payments, real wages and unemployment. By contrast, United States studies in the economics of immigration are often more microeconomic, focusing especially on labour market consequences. They typically examine particular industries, occupations or regions, or focus on immigrants as individuals and review issues such as employment substitution between natives and immigrants and wage assimilation of immigrants.

Reasons for such a difference in emphasis are speculative, but include: the stronger influence of non-neoclassical theories and approaches in Australian economics; the higher per capita immigration rate in Australia and greater national dispersion of migrants; a greater coherence, centralization and executive discretion in immigration policy formulation in Australia; a greater tradition of links with central policymakers for Australian economists; and a tradition of more complete national statistical collection over time in Australia, perhaps as a legacy of longer British colonial administration, as opposed to better micro-level data sets in the United States.

Each of these propositions deserves detailed development and justification, but the interesting question is whether any consequent differences in research findings are of style or of substance. Putting the matter another way, do the results from different methodological emphases fundamentally differ or are they consistent—after making due allowance for various national practices and structures? A full answer to this question is necessarily elusive, since the differing perspectives on research issues in the two countries make direct comparison of results the exception rather than the rule. Nonetheless, the next chapter does provide useful insights on labour market aspects, and the present one is similarly instructive from the aggregate perspective.

By virtue of the evident balance in research priorities between the two countries, the present chapter is inevitably shaped by Australian issues and analysis, though there are equivalent United States findings available in several areas. In the next section the effects of immigration on the various elements of aggregate demand and supply are considered, encompassing household, investment and government sector demands, and savings and other sources of supply. Also included is a brief outline of the recent debate in Australia on possible external sector effects of immigration. Next, the impacts of immigration (through the interaction of demand and supply) on unemployment, wages and inflation are discussed, together with updated examples of some econometric analysis on which the Australian conclusions on these questions are based. Then the effects of immigration on growth in output per capita are considered (including discussions of Australian model-based results), of the likely sources of such growth, and of certain distributional and welfare implications. Finally, some concluding comments are offered on possible commonality and difference between Australia and the United States implied by the aggregate level economic results and national policies towards immigration.

The outline of research findings in the two countries presented here is very much based, as in the next chapter, on the contents of several recent reviews. Wooden (1990) and Foster and Baker (1991) together provide quite detailed general coverages for Australia. Sources of information on aggregate economic consequences are more diffuse for the United States, though Greenwood and McDowell (1986), Papademetriou et al. (1989), Simon (1989) and Borjas (1990) each contains useful information on different aspects. Only where the present chapter goes beyond this literature are additional references supplied.

The aggregate analysis is largely conditioned by past and present policies. Some simulations (Hamilton and Whalley 1984) indicate that if all restrictions on international migration were removed there could be a very substantial increase in world gross domestic product (GDP)—perhaps doubling. National exclusiveness, however, means that hasty or wholesale dismantling of such barriers is unlikely. The practical policy question is more that of just how far countries of immigration, such as the United States and Australia, should open their doors. In deciding this, concern for aggregate economic effects of immigration has a role to play.

Figure 6.1 Rates of natural increase, total increase and net migration, 1900–86

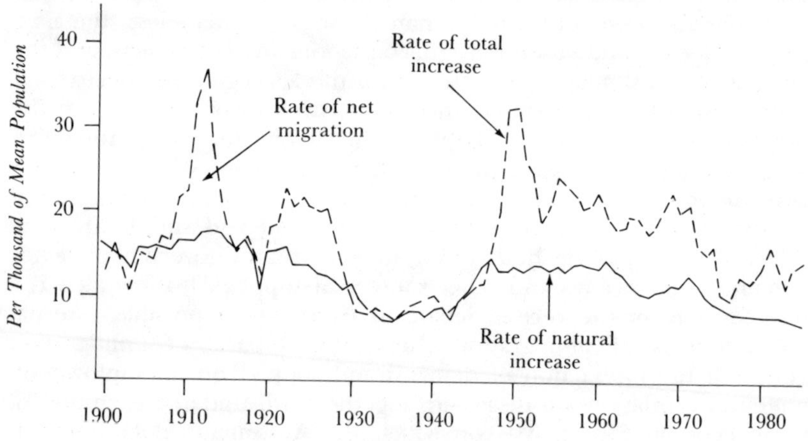

Sources: Commonwealth Bureau of Census and Statistics: demography bulletins; Australian Bureau of Statistics: year book and population and vital statistics

AGGREGATE DEMAND AND SUPPLY

The potential importance of an aggregate approach to immigration in the Australian context is readily seen in the fact that almost 60 per cent of post-war labour-force growth in Australia has come from immigrants or the children of immigrants. The contribution of immigration to United States population and labour-force growth, while increasing again in recent years, remains much less; the foreign-born constitute only six per cent of the United States population, compared with over 20 per cent in Australia.

A useful starting point in looking at the aggregate consequences of immigration is to consider the effects in terms of the major components of national product. Studies focusing on immigration and consumption, on savings and investment, on the government budget, and on the balance of payments have together in Australia provided a useful overview of the short and medium-term impacts. But several of these components have their own particular salience. The effects on consumption and investment patterns, and their associated resource use and pollution externalities, are central to the debate on ecologically sustainable growth. The effect on investment is also important for long-run growth analysis. The impact on the government budget becomes a highly emotive component of the immigration debate in terms of whether migrants are a source of fiscal burden to other taxpayers; on this point there are useful United States contributions. As well, the balance of payments effects and their implications for foreign debt are at the heart of recent policy concerns in Australia that the national economy cannot 'pay its way' and is heading for 'banana republic' status. It is therefore appropriate to look at the state of knowledge on each of these aspects.

Household Consumption

There are several reasons why immigration need not generate the same growth in household consumption demand that it does in underlying population. First, at the individual or household level, consumption expenditure can differ between otherwise comparable immigrants and non-immigrants, both in absolute terms and in its pattern by commodity. Second, at the group level, differences between immigrants and non-immigrants in age and income patterns, for example, can generate different aggregate patterns of spending behaviour.

Recent Australian data in fact suggest relatively little intrinsically different consumption behaviour by immigrant status at the individual level, once basic variables such as age, family structure and income are accounted for. While immigrant household expenditure does exceed that of non-immigrants, this is basically a function of household size, with average expenditure by overseas-born individuals very similar to that of the locally born. Recent arrivals, supported by funds brought with them, are relatively high spenders, with a steady decline observed over longer periods of residence—though even this trend moderates once other variables, such as age, are accounted for. Apart from the initial burst of high spending, neither period of residence nor birthplace contribute in any significant sense to individual differences in total expenditure. But the evidence does suggest some influence of such 'immigrant' variables on individuals' patterns of expenditure by commodity. After controlling for appropriate demographic variables, the overseas born still spend proportionately more than non-immigrants on, for example, food and current housing costs, the difference in the latter again particularly evident for recent immigrants.

Though consumption differences at the individual level are not striking, different demographic structures between immigrants and non-immigrants do generate correspondingly different spending patterns in aggregate, especially for new immigrants. This overall difference in economy-wide spending patterns between immigrants and non-immigrants has been shown, under recent Australian modelling, to be positive in itself for aggregate demand and output. Australian immigration is thus expansionary in economic terms, not simply on account of its obvious population augmenting effect, but also by virtue of the characteristic demographic structure and expenditure patterns of immigrants as a group.

Investment

One important element common to both household expenditure and immigrant investment is housing. Recent Australian data indicate that immigrant spending for housing-related purposes is some 10 per cent higher than for non-immigrants, though for the overseas born of more than a decade's residence there is virtually no difference. Investment in housing is particularly significant in the first year or so after arrival, and also after around six or seven years; some immigrants are evidently able to purchase immediately, while others require a period of financial consolidation, a pattern confirmed by home ownership data. Overall home ownership is very similar for the overseas and Australian born, though ownership rates do vary quite widely by birthplace, the highest being among immigrants from continental Europe.

Investment demand is also generated in a less specific sense, in that the foreign born ultimately require access to a comparable amount of social and industry capital per head to that of the non-immigrant population. The amount of investment needed to increase the overall capital stock by such a margin has given rise to well-documented concerns in both the United States and Australia on possible economic costs thus attributable to immigration. In Australia, for example, the fear has been that living standards (as proxied by output per head) would fall if the investment required to maintain established levels of capital per person was not forthcoming. Even if it was, it has also been noted that any domestic shortfalls in investment funds must then be met from overseas. This has undesirable implications for Australia's external balances and already high foreign debt, particularly in the current economic setting. Another dimension of concern among observers in both countries has been that providing more people with similar amounts of capital (capital 'widening') would seem less productive than investment effectively increasing capital per head (capital 'deepening').

While such issues obviously merit serious consideration, two important qualifications should be made in relation to the above. First, strict retention of pre-immigration capital to population ratios is not necessary to sustain a given quality of life. Falling values for that ratio may, for example, simply reflect greater efficiency in production. New investment, whatever its purpose, will generally embody better technology so that cost efficiency can rise, to consumers' benefit, even though capital per head may not. (As a corollary, the apparent dichotomy in productivity between 'widening' and 'deepening' investment is misleading and should not be overdrawn.) Economies of scale can reduce investment costs below the levels implied by simply factoring up the capital stock for population increase—lower marginal costs of investment reduce the average value of capital per head, again at no necessary loss to quality or service. Some large capital items may indeed have unused capacity for ready application to a larger population, under no added investment. Also, the additional labour available under immigration may encourage less capital intensive methods of production, again at no necessary cost to living standards.

A second major qualification concerns timing. Immigration-induced investment is neither required nor can be forthcoming immediately on migrant arrival. Indeed, recent work in Australia suggests that the annual peak in investment induced by a given migrant intake is not reached until several years after arrival, by which time immigrants' own productive contributions are helping to meet those investment demands. We will return to these matters in discussion of the implications of immigration for the host country's external account balances.

The Government Sector

At government level the short-term economic demands of administering immigrant selection and settlement are not great. Over the longer term, though, the age structure of the intake can affect the pattern of demand and expenditure required for major budget items, such as health, education and welfare. In Australia the median age of recent settler arrivals has been around five years below that of the non-immigrant population. Research in that country demonstrates that continued immigration with a similar concentration in the younger age groups does generate over the longer term increased demands per capita and per worker on education, but reduced demands for both social security and health (the impact is muted if only immigration levels—rather than rates—are maintained, since then immigration inflows have a proportionately reducing impact). The same general effect, other things being equal, of immigration on these major items has been noted in the United States, though such scenarios are always vulnerable to behavioural, socio-economic and policy change.

Evidence from both countries suggests broadly similar usage patterns in public transfer items among immigrants and non-immigrants. In the United States, for example, general immigrant use of social insurance and welfare programmes does exceed that of non-immigrants on average, but, again if demographic variables such as age are accounted for, usage levels become very similar when otherwise comparable cases are considered. This pattern is reflected quite specifically in welfare assistance, with female-headed households and more recent arrivals (in particular from Latin America), for example, being associated with relatively high usage rates and helping to contribute to greater immigrant usage overall than among non-immigrants. But despite this, it has also been shown at the individual level that immigrants do not use disproportionately more public welfare assistance than demographically comparable non-immigrants (and may even use less).

Recent Australian data on government pension or benefit use indicate that such transfer payments constitute the principal source of income for a slightly higher proportion of overseas-born income units than for the Australian born. Differences do occur, however, across the various individual pensions and benefits, even when age and eligibility conditions are taken into account. There is a relatively high take-up rate for the Age Pension among the eligible overseas-born, for example, offset to some extent by relatively fewer immigrant aged depending on other payments, such as the Veterans' Affairs Pension. However, a relatively lower proportion of the overseas-born unemployed depend on government transfers (reflecting, among other things, different patterns of asset ownership and private income among the respective unemployed groups).

Sources of Supply

An immediate source of supply to meet these various demands are the funds immigrants bring with them as part of the migration process. These have been estimated in Australia to be quite substantial, with one part of the official immigration programme specifically intended to stimulate this source of capital. Immigrants also make important contributions by bringing human capital—the host society avoids the costs incurred by source countries in prior education and training of newcomers.

Investment funds are of course generated through savings, at household, business and government levels. Little information is available on immigration and business savings in either country, but Australian data indicate that immigrant households save less than non-immigrant households. Interestingly, the pattern in household savings ratio (reflecting the propensity to save rather than consume) with period of residence appears to have changed in recent decades. In the 1970s the ratio decreased with time since arrival, but more recently it has increased with period of residence, with savings by immigrants in their early years after arrival being particularly low. As noted in the next chapter, caution must be exercised in interpreting any apparent effects of period of residence based only on cross-sectional data. However, it may be surmised that more substantial amounts of funds brought by recent intakes have allowed relatively higher early spending in relation to income, though other factors such as intake age patterns and changing attitudes to personal finance may play some part.

Superannuation has become an important form of personal saving in Australia, in terms of both coverage across individuals and aggregate funds generated for investment. Recent data suggest that superannuation coverage among the overseas-born employed lags within most age groups well behind that of the Australian born. For wage and salary earners only, the overall margin narrows, but continues to reflect structural factors such as the relatively low concentration of the overseas born in public sector employment, where superannuation coverage is traditionally strong.

On government savings, studies in both countries suggest that immigrants and non-immigrants pay on average quite similar amounts of income tax. For Australia, net transfers to government from the margin of income tax over pensions and benefits paid out are slightly higher on average for the overseas born than for the Australian born. Corresponding comparisons have not been formally undertaken with outlays for health and education also included, but life cycle considerations (in particular that immigrants arrive on average after their basic schooling years) suggest that immigrants overall make greater net contributions to government than non-immigrants. This position is also evident in the United States literature, where it is suggested that immigrants pay relatively more taxes and use fewer government services than non-migrants because of their younger age profile and higher worker/dependent ratio.

Whatever its source, though, investment per capita does appear to respond positively to the prospect of a growing population following immigration-based demands for industry and infrastructure capital. Recent Australian analysis of investment and population growth over the period 1901 to 1970 shows that net migration changes have been significantly associated with subsequent movements in per capita investment, and in the same direction. However, not all such investment funds may be available domestically, so that the implications of immigration for the host country's external accounts also become important.

The External Sector

Immigration can influence exports in several possible ways, though the various effects have not been thoroughly examined or quantified in either Australia or the United States. One fear in Australia has been that in a country heavily dependent on raw materials and food products in its export pattern, increasing population through immigration will increasingly divert such production from a limited effective land area to domestic use. Against that, any impetus to greater efficiency in Australian industry from immigration (to be discussed under the heading 'Output Growth Per Capita'), whether through scale effects, migrant skills, entrepreneurship or technological progress, should be reflected in a more effective export performance. In particular, a growing domestic market can generate scale economies in at least some export industries, so reducing unit costs and enhancing international competitiveness. This 'launching pad' effect for better export penetration has indeed been increasingly emphasized in recent times in the international literature as regional trade boundaries are reshaped. Finally, at the most immediate level, migrants can clearly assist in exporting through their personal contacts and knowledge of language, culture and tastes in foreign countries.

On imports, immigrants may have a relatively high propensity to consume some imported goods, particularly from their origin countries, but there are no direct data available on which to test the hypothesis. In Australia, of the main areas where the overseas born spend proportionately more than non-immigrants—food and housing related items—the former may incline migrant spending somewhat towards imports, but the latter do not generally have a high import component.

As noted, there has been vigorous recent debate in Australia on the implications of the investment demand generated by immigration for the current account deficit and foreign debt. Recent Australian research on the issue has more clearly recognized the time dimension implicit in the induced investment consequent on immigration. The peak period of investment demand associated with a given immigrant intake has been projected to occur around two to five years after arrival, with a subsequent tapering back to zero within a further four or five years. Migrants' own funds provide an immediate offset to the relatively low capital requirements in the very first years after arrival, but to the extent that continuing investment demand exceeds the domestic sources of supply attributable to immigration at around the peak demand period, a corresponding current account deficit is implied. As investment demand declines in subsequent years, it is again accounted for through immigrant contributions to the economy, with the implied current account deficit eventually turning to surplus.

Beyond this profile of changing impacts, however, the net effect of any given intake is not known. It is not yet clear how the negative and positive external effects balance over time. In particular, it is not clear how the various effects of earlier intakes combine at a given point in time, though it is quite evident that, under the time profile associated with a single intake outlined above, reasonable stability in immigration programmes will ensure that any medium term influence on the current account of recent intakes will be well dampened by offsetting longer term effects of earlier ones.

Finally, the longer-term benefits from the induced investment, which are crucial to this perspective on immigration's economic impact, will always depend upon how effective are the investment decisions of business and government. If these decisions are flawed, however, the host country clearly has problems well beyond any apparent contribution thereto from immigration.

UNEMPLOYMENT, WAGES AND INFLATION

How do the various demand and supply side influences discussed above work themselves out in terms of inflation and unemployment? These are the aggregate welfare indicators that are particularly focused upon in short-term stabilization analysis, and they can carry heavy political significance. Economists who model the political business cycle indeed find that these variables provide major explanations of political behaviour, reflecting voter concerns over their magnitude.

Any potential consequences of immigration for unemployment and inflation are likely to be linked through wages, the various theoretical relations between the latter variables being well established in the vast economic literature on unemployment and inflation. It makes sense then to consider the impacts of immigration on each of unemployment, wages and inflation.

Unemployment and the Real Wage

A popular fear historically in both the United States and Australia has been that immigration threatens the job prospects of non-immigrants and raises domestic unemployment. Though the relationship between immigration and overall unemployment has been the main source of concern, it has also been argued that immigration could have a favourable effect on at least some part of unemployment, specifically its frictional and structural components. However, despite the possibility that immigrant skills, physical mobility and relative willingness to accept unpleasant jobs might increase labour market flexibility and contribute to a more efficient matching of jobs with workers, Australian analysis can offer no empirical support for this proposition.

As noted in the next chapter, United States research into the effects of immigration on unemployment has focused particularly on the impact of immigrants on the employment prospects of non-immigrants in particular regions and industry sectors. The general conclusion is that any such effects are sufficiently isolated, small and mixed in direction to deny any significant general relationship between immigration and non-immigrant employment. Though the issues are conceptually distinct, this does suggest a similar lack of impact of immigration on unemployment rates, both for non-immigrants and in aggregate.

In Australia major efforts have been devoted in recent years to properly assessing the net impact of immigration on the aggregate unemployment rate, and a strong series of both qualitative and empirical studies appears to have formally resolved the issue. The key question here is the extent to which the aggregate expenditure effects of immigrant-based population increase have generated employment opportunities to match the corresponding growth in labour supply, leaving the aggregate unemployment rate effectively unchanged. The significance of immigration has accordingly been tested in a variety of sophisticated models of Australian unemployment incorporating many theoretical elements, using quarterly and annual data over varying time periods, and with different migration variables. The consistent result has been that immigration increases cannot be associated in any significant sense with subsequent increases in unemployment over at least Australia's past range of economic and immigrant experience.

Given Australia's research focus on the aggregate effects of immigration, both for unemployment and other economic variables, it is useful at this point to convey the flavour of at least some empirical work on which the Australian conclusions are based. Table 6.1 summarizes the statistical results for various 'causality' correlations between net migration rates and two important labour market variables (the unemployment rate and the real wage) and a third key variable that underpins Australia's material standard of living (gross domestic product per capita), based on data over the period since Federation. Put simply, the table portrays the extent to which current values of one variable from each pair considered (in column one) can be significantly related to, or 'caused' by, current or past values of the second variable (in column two). The statistical strength of each relationship is conveyed by the test statistics in the final two columns, and summarized by the use of asterisks—the lack of an asterisk indicates no statistically significant 'causal' relationship, while three asterisks indicates a particularly strong relationship running from the one variable to the other.

The test statistics indicate a modestly significant relationship from migration to unemployment—but one that the relevant underlying coefficients (not shown) indicate is in fact negative, suggesting a small net job creation effect. The reverse causality from unemployment to migration is, however, strongly negative, confirming the familiar observation that immigration has tended to fall with recession (for reasons of both policy and market forces).

A second historic source of labour market concern in both countries has been immigration's perceived effect on the price of labour, or the real wage. Table 6.1 thus also incorporates tests of the causality relationship between immigration and the real wage in Australia. This relationship is found not to be statistically significant. Taken with the unemployment result, the implication for Australia is that labour market adjustment generally takes place through changes to the quantity of labour, with the real wage being effectively exogenous. Such a

Table 6.1 Causality tests: immigration effects, Australia 1901–86

Dependent variable	*Causal variable*	*Causal lag (yrs)*	*Test statistics*	
			F	*log l'hood ratio*
Unemployment				
URC	NMR	0–2	3.8**	12.0**
NMR	URC	0–2	7.7***	22.1***
Real Wages				
RWC	NMR	0–5	1.1	8.0
NMR	RWC	0–5	0.8	5.7
GDP Per Capita				
RYC	NMR	0–10	8.0**	23.7**
NMR	RYC	0–10	0.7	10.0

Notes:

NMR net migration rate
URC unemployment rate changes
RWC real wage changes
RYC real income per capita changes

* significant at .10 level
** significant at .05 level
*** significant at .01 level

conclusion might not be surprising in a country with one of the most highly regulated wage-fixing systems of the industrial nations—a system of judicial arbitration of wages. At the same time it is possible to argue, historically, that the establishment of that unique wage-fixing system in the early twentieth century had as a pre-condition the earlier success of the labour movement, aided by an ailing economy, in obtaining a turning away from mass migration for some decades after 1890.

There is also a statistically insignificant reverse causation result from real wages to migration, which is consistent with much previous work in Australia and elsewhere. There has been a remarkable inability to find significant relative wage (or even income) effects in international migration analysis, with a consequent tendency for the historical literature, at least, to fall back into 'push' or 'pull' debates in quantity adjustment terms. The Australian evidence is consistent with a significant 'pull' effect, but also with a tightening of assistance and admission policy in times of high unemployment. The latter policy explanation would indeed be of increasing importance for Australia into the twentieth century.

Wage and Price Inflation

Research in both countries has addressed the possible effects of immigration on nominal wages or earnings. Immigration could conceivably influence nominal wages in either direction. By allocating mobile workers to occupational bottlenecks, it could relieve wage pressures in those areas and so perhaps also in the broader economy. Low-skilled (including illegal) immigrants could undercut prevailing wage levels in certain industries or localities, feeding through to more general wage effects. On the other hand, if migrant demands on infrastructure and government spending are thought (correctly or not) to retard growth in living standards for non-immigrants, the latter may seek compensation through higher wages.

United States researchers have looked hard at the possible effects of immigrant workers on the earnings of non-immigrant groups in particular regions and industry sectors. As with the employment question, however, the overall conclusion is essentially benign. Though there are undoubtedly earnings effects within particular firms or industries, especially during periods of adjustment to new domestic and international competition, there is no evidence that these impacts are felt beyond the industries concerned, with no discernible effect on aggregate wage levels. In Australia growth in nominal wages has been modelled in various, more direct ways, and the significance of net migration for wages growth tested. A range of estimations have been performed using different combinations of migration and other economic variables over the post-war period, the consistent result being that immigration makes no statistically significant contribution to aggregate wage change.

Similar empirically-based econometric work in Australia has found no evidence of a significant link between immigration and price inflation. Again, a wide range of migration variables, econometric models and time periods have been used in testing, with the same consistent result, yet again, that immigration makes no significant contribution. Causality analysis has also supported this conclusion, on the basis of a further very broad range of pairwise tests.

The separate results for nominal wages and inflation are thus helpfully in accord with the result for real wages. And the upshot of the current state of knowledge in Australia on immigration, unemployment, wages and prices therefore is that, contrary to traditional opinion, no major link exists between changes to immigration and changes to any of these aggregate short-term stabilization variables.

OUTPUT GROWTH PER CAPITA

A summarizing standard often adopted by policymakers and economists in assessing the ultimate effects of a given policy is the consequent impact on output growth per capita as a proxy for domestic living standards. The longer-run effects of migration on changes in gross domestic product per capita are clearly of importance if government is interested not only in short-term demand side considerations, but also in matters of expansion of production potential relative to workforce or to population. Certainly, the 1986 US *Economic Report of the President* says that 'for much of the nation's history, U.S. immigration policy has been based on the premise that immigrants have a favourable effect on the overall standard of living and on economic development' (p. 234).

The result for output per capita has also been emphasized in aggregate immigration analysis in Australia. The effects of immigration on this measure have been examined from several different standpoints, the generally consistent conclusion being that over the long term immigration does generate positive (but quite moderate) economic results for output per person. Beyond the basic finding, however, it is also important to ask what the likely sources of this gain are, and what associated welfare and distributional consequences might be relevant—and each of these aspects is considered in this section.

Model Results

In sampling some Australian results, note first that Table 6.1 also contains results on the long-run 'causality' relationship between immigration and gross domestic product per capita. The relationship is clearly significant and the sum of the underlying coefficients is small but positive, which provides preliminary confirmation for post-federation Australia of the United States presumption, cited above, that immigration has indeed been favourable for overall living standards. However, such simple a-theoretical causality analysis has limitations, including its inability to appropriately account for the influence of other variables beyond the pair under consideration.

Broader econometric approaches to immigration's effect on output per head can be pursued within the neoclassical growth model framework. One recent example in Australia incorporated the joint effects of population growth on employment growth per head, of immigration on the rate of technological change, and of immigration on capital per head, to yield a final quadratic form for growth in output per head in terms of population growth, whose maximum could be easily derived. This particular model was characterized, interestingly, by a wide range of implied immigration intakes around the derived optimum with relatively little effect on realized output per head. Australia's post-war immigration experience fits quite well within this range, suggesting generally positive effects of the programme over that period; but for intakes outside that derived range the model suggests a sharp deterioration in growth in output per head.

Another common econometric approach is simulation analysis using large-scale economy-wide models. In looking at effects on per capita output, Australia's two biggest econometric models, ORANI and IMP, though different in many fundamentals, give generally similar answers.

ORANI is a computable general equilibrium model, where IMP assumes that the economy will not necessarily or readily return to equilibrium when disturbed. ORANI essentially provides comparative static scenarios, the short and longer terms being distinguished by rates of return on capital varying for the former, but returning to long run equilibrium values in the latter (with the capital stock adjusting). IMP is time specific, with short run applications analysing whatever disequilibria do arise (in the absence of strict assumptions on competition and market clearing), while various policy instruments including tax rates, tariffs, government spending and interest rates are applied over the longer run to restore balanced growth. ORANI embodies constant returns to scale in its basic form (though this can be varied in running the model by user assumption), while IMP's structure does permit scale effects. The models are very powerful, and both have been widely used in recent years in Australian academic, industry and policy analysis, including on the effects of immigration.

Early applications of ORANI showed little impact of immigration on gross domestic product (GDP) per head, with a slight negative effect on gross national product (GNP) per head (due to implied changes in foreign ownership of Australian assets). Assuming modest positive returns to scale, however, immigration's effect was clearly positive on both measures. Later applications confirm that immigration has marginally favourable effects on output per head. Both early and recent applications of IMP give very similar results for output per head to ORANI—small but positive effects from immigration.

Sources of Growth

If immigration does generate a positive effect (albeit small) on output growth per capita, it is then relevant to ask what the sources of that growth might be. The appropriate starting point here is migrant skills. It has been common in host countries for the composition of immigration to have changed significantly in recent years (raising the possibility of bias in empirical results using measures of migration that are not quality adjusted), with the recent United States and Australian experience referred to in the next chapter. Although there has been considerable debate on skills in United States analyses, the discussion has generally had to rely upon imputed measures of skill.

More direct measurement is, however, possible for Australia. Given the importance of skills in assessing the economic effects of immigration (at both aggregate and microeconomic levels), the basic data and results are usefully illustrated in Table 6.2. Adopting an occupation-based approach, estimates of average skills content are thereby derived for migrant arrivals to Australia for individual years over the post-war period. The occupation data are compiled from official sources, and provide ten categories broadly allied with skill in the sense of education and, importantly, earnings. Average earnings are then used to convert these skill distributions into a skill index. The results show a significant upward trend in the skill composition of immigration to Australia in the post-war period, despite significant numbers in the social and humanitarian admission categories. Of course, elements within these seemingly 'non-economic' categories can still be highly selective, and skill is a major selection criterion.

However, social and humanitarian migrant entry can be important in affecting realized skill benefits via a changing dependency ratio. Indeed, the share of workers in migrant arrivals has steadily declined in post-war Australia, so tending to offset apparent skill gains. Nevertheless, for almost all of that period the intake worker share has been above resident levels, as has skill composition, which suggests overall a jointly beneficial impact on per capita income growth. Indeed, on this basis, for the overall effect of immigration on per capita output to be negative, there would need to be a substantial deficiency in capital growth (which has in fact been higher than population growth until very recently) and substantial diseconomies of scale.

Figure 6.2 Skill index and worker ratio migrant arrivals, 1951–86

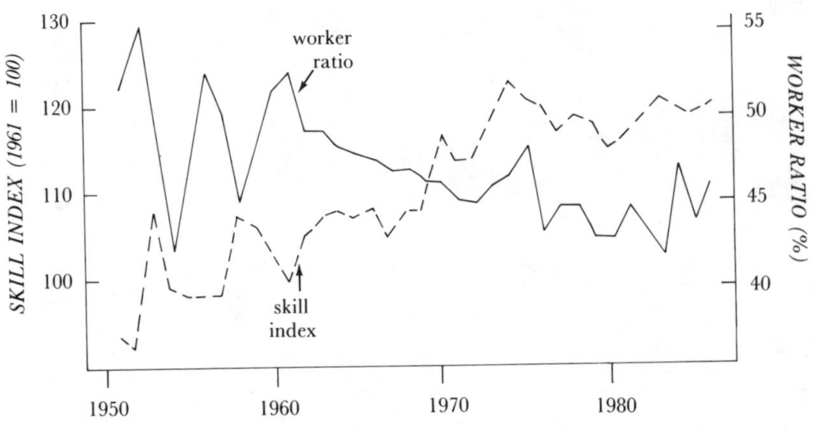

Source: Table 6.2

Beyond skills, strong empirical guidance on the roles of other contributing factors to the positive result for output per capita with immigration is generally lacking. It is not particularly clear what the relative contributions of such efficiency-oriented aspects as occupational (and entrepreneurial) skills, scale economies and technological development through immigration might be. Real methodological

Table 6.2 Occupational distribution of migrant arrivals, Australia 1951–86

Financial year	*Occupations (percentages)*								*Total workers ('000)*	*Skill index (1961 = 100)*	*Worker ratio (%)*
	1	*2*	*3*	*4*	*5*	*6*	*7*	*8*			
1951	6.9	29.3	14.1	14.9	6.8	13.0	8.6	6.1	80.2	93	52.3
1952	6.1	25.1	13.1	14.1	7.1	13.5	15.5	5.2	72.7	92	55.7
1953	7.7	20.8	15.2	11.5	7.4	15.9	16.9	4.3	47.6	108	49.7
1954	9.9	24.9	16.4	11.3	6.8	14.7	10.8	4.7	37.1	99	42.9
1955	6.9	22.9	12.5	13.3	9.2	16.3	12.6	5.9	60.1	98	48.4
1956	6.5	21.2	13.0	13.4	10.4	17.1	11.3	6.7	70.4	98	53.1
1957	8.5	21.7	14.7	16.0	13.9	9.5	7.7	7.6	61.1	98	50.7
1958	10.2	23.3	19.0	16.4	15.4	5.0	4.6	5.8	49.4	107	45.7
1959	10.5	23.8	18.7	14.5	14.8	4.9	7.4	4.9	57.3	106	49.1
1960	9.4	24.1	17.4	13.0	10.8	5.9	12.4	6.6	69.5	103	52.0
1961	7.1	27.3	12.7	10.8	12.5	7.1	14.0	8.1	57.5	100	53.1
1962	9.0	19.6	13.2	11.1	24.8	5.8	11.8	4.5	42.8	105	49.9
1963	8.9	21.8	15.2	10.8	15.0	7.0	15.7	5.3	50.8	107	49.8
1964	9.6	24.2	16.4	10.8	13.9	7.1	12.2	5.5	59.7	108	48.8
1965	9.3	23.0	17.4	13.2	11.9	5.7	12.6	6.5	67.8	107	48.4
1966	9.5	22.2	17.4	14.0	11.6	4.9	13.5	6.6	69.2	108	48.0
1967	10.2	23.2	19.3	14.4	10.0	3.8	14.1	4.8	65.7	105	47.4
1968	11.0	24.3	19.5	13.8	9.0	3.3	13.4	5.3	65.2	108	47.4
1969	12.0	23.2	19.6	15.0	8.9	2.7	11.7	6.6	82.0	108	46.7
1970	11.6	21.4	19.0	17.6	8.3	2.3	14.8	4.8	85.9	116	46.4
1971	13.8	20.0	18.9	17.7	8.5	2.0	12.5	6.2	77.1	114	45.4
1972	16.6	20.2	20.9	15.3	9.0	1.6	9.5	6.5	60.1	114	45.3
1973	17.6	20.9	23.1	14.0	9.0	1.5	8.5	5.0	50.0	119	46.5
1974	17.4	20.5	22.7	13.5	7.5	1.4	9.2	7.5	53.1	123	47.1
1975	23.0	19.5	23.3	10.2	6.0	1.2	6.6	9.9	43.1	121	48.4
1976	26.4	23.4	20.4	5.4	5.7	1.1	4.6	12.6	23.0	120	43.7
1977	22.4	23.3	17.2	6.0	5.2	1.3	6.8	17.3	32.1	117	45.2
1978	22.9	22.4	21.2	6.4	6.0	2.3	5.6	12.9	33.0	119	45.1
1979	19.8	19.2	20.5	9.0	5.6	2.0	13.5	10.1	29.1	118	43.3
1980	29.5	16.5	4.7	16.1	4.5	1.2	19.9	7.3	34.9	115	43.2
1981	30.8	17.7	5.1	18.6	4.9	1.5	18.1	3.1	49.8	117	45.0
1982	32.2	20.1	4.5	19.0	4.7	2.1	12.9	4.2	51.4	119	43.5
1983	33.8	22.0	4.1	18.5	4.1	3.3	6.4	7.7	39.8	121	42.3
1984	30.5	9.3	3.9	16.9	4.6	2.8	6.8	25.2	32.5	97	47.2
1985	38.1	10.1	5.4	21.7	6.8	2.8	7.0	7.9	34.1	119	44.0
1986	40.5	11.9	5.4	20.4	7.1	2.5	4.9	7.5	42.8	120	46.2

Keys to occupation groups:

1 Professional, technical and related occupations/Total workers
2 Trades occupations/Total workers
3 Clerical, commercial and administration occupations/Total workers
4 Other semi-skilled/Total workers
5 Service occupations/Total workers
6 Rural occupations/Total workers
7 Labourers/Total workers
8 Occupations not stated/Total workers

Sources: Department of Immigration, *Immigration: Consolidated Statistics*, annual; CBCS, *Labour Report* and ABS, *Labour Statistics*, annual; Department of Immigration, unpublished data, 1983–86.

difficulties exist in separating the various productivity augmenting effects (including the above) that may contribute to observed growth in national productivity over time. Accepting this empirical difficulty, one recent Australian study, using the IMP model, derived indices reflecting the contribution of greater scale to the Australian economy over the last two decades in a general sense, incorporating the combined effects of 'pure' scale, embodied technology, and other factors including specially enhanced skill levels through migration and better access to foreign markets.

Though derived separately for different Australian industry sectors, the index in aggregate suggests that a 10 per cent increase in inputs generates around a 13 per cent increase in output. Though immigration is obviously important to general input growth (as a component of population growth), and thus to the observed positive result, correlations between the index results for various sectors and associated proportions of overseas-born employed give a somewhat ambiguous picture on any more specific role of immigration. Within manufacturing, those sectors with high index values did tend also to be those with high concentrations of overseas-born employment, but no such association applied across the various major industry groups (where manufacturing is included as a whole).

Turning specifically to scale effects at the firm or industry level, it might be expected that unit costs of production would tend to decrease with greater population and domestic markets. One popular view in the United States, however, is that economies of scale in that country ceased being generally available by early in the present century. Though the corollary—that scale economies did apply prior to that point—offers encouragement for the very much smaller Australian economy, population growth as a source of scale gains is often played down in Australia by comparison with other approaches, such as rationalizing the structure of domestic industry or export market expansion. However, the 'launching pad' effect noted earlier, whereby industry becomes better equipped to tackle foreign markets through efficiency gains from domestic market growth, is receiving renewed attention today, particularly by management and business analysts. Overall, there is little research with which to assess the present relevance of scale economies in Australia, though some historical studies have claimed empirical support for positive scale effects in manufacturing, or in general non-rural production. At another level, Commonwealth Grants Commission relativities imply that scale economies do apply in the provision of government services to the smaller states, but only up to a population of around 2.5 million. More work is certainly needed to pin down the 'pure' scale effect, but nowhere does the Australian evidence legitimately suggest that scale economies do not exist or are not important.

On the related matter of technology, while there are persuasive prior reasons for immigration accelerating the rate of technological change—such as through technology-embodying investment, or through directly imported technical expertise and its spillovers to local workers, or through 'knowledge' scale effects raising the chances of both gifted individuals appearing and of a more effective scientific infrastructure—there is only limited empirical evidence on immigration and technology as such. There has been a stronger focus on these possibilities in the United States than in Australia, with opinion being generally positive, but findings not yet definitive.

Immigration and Welfare

It is probably true to say that the result that immigration within traditional parameters need not create net unemployment for residents is now widely accepted among Australian economists. There is also associated evidence that immigration has not retarded real wage growth nor exacerbated inflation, and that it may have enhanced per capita output growth over the longer term, and therefore positively affected growth in incomes per capita as well.

A related point is also increasingly recognized: there are significant and highly pertinent deficiencies in using per capita GDP growth as a welfare indicator in the presence of substantial immigration. By convention, inter-temporal welfare gain is generally proxied by changes in real GDP per capita. This has some merit for continuing residents of an economy, but it can be quite insufficient and inappropriate for immigrants. For a full welfare analysis, review of income of immigrants prior to arrival is essential to inter-temporal assessment. The point is also important if comparison of per capita growth performance is made across countries. For example, a country (such as Japan) which draws on internal migration from low productivity agriculture to high productivity manufacturing will record a boost to its GDP per capita growth that is not similarly available to another country (such as Australia) drawing on external migration from a separate low productivity agricultural economy.

Australian research indeed shows that migration has provided a major real income gain for most immigrants, relative to their home country. It has been estimated that, for immigrants overall, moving to Australia has doubled their real income growth in the post-war period relative to the average for their home countries. Interpretations of immigration as 'exploited labour' need to be heavily qualified in the light of this outcome, at least for Australia.

There is an associated debate in Australia on whether the assumption of benefits from immigration to previous residents can be sustained. In this context, the Berry–Soligo (1969) theoretical results have been revived to demonstrate formally that residents' per capita income must rise with immigration unless there are major diseconomies of scale or extensive foreign ownership of the national capital. Since empirical evidence exists of real per capita income rising with immigration and without effect on real wages, the conclusion seems possible that it is domestic asset-owners who benefit most from immigration, together with the migrants themselves.

As well as distributional matters, a question also arises of externalities not being reflected in per capita income measures. Recent Australian debate has strongly emphasized the possible negative consequences of immigration for the urban and natural environments, primarily through the general population scale effects rather than through immigrant-specific characteristics. This issue takes us well beyond the narrower economic scope of this chapter and deserves separate full treatment elsewhere. Australia has produced a lively literature on this issue, which is well summarized in Fincher (1991).

CONCLUSIONS

The contents of this chapter are dominated by Australian economic issues and results. Can such results be transferred to the United States? Recalling the unemployment and real wage discussion, it bears stressing that Australia has had a unique arbitral court-based wage-fixing system since early in the twentieth century. There are debates over the extent to which legal minimum wages emerging from Australian arbitration have effectively replicated the market. To the extent that greater downward rigidity of wages has resulted, however, there will be a systematic bias towards accentuating any negative employment consequences and understating any negative nominal wage effects of immigration. On this basis, countries like the United States with more wage-flexible labour market systems might see relatively more net employment generation and more nominal wage retardation through immigration.

With respect to real wages, the Australian economy is small and has been protected by distance and tariffs. Larger or more open economies such as the United States may well reap less from immigration by way of scale economy and tariff-leaping effects. If so, this would imply the possibility of a negative rather than independent relationship running from immigration to real wages for such economies. Indeed, just such a relationship has been hypothesized for the United States by Williamson (1974) and confirmed empirically by Geary and O'Grada (1985) using causality analysis. The Geary–O'Grada study covers the period 1820–1977 and, in sub-period analysis, finds the negative effect weaker in pre-World War II data, as the scale economy hypothesis would require. Positive per capita income effects overall, however, may still be plausible for non-immigrants, allowing for increased returns to owners of assets.

Finally, the social accounting point is readily transferable. All that is required is that immigrants improve their income compared to their source country position. This will characterize much immigration (indeed probably most immigration), and this is perhaps very much the point of the economics of international migration. Removal of all restrictions could substantially enhance world GDP, but the distributional and other non-economic implications of such dramatic liberalization are likely to limit its pursuit. Instead, countries such as the United States and Australia at least allow some substantial entry, so permitting an increase in the welfare of new citizens without generally disadvantaging the economic position of most of their own residents while substantially benefiting many. To economists reared on Paretian principles this would seem an achievement worthy of their endorsement. Yet it is a policy not universally accepted. Countries such as Germany are anxious to repatriate foreign workers, and others such as Japan very forcefully exclude significant numbers of foreign permanent residents. The commonality of view between Australia and the United States, in contrast to these other countries, is striking. Despite different research traditions and approaches (for example, aggregate versus microeconomic), and in spite of major differences in scale, institutions and economic structure, there is overall a striking convergence of broad research results, policy discussion and debate, and policy direction and commitment.

Due allowance must be made for the differences in labour systems, welfare systems, product markets, international integration, governmental structure and the like. Even within the immigration arena it must be recognized that there are major differences, such as greater illegal immigration and relatively less skilled immigration to the United States (as highlighted in the next chapter). But the sorts of overall conclusions on immigration's economic effects reached in recent Australian reports match well those of equivalent United States surveys, despite the different research base. The kinds of sentiments on the economics of immigration in the 1988 *Report of the Committee to Advise on Australia's Immigration Policies* seem remarkably similar to those of the 1986 *Economic Report of the President.*

In the United States specific regions of immigration such as California, New York and Florida represent economic units the size of national economies elsewhere, including Australia. Their rates of immigrant inflow are generally comparable to those of Australia. In the broad, therefore, it is gratifying that the 'disaggregate' analyses of the United States are possibly not too divergent from the 'aggregate' analyses of Australia, and that our policies, for all their interesting differences, have moved and continue to move along similar paths.

7

THE MICROECONOMIC ANALYSIS OF IMMIGRATION IN AUSTRALIA AND THE UNITED STATES

Peter J. Dawkins, William Foster, Lindsay Lowell and Demetrios G. Papademetriou

This chapter focuses on the economic effects of immigration on Australia and the United States. Whereas the previous chapter emphasized immigration's consequences for the economy as a whole, this chapter examines its labour market effects, that is, at the individual or firm level. Though this is a useful division, the chapters overlap in several areas. For example, although this chapter examines immigrant occupational skills and their implications for individual labour market outcomes, the skill content is also important in determining economy-wide effects.

The two chapters draw on a substantial and growing research literature in both countries on the economics of immigration. Comprehensive reviews have recently become available—in particular by Greenwood and McDowell (1986, 1990), Papademetriou et al. (1989) and Borjas (1990) for the United States, and by Wooden (1990) and Foster and Baker (1991) for Australia—and these form the basis for discussion of the issues and findings in the two countries, and for comparisons between them.

To provide some brief but useful background, we first outline several notable differences in perspective in the research and then recall some basic descriptive information on recent immigration to the two countries. Other topics then considered include the key issue of immigrant skills; labour market outcomes for immigrants and non-immigrants; immigrant self-employment and possible contributions to host country entrepreneurship; the economic and labour market effects of immigration at the industry level; and regional economic effects. Finally, we draw some broad conclusions.

RESEARCH DIFFERENCES

There are interesting and important differences in emphasis in recent research on the economics of immigration in Australia and the United States. The much stronger contribution of immigration to population growth in Australia and its relatively small, highly urbanized population have contributed to a much keener focus on immigration's aggregate, economy-wide effects. Indeed chapter 6 is much shaped by the Australian research perspective and findings. By the same token, the size and diversity of the United States economy has generated a broad range of disaggregate industry and regional labour market analyses of immigration of a kind virtually absent in the Australian literature. Much of this chapter focuses on the American perspective and findings.

At the microeconomic level, other important differences are apparent. United States research focuses very much, for example, on immigration's effects on the earnings and employment of non-immigrant groups. In Australia the focus is almost exclusively on the labour market outcome of immigrants themselves. In the United States the effect of illegal immigration has been an important issue. In Australia geography and centralized entry processes have meant that, at least until recently, illegal immigration has been relatively minor. Perhaps most important, however, is the difference in emphasis in issues and research arising from the countries' different perspectives on immigrant skills.

DESCRIPTIVE BACKGROUND

The contribution of immigration to Australian population growth has been over 40 per cent in recent decades, and the overseas born in the 1990s account for over 20 per cent of Australia's population. In the United States the overall demographic impact is much less. Though more than in previous decades, the contribution of immigration to overall population growth in the 1970s was still around 20 per cent, with just 6 per cent of the United States population being foreign born.

There are important differences in intake composition between the two countries. In particular, the skilled, or economically oriented, component of immigration has been more prominent in Australia. While family reunion entry into Australia is the largest component of the intake, fluctuating over the 1980s between around 40 and 50 per cent of annual settlers, immigration specifically on economic or skill grounds constituted around 30 per cent of the intake at both the beginning and end of the 1980s, after a temporary, quite sharp fall in the early part of the decade. Humanitarian (or refugee) entry approximately halved to around 10 per cent of the intake over the 1980s, with the balance of some 15 to 20 per cent consisting almost entirely of unvisaed New Zealanders.

Immigration to the United States is dominated by family reunion entry, which has accounted for around 70 per cent of the intake in recent decades. Of the other main entry components, the refugee proportion was larger in the 1980s than in the previous decade (around 18 per cent compared with 12 per cent), while the specifically economic or skill-oriented entry categories continued to account for only around 10 per cent of entrants.

Both countries have experienced recent shifts in their pattern of immigrant source countries. In Australia there has been a continued reduction in the proportion of immigrants from the traditional source region of Europe, particularly from the United Kingdom and Ireland, with a corresponding shift over the last two decades towards settlers from Asia and New Zealand. For the United States, the major shift has been to a much greater concentration of newcomers from Central America, principally Mexico and the Caribbean, and from Asia, principally the Philippines, Korea and Vietnam.

IMMIGRANT SKILLS

The difference in the proportion of skilled or economic category immigrants in each country's intake suggests there should be a corresponding difference in overall skill content. In both countries the average skill level of economic category entrants lies well above that of family and humanitarian settlers. However, the latter two categories also contribute importantly to overall intake skill levels. Changes in skill content within family and refugee groups, and changes in their intake proportions, will naturally affect overall skill content.

Over time, occupational data indicate that intake skill levels have increased through the post-war period in Australia, while probably decreasing in recent years in the United States. Though earnings-based skill indices should be interpreted with some care (since, for example, earnings is only one reflection of skill, and the occupation accorded immigrants on entry may not properly reflect their ultimate skill contribution after arrival), their application to Australian data suggests that intake skill levels increased by around 15 to 20 per cent in the three decades to 1980. Comparisons with corresponding indices for non-immigrants suggest that the immigrant skills content in fact exceeded that of the concurrent non-immigrant workforce by at least five per cent over the same period. More recently, simple inspection of occupation data suggests that intake skills also increased over the 1980s.

For the United States, however, life-cycle earnings estimates suggest a steady decline in the average skill level of immigrant men between

1950 and 1980. By the mid-1980s around one-half of immigrant labour force entrants moved into semi- or low-skilled occupations, compared with one-third of all United States employed being in such occupations (though the distributions were broadly similar at the highest skill levels).

This apparent contrast in recent experience in skills content between Australian and United States immigration has been confirmed through more direct comparisons of imputed earnings by birthplace. Borjas (1988) explicitly compared the labour market performance of immigrants in the United States, Australia and Canada, incorporating an analytical framework whereby immigrants choose their destination according to relative advantage among the different alternatives, subject also to host country immigration policy. In this study Borjas found that the skill level of immigrants to Australia, relative to non-immigrants, appears to have increased in recent decades, while the comparable measure had declined for the United States.

Educational attainment data also support the general contrast. In Australia around 40 per cent of overseas-born adults in 1987, for example, had post-school qualifications, compared with 35 per cent for the Australian born. Recent immigrants tended to be more highly qualified than earlier arrivals, with around 48 per cent of those in Australia for less than five years having post-school qualifications. In the United States much greater proportions of immigrants than non-immigrants are to be found at both the highest levels of qualification and the lowest levels of education. However, while the average school years of adult male immigrants did increase through the post-war period, the measure has moved from lying above that for all adult males in the United States in 1960, to slightly below in 1970, and further below in 1980.

These recent skill and education trends can be related to corresponding changes in intake pattern. In the United States, for example, the proportion of humanitarian immigrants has increased and is now much higher than in Australia, where the recent trend has been downwards. The average skills of this group lie below those of family reunion immigrants in both countries, so that the overall effect is to reduce United States intake skills relative to Australia. Recent changes in birthplace pattern are also relevant. For the United States, Asian immigrants are much more likely to have high-level college qualifications than those from North and Central America (including the Caribbean), and indeed than the United States adult population as a whole. At the other extreme, a much greater proportion of North and Central American immigrants have low levels of elementary schooling than of both Asian immigrants and all United States adults. Though increased Asian immigration may thus have tended to increase the intake of education and skill levels, the effect will be strongly offset by recent shifts to

Mexican and Caribbean immigrants. In Australia, however, the medium-term movement towards greater proportions of immigrants from Asia and New Zealand would appear, given prevailing patterns of education and occupation, to have made a clear, positive contribution in immigrant education and skill trends.

The Australian emphasis on immigrant skills has indeed led, from time to time, to concern by some that government and industry commitment to the domestic source of skills, the education and training system, may be undermined as a result. However, there is no available evidence, economic or otherwise, on which to properly assess this proposition, and others argue that any perceived shortcomings in Australia's education or training commitment should be addressed directly, rather than through an unproven and indirect link with immigration. Comparable arguments have been put in the United States, for example in relation to its recent influx of foreign-born engineers, but not with the apparent strength or consistency evident in Australia.

LABOUR MARKET OUTCOMES

The two obvious groups for whom the question of the effects of immigration on individual labour market outcomes has immediate relevance are immigrants themselves and non-immigrants. In the United States research has looked at the effects for both groups. In Australia the emphasis has been very much on the labour market experience of immigrants alone, though a strong recent focus on aggregate effects (see ch. 6) also enables some indirect inference on the experience of non-immigrants. This section discusses the evidence on immigrant labour market outcomes and then the effects of immigration on non-immigrants.

Immigrant Outcomes

Labour market experience can be summarized in terms of a number of key indicators, including labour force participation, unemployment and, for the employed, earnings and occupational status. In the 1990s in Australia the participation rate of the overseas born lies below that of non-immigrants, though it was comfortably above at the start of the 1980s. Unemployment is higher among the overseas born, though there is considerable variation by birthplace. By contrast, incomes for the overseas born are on average slightly above those of non-immigrants. Finally, while the two groups are similarly represented in high-status managerial and professional occupations, the overseas born are more heavily represented in the lower-status categories (operators, drivers, labourers, etc.), suggesting some overall margin in occupational status in favour of non-immigrants.

In the United States the general picture is quite similar. Labour force participation among foreign-born males was slightly higher in 1980 than for non-immigrants, though participation for both males and females is strongly associated with regional and ethnic factors. Unemployment among immigrant males was also slightly higher, though there was again considerable regional variation, with immigrants tending to have greater relative rates of unemployment in depressed areas. The 1980 Census indicates that hourly wages of foreign-born males were marginally below those of non-immigrants. A more significant shortfall in hours worked then generates a quite substantial difference in annual earnings. Finally, the occupational distributions of the foreign-born and non-immigrant groups are similar, though (as in Australia) the foreign born are represented rather more in lower-status occupations.

A major series of studies has been undertaken in both countries comparing the labour market outcomes of immigrants and non-immigrants, and investigating the reasons for any differences. These studies attempt to account appropriately for the influence of such variables as age, sex, occupation, birthplace, language and period of arrival in governing individual labour market outcomes. On participation, for example, Australian studies suggest that after an initial period of lower participation, male immigrants do not significantly differ in their rate from non-immigrants of similar age, education and other characteristics. However, for females, after initial adjustment, participation appears to be greater than for comparable non-immigrants. Similar United States analysis suggests that the foreign born have intrinsically greater labour force attachment than non-immigrants, although female immigrants do not participate as strongly as their male counterparts.

Studies attempting to account for the relative importance of various possible factors in influencing unemployment, earnings and occupational status by birthplace have mostly applied human capital theory to cross-sectional (mainly Census) data. Within this framework, specific allowance is made for demographic and productivity-related differences in observed labour market outcomes. The Australian results consistently stress the importance of three particular variables in accounting for observed differences in unemployment, earnings and occupational status—English language ability, period since arrival, and education. United States studies have focused mainly on the determinants of earnings differences by birthplace, but have identified essentially the same set of key variables.

Thus good English is associated with lower unemployment, and higher earnings and occupational status. The various studies indeed more formally confirm what can be clearly observed in aggregate Australian data on these variables—that the data patterns for employment prospects for overseas-born persons from English-speaking countries and for the Australian born are very similar, but that the employment outcome for the non-English-speaking overseas born is significantly worse.

The second key variable from the various studies is that the longer the period since arrival, the better is the apparent outcome for unemployment, earnings and occupational status. Given that most immigrants arrive without sponsored employment, it seems only reasonable that labour market outcomes in the early period after arrival should be worse than for both non-immigrants and immigrants of longer standing. But beyond this, the broader issue of labour market assimilation over time in their new country is in fact more complex than much recent research suggests. Unfortunately the plausible proposition that the labour market experience of immigrants converges with that of non-immigrants cannot be supported on the basis of just one source of cross-sectional data, as applies to many such studies in both countries.

The basic reason is that an apparent duration effect detected in cross-sectional data may simply reflect differences in characteristics or subsequent experience of immigrant groups arriving at different times. For example, differential rates of emigration by birthplace over time confound the testing of the assimilation hypothesis if the latter is based simply on observed demographic and skills profiles and labour market outcomes of the various groups identified by period of residence at a given time. A second complication is that entrants from different cohorts may confront very different labour markets on arrival. If earlier cohorts find initial jobs more readily than later groups simply because the economy is healthier when they arrive, a misleading impression of labour market adjustment may be observed from a subsequent cross-section. A further possibility that might also contribute to a misleading impression of labour market assimilation is that of differences between arrival cohorts in characteristics—such as motivation—that are unobserved or otherwise unaccounted for in the relevant cross-sectional analysis.

An apparent gain in earnings over time may thus actually indicate greater (unobserved) labour market 'quality' among earlier immigrants relative to more recent arrivals. Indeed, by comparing earnings over time for same-birthplace immigrants from the 1970 and 1980 United States Censuses, it has been shown that 1970s entrants realized less return to their skills and time since arrival than earlier arriving cohorts. Late 1970s arrivals, for example, do not attain over time the earnings of comparable non-immigrants, whereas immigrants from the early 1960s do, suggesting that the relative 'quality' of immigration may, in some sense, have dropped. In Australia a similar application of two cross-sectional data sets, for 1973 and 1981, suggests that period of residence has in fact only a minor effect on earnings differences.

The third key variable in the various studies is that better educational qualifications and labour market experience, acquired before or after immigration, also contribute to better labour market outcomes. Some interest has focused on the relative effects of education prior and subsequent to arrival, with the United States literature showing no unanimity on whether the positive returns to education obtained after immigration exceed those for education acquired before. In Australia it has been found that while higher levels of pre-immigration education are generally associated with better labour market outcomes, the relative position of the overseas born deteriorates with higher educational qualifications, particularly for those from non-English-speaking backgrounds. Transferability of foreign qualifications is evidently limited at higher, more specialized levels. There is presumably an increasing content in higher-level qualifications that is specific to both country and educational institution of origin, so that some overseas qualifications may indeed not be particularly applicable to a new labour market. Alternatively, some higher-level education or training may simply be of better quality in the host country. The greater concern in Australia, however, has been that quite adequately transferable qualifications are not accorded their appropriate labour market position, due either to employer oversight or to inadequate processes for formal recognition of overseas-based qualifications (which can particularly discriminate against immigrants from non-English-speaking backgrounds). This possibility is clearly wasteful economically for both the immigrants concerned and the nation.

Non-Immigrant Outcomes

The effects of immigration on the labour market prospects of non-immigrants has been a major focus of research and debate in the United States, in contrast to Australia. Many empirically-based United States studies have been undertaken to assess the manner in which mainly low-skilled or illegal immigrants complement or substitute for non-immigrant groups in employment, with any corresponding implications for earnings. Some specific findings will be noted in later discussion of industry and regional studies, but the general conclusion is that while immigration may cause some decrease in employment and wages among low-skilled non-immigrants, depending very much on the region or industry examined, these effects are small. Immigrants (and illegals) tend towards only weak substitutability or complementarity with non-immigrant groups, with the overall result being essentially benign. At the same time, some evidence exists that newcomers can affect the labour market outcomes of earlier immigrants to a greater degree.

In Australia the issue of labour market impact on non-immigrants has been much less explicit, with a lack of regional and industry studies comparable to the United States research effort. The question receiving greater attention in Australia has been the effect of immigration on aggregate, measured unemployment and wages. The conclusion on this can be stated briefly. As discussed in the previous chapter, a broad range of empirical studies shows that changes in immigration cannot be associated in any statistically significant sense with concurrent or subsequent changes in either the aggregate unemployment rate or wages. One corollary of this result is that, given the relatively high unemployment of immigrants, particularly in their early period after arrival, the employment prospects of the non-immigrant unemployed may in fact be assisted by immigration.

IMMIGRANT ENTREPRENEURSHIP AND SELF-EMPLOYMENT

The extent to which immigration affects the incidence and nature of entrepreneurship in the host country—as judged by the successful introduction of new business ventures, activities, methods and products—has been an important source of conjecture in both countries. The basic intangibility of entrepreneurship and its underlying attributes, however, make any association with immigration very difficult to detect. For example, entrepreneurial skills cannot be identified on entry (and after) in the same direct manner as occupational skills. Despite much anecdotal evidence, relatively little data and research exists on which to assess systematically the economic implications of immigration for entrepreneurship.

One convenient indicator of entrepreneurship is self-employment or employer status among those surveyed as being in employment, though the measure is not completely adequate—some measured self-employment, such as for Australian textile industry outworkers, reflects disguised wage employment rather than entrepreneurship. Accepting such limitations, though, the observed incidence of self-employment has been very similar in recent years for the overseas born and non-immigrants in Australia. Moreover, recent research can find no statistically significant difference in the tendency of the overseas born and non-immigrants to be self-employed, and no particular pattern across birthplace groups among the overseas born. However, an apparently greater tendency to self-employment among immigrants as period of residence lengthens is suggested (though again caution must be observed on the true role of the latter variable).

In the United States, though, immigrants have traditionally been more likely to be self-employed than non-immigrants. Indeed a notable increase in self-employment in the United States through the 1970s has been associated with the increased immigration of that decade, with more recent cohorts of immigrants showing a greater propensity to self-employment than earlier groups. In 1980 the proportions of self-employment among the total employed for immigrants and non-immigrants were around 11 per cent and nine per cent respectively (being similar in magnitude to the comparable Australian rates at around 10 per cent), and this margin remains even after controlling for demographic and other characteristics. Census data from 1970 and 1980 also suggest that immigrants are more likely to be self-employed the longer they have been in the United States.

Immigrants can become self-employed for various reasons. They may be inclined towards entrepreneurship by virtue of particular attitudes and abilities. They may also be influenced by cultural factors, such as the traditional roles of some immigrant groups in certain forms of business, and the presence of relatively large ethnic groups, or enclaves, which can provide capital and other resources, as well as natural markets for immigrant business. Research in both countries points to the importance of these sorts of factors, the Cuban community in Miami providing a particularly good case study. Self-employment can also serve as an economic refuge, effectively a form of under-employment, for immigrants with some start-up capital but otherwise relatively low wage options due perhaps to language or skill recognition difficulties. The United States literature suggests that such economic considerations may be significant in self-employment in that country, though Australian research finds no such formal connection.

Perhaps this last point helps explain why immigrant-owned small businesses in Australia appear to be more successful than non-immigrant businesses. Recent evidence suggests that they are more likely to remain in business in the crucial early years, and are more successful than non-immigrant businesses in achieving growth in employment, sales revenue and net profits—they typically start smaller and mature into larger enterprises. In Australia, therefore, while immigration may not increase the overall incidence of entrepreneurship, it may raise its quality.

The economic place of immigrant self-employment in the United States is less clear-cut. The data suggest that the immigrant self-employed earn less than demographically comparable immigrant wage earners and, in contrast to the Australian case, immigrant-owned businesses have very high failure rates. Yet foreign-born entrepreneurs in the United States are a major source of employment for immigrants of the same ethnicity. For example, a substantial proportion of Mexican businesses in south-western cities tend to hire Mexican immigrant employees. The hiring tendencies and products of ethnic businesses indeed provide valuable stability in 'enclave' communities which offer important—albeit difficult to quantify—resources assisting first generation workers to adapt to the United States.

INDUSTRY EFFECTS OF IMMIGRATION

The size of the United States economy and its breadth of industry have led naturally to a wide range of studies, with no research parallel yet in Australia, assessing the role of immigration in specific industries and its effect on non-immigrant workers. These investigations have focused very much on industries and regions with a significant immigrant presence, whether legal or illegal, and have been primarily based upon intensive case studies in particular localities, often supported by extensive field observations. A wide span of agricultural, manufacturing and service industries have been examined, with several themes emerging. However, any effects of immigration should be particularly visible in these sorts of studies, since firms and industries are typically selected precisely because of a significant immigrant presence. Also, industry-specific effects are limited if considered in themselves, since the consequences of immigration for particular firms or industries always flow through to the broader regional economy (studies from this perspective are discussed in the following section).

One theme concerns the apparently major role of low-skilled, low-cost immigrant labour in industry adjustment to competitive pressures from both overseas and home. Employment of illegal immigrants was an important element, for example, in the transition to more capital-intensive methods among automotive parts firms in Los Angeles in the early 1980s. In electronics companies in southern California immigrant workers have also been part of a conscious competitive strategy in the face of strong international pressures—at least one-third of their labour force consists of foreign born, with the Mexican born providing a ready supply of low-cost workers. Garment manufacturing also faces intense overseas competition, and relies on a continuing flow of newcomers. In furniture and poultry processing the competitive pressures are more domestic than international. Again, however, the evidence suggests that new and illegal immigrants have enabled some struggling firms to survive through lowered wage costs.

Further themes are evident in these studies. For example, immigrants have been important in other forms of adjustment. As the meatpacking industry has shifted from urban to rural areas, declining union involvement and lower wages have been associated with increased hiring of low-cost immigrants. In Los Angeles during the 1980s medium-sized contract cleaning firms initiated a structural shift in their industry by using mostly temporary immigrant workers to undercut larger unionized establishments. In other industries, such as textiles and shoe manufacturing, particular forms of immigrant labour have been important through lack of appropriate domestic training. For example, skilled Colombian loom fixers have assisted Massachusetts textile mills to continue, and low-wage Mexican immigrants, including illegals, have meant the survival of many shoe manufacturing firms in southern California.

At higher skill levels the foreign born do command good jobs, and there is little direct evidence of non-immigrant job displacement. Immigrants tend to complement the prevailing skill mix and function indistinguishably from non-immigrant workers. However, there is also evidence of immigrant niches emerging in some professions, with immigrant jobs seen as less desirable than those of non-immigrants. Among the 15 per cent of foreign-born physicians in the United States, for example, there appears to be some clustering in less desirable residency programmes. In nursing, where shortages are increasingly met by immigrants, particularly from the Philippines and Korea, the newcomers are disproportionately found in lower status positions. This phenomenon is also suspected in engineering, where there has been a rapid growth in the foreign born, their proportion of all engineers approximately doubling (to some 17 per cent) through the 1970s.

Beyond these general themes, the precise effect of immigration in different industries depends on a number of factors. For example, as suggested above, the nature of competition faced has an important bearing—competition from low-cost international manufacturers is typically more intense than from domestic businesses. Firm size can be an important determinant of the general quality of immigrants' jobs. In the furniture, garment and contract cleaning industries, larger unionized firms appear to treat immigrant workers equitably with natives, in contrast to smaller firms where illegal immigrants in particular can be paid much less. The vitality of the industry concerned is important also in its ability to absorb immigrants without affecting native workers. For instance, growth spurts in construction and constantly increasing demand for medical services make it possible to accommodate entrants more readily there than in less stable industries such as automobile parts manufacturing.

Though immigration has enabled some firms and industries to adjust and survive, its effect is regarded in the literature as something of a mixed blessing. The clear implication of many United States industry studies is that, in assisting firms to survive, immigrant labour has adversely affected the wages and employment of other workers. In unskilled jobs in particular new immigrants are targeted by firms hoping to underbid established businesses, such as in the Los Angeles contract cleaning industry. In other industries the effects may be more diffuse. For example, in the furniture and poultry industries, interregional competition may be effectively transferring jobs from domestic workers in the South and East to immigrants in southern California. Little hard empirical evidence exists for such effects, though, and what evidence there is suggests the quantitative effects are not great—research on the impact of Mexican labour on non-immigrant earnings in the Los Angeles apparel industry reveals virtually no discernible impact.

Other undesirable effects have been attributed to the use of immigrant labour. Some assert that in the southern Californian fruit and vegetable industry relatively cheap immigrant labour has retarded mechanization, dulled industry responsiveness to consumer tastes, and inflated land values. The recent preponderance of foreign-born engineers is thought to have undesirable implications for secondary education in science and mathematics. Also, the availability to the textile industry of specialized immigrant labour, otherwise lacking in the United States, and the availability of foreign-born nurses is thought to delay inevitable and necessary structural reforms in those sectors through capital upgrading and changed methods.

There are virtually no Australian studies yet available on the effects of immigration at the specific industry level. Industry issues, however, have been debated in the broader sense in Australia, particularly the extent to which immigration might assist or retard industry restructuring. No convincing economic evidence exists either way on this question, but clearly sectoral research along the United States lines would assist. The United States message that the 'industrial' impact of immigrants varies strongly by establishment and locality may well extend to Australia, even if its more structured wage system should reduce the likelihood of specific wage and employment effects. Some Australian observers assert that industry policy may have been politically inhibited by an immigrant presence in assisted industries. However, since the overseas born are also present in sectors likely to benefit from restructuring, the net effect on employment by birthplace is unlikely to be significant, and any such inhibition, even if proved, would appear to be misplaced.

REGIONAL EFFECTS

While there has also been substantial research on the regional effects of immigration in the United States, there has again been much less emphasis on this dimension in Australia, though several regional studies are now under way. This difference in emphasis stems from the geography of the two countries, with the foreign born very much more concentrated in specific states and cities in the United States than in Australia. This raises the potential for immigration's labour market impacts to be focused in a relatively few areas and thus to be generally uneven in incidence and nature.

In 1980 in the United States around two-thirds of the foreign born lived in just six states, which together accounted for 37 per cent of the total population. In Australia, New South Wales and Victoria together account for around 63 per cent of the overseas born, but this is only slightly above their share of total population (around 60 per cent). Immigrants in both countries exhibit a similar propensity for city living, with over 90 per cent of the foreign born in each to be found in metropolitan areas, compared with 75 per cent of the total population in the United States and 84 per cent in Australia. The 25 largest metropolitan areas indeed account for around 40 per cent of the United States total population, but over 75 per cent of the foreign born; in Australia the five largest cities account for 60 per cent of all Australians, and around 80 per cent of the foreign born.

In recent years immigrants have increasingly entered the United States across its southern and western borders into Florida, Texas and California, which with New York are now the main regions of foreign-born residents. In Australia, New South Wales and Western Australia have recently attracted a disproportionately high share of immigrants, given their stock, a shift associated with Australia's changing pattern of immigrant sources, particularly towards Asia and New Zealand. By contrast, South Australia's relatively low share of the recent flow represents a reversal of its success in the 1960s in attracting European immigrants into manufacturing employment using assisted passages and housing subsidies, with the consequent chain migration through family reunion having now largely disappeared.

In both countries, but particularly in the United States, the regional concentrations of the foreign born suggest that immigrants are strongly influenced in their choice of destination by the presence of established family and ethnic ties. Economic factors do, of course, play some part, as the South Australian experience suggests. In the United States illegal immigration, which is mainly concentrated in California, also appears to be more responsive to economic conditions than legal entry.

The United States research has highlighted broad regional variations among the foreign born in such indicators as occupational pattern, education, labour force participation and earnings. In the West and in Texas, for example, immigrants are to be found more in low-status occupations than elsewhere, with the growing concentration of Mexican immigrants associated also with relatively low averages in skills, education levels and earnings.

Studies of the local effects of immigration cover a wide range of areas across the United States, though the majority focus on New York and Los Angeles. New York has been the traditional entry point for European immigrants to the United States, and despite the recent shift to increased immigration from Central America and Asia, the influence of immigration continues to be great. During the 1970s both New York and Los Angeles experienced high levels of White out-migration together with large-scale net international immigration, resulting in Blacks moving into public sector and white-collar occupations, and immigrants into small business and manufacturing. Other major immigrant localities and regions that have been studied include Chicago, Miami and Texas.

The prime focus of these locally based studies is again the likely effects of immigration on non-immigrant employment and wages. In New York, for example, it has been concluded that though in the 1970s immigration may have depressed wages in some sectors, the effect was neither substantial nor permanent. In Los Angeles, in the same decade, immigration appears to have had no adverse effects on the employment of White or Black non-immigrants, though earlier cohorts of Mexican entrants may have been affected. In Texas immigration may also have affected earlier Mexican entrants, but research on San Antonio has concluded that illegal immigrants have only a small effect on the wages and employment of other groups there. A major influx of unskilled Cubans into Miami in the early 1980s resulted in a virtually immediate increase of around seven per cent in Miami's labour force, but no significant difference in non-immigrant wages and unemployment was subsequently discernible from concurrent changes in other cities such as Los Angeles, Houston and Atlanta. In summary, while the broad range of regional and local labour market studies does provide evidence of wage and employment effects with immigration, taken overall these are relatively isolated and small, with immigration playing a secondary role to other factors. The labour market impacts thus do not appear to be particularly uneven across different regions.

As noted earlier, a similar conclusion on wages and unemployment has been reached in Australia, but at the aggregate level rather than specifically for non-immigrants. However, though Australia lacks the regional diversity in immigration background so obvious in the United States and a corresponding tradition of regionally focused studies, there may still be instructive labour market differences in immigration's effects within the major cities, and a greater local and regional dimension is warranted in Australian immigration research.

CONCLUSIONS

This chapter has reviewed a variety of microeconomic and labour market effects encompassing often quite different methodologies in Australia and the United States. The underlying reasons for the different focus and methods of research in each country have been touched upon, and their effect is to make direct comparisons difficult. Overall, however, both countries demonstrate an ongoing capacity to successfully integrate newcomers into varied and dynamic immigrant societies, though differences exist between the two. Various broad conclusions can be drawn from the main points in each section, and these, including the key differences, are summarized below.

First, there is an important contrast in recent trends in immigrant skills content for the two countries. The evidence suggests that the average skill level of immigrants has increased through the post-war period in Australia, but decreased in recent decades in the United States. Such variation is clearly associated with changing patterns of entry category and birthplace among immigrants to the two countries.

The labour market outcomes of immigrants depend most upon a similar set of productivity-related factors in both countries, incorporating educational status and qualifications, work experience, and English language facility. While some studies suggest that period of residence also significantly improves immigrant outcomes, for methodological reasons labour market assimilation cannot be established through just one source of cross-sectional data (as applies in many studies). Indeed research in both countries linking different data sets suggests that labour market outcomes for a given migrant cohort do not necessarily 'catch up' with those of demographically comparable non-immigrants, so assimilation cannot be generally assumed.

Clear differences exist in the association of immigration and self-employment in the two countries. In the United States immigrants are more likely to be self-employed than non-immigrants, but immigrant-owned small businesses tend to be less successful than non-immigrant businesses. In Australia, on the other hand, the overseas born appear no more likely to be self-employed, but evidence suggests that their businesses are the more successful.

There has been substantial research in the United States on the effects of immigration on specific industries, and within specific localities and regions. In Australia these dimensions have been much neglected in immigration research. The United States literature focuses mainly on the role of immigrants in industry adjustment and their effects on the wages and employment of non-immigrants both within any industry examined and more broadly. Low-skilled or illegal immigrants have clearly facilitated adjustment in certain industries, particularly as a low-cost response to intensifying international and local competition. Also, as a source of relatively flexible, low-wage labour, such immigrants have inevitably affected prevailing wage levels and the employment prospects of non-immigrants, though no evidence exists that such impacts are felt beyond the industries concerned.

The regionally based studies confirm the likely limited nature of immigrant wage and employment effects. Immigrants in both countries, but particularly in the United States, cluster together in relatively few localities, suggesting the importance of established family and ethnic ties in locational choice, perhaps more so than purely economic factors, and raising the possibility of uneven labour market impacts of immigration across each country. However, the United States literature indicates that, while in some regions or localities there may be specific effects of immigration on non-immigrant employment or earnings, these effects are isolated and small. The overall conclusion is that, to all intents and purposes, there is no significant impact of immigration on non-immigrant wages and employment.

In Australia a parallel conclusion has been reached for the effect of immigration on the unemployment rate and wages at the aggregate level. The impact of immigration specifically on the wages and employment of non-immigrants has not been addressed through studies of particular industries or regions. However, despite Australia's different demography and more structured wage-setting system, the United States literature suggests there may well be useful labour market lessons for Australian researchers in undertaking more focused industry and regional studies, particularly in the current era of industry challenge and adjustment.

Underlying this general picture, though, in terms both of accounting for specific findings and of framing research agendas in the two countries, are issues of intake skills. The recent trends in skill content may help explain specific empirical results for the two countries, such as the apparently greater success of Australian immigrants in self-employment, and the apparently stronger role of ethnic enclaves in United States small business. But beyond this there also appears to be a noticeably more positive tone in the Australian research perspective on the microeconomic effects of immigration, based upon the different place of skills in the two countries' immigration experience, with recent movements in intake skills content tending to crystallize this fundamental difference.

Economic selectivity has always been a key aspect of Australian immigration policy and, despite occasional fluctuations, policy makers continue to see an important role for immigration in providing economically needed skills. The proportion of skill-category immigrants in the Australian intake in recent decades has been well above that for the United States, with the margin in overall skill content apparently widening. This traditional emphasis may have contributed to a special consciousness in Australia, relative to the United States, of the skills aspects of immigration, particularly at the higher end of the skills range. Thus, in Australia concern often focuses on specific implications of skilled immigration, including the possible impact of immigration on the domestic education and training commitment, transferability and apparent non-recognition of immigrant skills, and how immigrant skills can be used to their full potential. These questions are also asked in the United States, but immigration's role as a positive source of skills seems much less explicit, with the recent perspective fixed more at the lower end of the skills scale. This focus has generated a correspondingly different framework of questions, such as how lower skilled immigrants assimilate into the United States labour market, what effects they might have on non-immigrant groups, and what role they may have in industry adjustment.

Immigration policy and control in the two countries is obviously fundamental to this difference in perspective. In Australia a relatively high degree of control continues to be exerted over the occupational skills and other characteristics of the immigrant intake through, in particular, the well-established points system. In the United States the official emphasis on immigration as a source of useful skills appears much less, with a greater role for family reunion and other considerations. On this basis, it will be interesting to observe, some years hence, the implications for research questions and findings if the United States intake does indeed shift towards a greater emphasis on skilled and employer-nominated immigrants into the 1990s.

PART III

IMMIGRANT SETTLEMENT

8

IMMIGRANT SETTLEMENT POLICY IN AUSTRALIA

James Jupp

Australia, usually in co-operation with Britain, assisted immigrants with their fares under various schemes between 1831 and 1982. As a corollary of such immigrant assistance, Australian authorities increasingly undertook a role in their settlement. After 1870, when the colonies took over final responsibility for assistance from the British Colonial Land and Emigration Commission, the public provision of temporary accommodation and onward fares on arrival became common. Voluntary agencies also adopted a role in assistance. This combination of basic on-arrival services, supplemented from the voluntary sector, was still relevant in the 1970s.

The state also had a role in ensuring that new arrivals were not exploited. An important difference between Australia and other immigrant recipients was the development of a strong trade union movement and an industrial arbitration system which created machinery for national wage determination with legal sanctions. While this was of no benefit to the unemployed, it established the principle that immigrants could not be used as cheap labour in urban employment. Essentially, most immigrant workers were employed under the same wages and conditions as native-born Australians. Strike-breaking by immigrants (which had occurred in the waterfront strikes of 1928) became impossible in the conditions of post-war full employment. While many non-English-speaking immigrants were employed in the less attractive industrial jobs, these were fully unionized and covered by legally enforceable awards. Indeed, the level of unionization of southern Europeans has consistently been well above that of native-born Australians, despite the strong position of the latter in the highly unionized public sector.

POST-WAR IMMIGRATION

All public policy between 1914 and 1947 was directed towards assisting and encouraging the British, discouraging and not assisting alien Europeans, and rigorously excluding all non-Europeans. The only significant exception was the acceptance of Jewish refugees from Nazism under the Évian agreement of 1938. Their settlement became the responsibility of the Australian–Jewish Welfare Society, an organization specifically and officially created for that purpose and still functioning today. This was the first example of co-operation between authority and what later became known as an 'ethno-specific' welfare agency. While self-help organizations did exist among other non-British immigrants, they received no official recognition.

The official encouragement of non-British immigration dates from 1947 and was based on refugees. These, like convicts and assisted immigrants in the past, could be selected, directed and assisted effectively because they were dependent on public support for their settlement in Australia. The settlement programmes for refugees had several objectives: to alleviate the material problems of the new settlers; to house them; to direct them towards suitable employment as determined by authority; to teach them the basic linguistic and cultural skills necessary for integration into majority society; to ensure their basic health; to equip them with skills and attitudes relevant to surviving as free settlers after the two years of bonded labour. The programme also aimed to influence public opinion: to persuade Australians that aliens would make good 'New Australians'; to argue that working conditions and housing for Australians would not be adversely affected by immigrants; to impress on aliens the need to assimilate rapidly to Australian culture; and to stress that refugee migration was an expedient which did not challenge the established principle of attracting settlers from Britain (Kunz 1988). All refugees were Europeans, and those who had fled to Australia from Asia during the war were normally returned home.

The objects of settlement policy were to ease the assimilation process, to avoid the creation of ethnic enclaves, to minimize public costs, to reduce majority anxieties, to use migrant labour for projects of national importance, and to ensure that immigrants became permanent settlers who would not differ too markedly from the average either culturally or socially. At this stage Australia saw itself as a homogeneous and egalitarian society, which was measurably true in many respects (though not, of course, in all).

The refugee phase was quite short but crucial in establishing methods for dealing with non-British arrivals. Camps were used for these and even for Commonwealth-nominated British immigrants who had no local relatives or sponsors. The camps were used again for refugees after the fall of Saigon in 1975, under the less alienating description of 'hostels'. Apart from the hostels, the other legacy of refugee settlement includes the Adult Migrant English (previously Education) Programme (AMEP). The AMEP was started in 1947 with the initial objective of teaching 'survival English' to new arrivals. It has developed as a major service and is, indeed, the only generally available provision for learning adult English as a second language other than by private tuition. In some states it is administered through the technical and further education (TAFE) system, but elsewhere it has teachers, courses and buildings of its own.

Previous reliance on voluntary agencies was extended by the creation of the Good Neighbour movement in 1949. This was funded by government to co-ordinate the efforts of charitable and religious agencies working with immigrants. As hundreds of thousands of Maltese, Italians, Greeks and Yugoslavs arrived in the major cities, the Good Neighbour movement found itself challenged both by its inability to communicate with those who did not speak English and by the rapid expansion of organizations and media based on the new arrivals. These arrivals predominantly became industrial workers who began to look towards the trade union and labour movement, whereas many in the Good Neighbour movement were established conservatives in sympathy with the ruling Liberal and Country parties. They accepted assimilation as a goal and were reluctant to give a voice to new arrivals either in their own organizations or in their annual citizenship conventions. The early 1970s saw the collapse of conservative political hegemony and the election of the first Labor Government for 23 years. They also witnessed a growing southern European revolt against the paternalism and assimilationism of the Good Neighbour movement.

THE GALBALLY SYSTEM

One watershed in settlement policy was marked by the admission of 170 000 refugees after 1947. The next was the adoption in 1978 of the report on migrant programmes and services (Galbally 1978). This moved away from assimilationism towards recognizing ethnic identity. It opened up the prospect of a greater investment of public funds and effort than had been thought appropriate under the 'survival' strategy of the past. Most of the basic Galbally programme is still in place, having survived a change of government, a shift in intake sources from southern Europe to Asia, a decline in the level of employment, a rise in the level of immigration, a shift from Keynes towards Milton Friedman and no fewer than nine Commonwealth Ministers of Immigration. While the Galbally provisions have not solved all the problems of mass immigration, they have appealed to the organized immigrant community. The history of settlement policy since has centred around the

Galbally approach—modified, eroded, expanded and contracted—but never openly abandoned.

The Galbally Report recommended expansion and improvements in the Adult Migrant Education Programme, which was further reviewed in 1985. This became the largest budgetary item for the Department of Immigration, although general reviews of services in 1986 and 1988 recommended its transfer to the Department of Education, without effect. Galbally also commended the Telephone Interpreter Service (TIS), which has been administered by Immigration since 1973 and serviced 362 235 calls in 1989–90 without charge to the user (DILGEA 1990). TIS still represents the best means for a non-English speaker to summon emergency help, and hospitals are major users. At the time Galbally reported, many on-arrival services were still being provided through hostels. In accordance with the philosophy of the governing Liberal Party, however, he argued that more reliance should be placed on voluntary self-help and less on directly provided public services. Supporting the withdrawal of funding from the Good Neighbour Councils, Galbally recommended an extension of grant-in-aid to ethnic associations, which had been receiving some small support since 1968. Such grants-in-aid in 1992 extended to 245 organizations in all states and territories. The normal provision pays for a full-time worker with office support, but there is a recent tendency to give half-grants for servicing the variety of small ethnic groups which have entered Australia since 1975. Another institution launched by Galbally was the Migrant Resource Centre (MRC). There are currently 25 MRCs located throughout Australia. The more enterprising have extended their sources of funds and some now employ 10 or more staff on various grants, while others are confined to the full-time worker and office staff normally provided by the Department of Immigration. The MRCs act as focal points for individuals and organizations, and some also engage in research and publication. They are managed by voluntary committees drawn mainly from the non-English-speaking population of the relevant district, but include a departmental representative.

Galbally extended his support to non-English broadcasting and what he called 'ethnic television', institutionalized as the Special Broadcasting Service in 1978. The only major institution founded by Galbally which has not survived was the Australian Institute of Multicultural Affairs (AIMA), abolished in 1986 after a series of reviews. AIMA's research function had to be recreated by the Office of Multicultural Affairs (1987) and the Bureau of Immigration Research (1989). Its demise was partly the result of too close an association with the defeated Liberal Party and partly of bureaucratic manoeuvrings within the Department of Immigration. The range of settlement and multicultural services initiated by Galbally otherwise remains and has been important in creating a body of interested individuals and groups who receive public funds. While such funds are much less than those devoted to Aboriginal services, they represent a significant basis of welfare support for ethnic associations. While Galbally's emphasis on self-help was attacked as reducing the level of professional service available, it proved very popular with ethnic organizations. Attempts to reduce the Galbally provisions in the mid-1980s were met with strong resistance.

ACCESS AND EQUITY

As Galbally had noted, the Department of Immigration services only touched upon immigrant lives at limited points. Areas such as education, general welfare or employment were the province of other Commonwealth and state departments. These tended to refer immigrants to the Immigration Department and to deliver their services largely or wholly in English. Thus they were not accessible to many hundreds of thousands of Australian taxpayers who had to rely on Galbally services such as grant-in-aid workers or MRCs—or go without. Within the Department of Immigration there was concern that a variety of services was being undertaken for which the Department was not always well equipped and which might overlap with the responsibilities of others. Such services included adult (but not child) migrant education; validation of qualifications; translating and interpreting; provision of hostels; welfare case work; support for ethnic organizations; monitoring migrant access to other services; and some language policy. The Department was seen as 'client driven', a criticism made by the FitzGerald review of immigration policy in 1988. While not wishing to contract its functions purely to a selection and exclusion role, some officers were not anxious to retain the welfare and provision role which Galbally had expanded.

The AIMA reviewed the Galbally provisions in 1982 and found them to be generally satisfactory (AIMA 1982). As Galbally had already noted, however, there were major problems in persuading public agencies other than those directly concerned with immigrants to acknowledge the changed character of their clientele. This limited access to mainstream services for those whose English was inadequate or who were unaware of what was available. Services of great importance to immigrants, such as employment and unemployment programmes, health, welfare, education, women's services, and aged care, were often unaware of the need to change or were reluctant to do so. Immigration, as a small and politically weak department, was unable effectively to implement the monitoring and advocacy role which Galbally had suggested.

Following the 1982 review, which was held under the Liberals, the new Labor Government began a series of reviews of the whole area of multicultural and immigrant programmes. Among these were reviews of AIMA (1983), the Special Broadcasting Service (1984), child ESL education (1984), Adult Migrant Education (1985), migrant and multicultural programmes in general (ROMAMPAS 1986), and immigration policy (CAAIP 1988). At the state level, too, there were important reviews in New South Wales (1978), Victoria (1983) and Western Australia (1985). Internal Immigration Department reviews continued in parallel, as did those of the National Population Council (1985 and 1988) and the Advisory Council on Multicultural Affairs (1989). These culminated in the publication of a National Agenda for a Multicultural Australia in 1989.

By 1990 most aspects of successful settlement were well understood and documented. What was less well mastered was the implementation of notions of access and equity which would ensure that all public services were equitably delivered and made available to those of a multiplicity of backgrounds and differing levels of English competence. This was a complex area (Jupp 1989). It involved challenging long-held beliefs and prejudices, not least those of some of the ministers concerned as well as their senior public servants. One model for monitoring progress and dispelling prejudice was the work of the Office of the Status of Women and its state equivalents. But women were more effectively mobilized and coherent and made up more than half the electorate. While excluded from many positions of influence, their role in parliamentary and bureaucratic politics was expanding during the 1980s more markedly than that of immigrants, whose sources of origin were changing rapidly and whose institutions were heavily dependent on government funds. The round of enquiries kept many ethnic activists tied up in seemingly endless consultations and submissions. Much energy had to be put into preserving threatened institutions, most notably the Special Broadcasting Service, and countering the attacks on multiculturalism and universal intake which characterized conservative politics in the later 1980s.

Among the issues canvassed during the 1980s were: the extent to which settlement services should be confined to recent arrivals; the degree of priority which should be given to 'new and emerging groups'; the division of responsibility between Immigration and other Commonwealth departments; the role of the states and local government; the relationship between ethnic-specific and mainstream services; the possibility and limitations of the user pays principle; the possibility of limiting services to citizens; the modification of existing services to meet the needs of new clients; the continuing validity of the Galbally approach; the special needs of refugees, women and the elderly; and the ever-present issue of costs and benefits. While a whole range of minor programmes have been instituted, usually on a short-term basis, there have not been the major innovations that characterized the immediate post-Galbally period. Most initiatives have come from within the bureaucracy, with the ethnic constituency often forced into the role of defending the existing provision. The main thrust of government policy has been to make mainstream agencies responsive to their diverse clientele, rather than to launch new departures.

The Commonwealth access and equity strategy was adopted in 1986 and extended in 1989. Its origins, though, lay in earlier initiatives at the state level, as developed in the New South Wales report *Participation* (1978) and the Victorian report *Access and Equity* (1983). The central concept of access and equity was endorsed by ROMAMPAS in 1986 and had been taken up by the National Population Council (the major advisory body on immigration) in the previous year (NPC 1985). This development reflects two influences: the desire of newly elected Labor governments to implement social justice objectives, and a bureaucratic concern that the Galbally strategy was too limited and had not sufficiently influenced departments other than Immigration. Some suspicion of the strategy arose among ethnic organizations, who feared that it threatened the ethno-specific approach of subsidizing their welfare activities. Initially the Government provided a major expansion of grant-in-aid, though this along with other services was limited after the 1986 budget cuts.

The access and equity strategy is monitored by the Commonwealth Office of Multicultural Affairs and the State Ethnic Affairs Commissions. Departments and agencies are expected to prepare and publish access and equity programmes which detail the means they will adopt to service clients from cultural minorities. In New South Wales this obligation has been extended to local government authorities. Such programmes include special language services, staff training and the targeting of disadvantaged groups. At first many agencies confused access and equity with equal employment opportunity, which also obliges them to report on the extent to which they employ and promote staff of non-English-speaking background (NESB), as well as women, Aborigines and the disabled. Some policy departments, such as Treasury and Finance, have been reluctant to admit that access and equity extends beyond the service delivery areas in which they are not engaged. Naturally the strongest focus and most elaborate programmes have been those of departments concerned with immigration, education, welfare, social security, health and employment.

The Commonwealth access and equity strategy was under review in 1991. It has not so far been used to replace ethno-specific services, although these have not expanded very rapidly in recent years. At the commonwealth and state levels government agencies are gradually becoming used to their obligations and now incorporate access and equity approaches in their staff training and operations. Language services (interpreting, translating and teaching) have all expanded and are currently under commonwealth review aimed at standardization and elimination of overlap. There has undoubtedly been improvement in many important areas despite bureaucratic and (less importantly) political resistance to what many regard as 'special treatment' for immigrants and cultural minorities. Cost is still used as an argument for not amending or expanding staffing arrangements. Some agencies, such as the Commonwealth Employment Service, have greatly improved their record, while some departments, such as Health, Housing and Community Services, have moved away from a previous insistence on undifferentiated 'mainstream' services. The publication of departmental access and equity programmes, which was recommended by ROMAMPAS (1986) and implemented by the Office of Multicultural Affairs, has been an important instrument in ensuring compliance. Weaknesses in service delivery now more frequently represent lack of resources rather than indifference or hostility to the multicultural clientele, though there is still much lip-service among agencies which do not deal directly with immigrant clients. Even so, such agencies have been obliged to take note of the multicultural reality of the Australian public.

As most services relevant to settlement of immigrants now lie outside the functions of the Commonwealth Department of Immigration, the adoption of an access and equity approach is potentially of great importance. This is particularly so as Immigration itself has shifted its focus towards recent arrivals. With a limited budget, of which settlement services take up the largest part, the Department was faced in the 1980s with a steadily rising number of immigrants from an increasing variety of sources. New South Wales and a small number of municipalities in Sydney were faced with the greatest obligations. As that state had been a pioneer in applying access and equity principles to its departments and local authorities, the methods were already in place for dealing with the influx. At the national level, concentration on new arrivals was endorsed by the FitzGerald committee on immigration policy of 1988. Its rigorous insistence on a two-year maximum period for settlement service eligibility was not endorsed by government. In effect though, the Department of Immigration now targets those arriving within that timeframe, with a special emphasis on 'newly emerging groups'—a euphemism for those from Asia and the Middle East.

The shift towards servicing new arrivals has created potential problems for many NESB Australians who come from earlier intakes. Many of these never became proficient in English. Now aging rapidly, many eastern and southern European communities traditionally looked to ethno-specific services funded through the Department of Immigration.

As long-established citizens, they were able to apply political pressure to slow down the process of transferring such services to new arrivals. The access and equity strategy held out the promise that other departments (especially Health, Housing and Community Services at the commonwealth level) would take over the responsibility. There was a major development in studying the needs of the 'ethnic aged' in the early 1980s, and this led to changes in policy towards subsidizing ethnic nursing and home care facilities. At the state level the emphasis on new arrivals has been less marked and ethnic affairs commissions do not differentiate their clientele in terms of recency of arrival, seeing themselves as 'ethnic' rather than 'immigrant' agencies.

ISSUES AND PROBLEMS

Australian settlement policies compare favourably with those of some other immigrant recipients, most notably Britain and the United States. They are comparable with many initiatives taken in Canada, although provincial variation and responsibility is more important there. The elaborate welfare states of Sweden and The Netherlands give more detailed attention to vulnerable groups such as refugees, using local government much more widely than would be feasible in Australia. Some Australian programmes have aroused interest and even admiration from elsewhere—most notably the Telephone Interpreter Service and some aspects of direct method teaching under the Adult Migrant English Programme. Most interchange of information has taken place with Canada (Hawkins 1989).

The relative success of immigrant settlement in Australia has tended to blur criticism of existing programmes or suggestions for their improvement. The 1986 review (ROMAMPAS) was largely vitiated by the budgetary cuts of that year and there was little new or relevant on settlement in the 1988 CAAIP (FitzGerald) review. However, as suggested above, within the bureaucracy there have been considerable shifts of priority towards new arrivals. No immigrant settlement programme can be altogether successful and some major problems are apparent to those who study this area, although they have scarcely surfaced as political or bureaucratic imperatives. Among these problems have been the following:

English Proficiency

The early concentration on simple 'survival' levels has left hundreds of thousands locked into illiteracy, unskilled employment and lack of effective citizenship. The recent emphasis on new arrivals does nothing for those neglected in the past. On the contrary, the shift of resources towards those settling within two years has disadvantaged those who have not previously acquired a reasonable level of spoken and written English. The official expectation that they might become the responsibility of the mainstream education authorities is quite utopian. A generation who arrived between 1947 and 1978 is still locked into unskilled manual employment; many have lost the ability to respond to rapidly changing employment patterns. Also it is not at all clear that the resources dedicated to the Adult Migrant English Programme are sufficient to train all those currently seeking its services (Campbell 1985). There are long waiting lists in the major immigrant centres. Most AMEP clients are unemployed or women in the home. Workers in regular employment are quite ineffectively serviced. Many recent arrivals, however, seem to be using their period of unemployment to acquire English skills, and the major clients are from Southeast Asia and Latin America.

Unemployment

Those arriving before 1972 had no problems in securing employment, even if it was not in jobs which they eagerly sought. Refugees were directed to employment in conditions of acute labour shortage. The rapid expansion of manufacturing in the 1950s and 1960s ensured factory jobs for southern European arrivals. Government agreements with countries such as Turkey (1967) and Yugoslavia (1970) were based on a desire to emulate Germany in attracting such workers, though as 'settlers' rather than as 'guests'. While there was always a degree of mismatch between skills, potential and actual employment, this happy state of affairs allowed new arrivals to maximize their income. The level of home ownership among southern European families is still well above the national average at virtually saturation levels of more than 90 per cent. Unemployment levels, however (which had rarely exceeded two per cent between 1947 and 1972), are now normally between six per cent and 10 per cent and are higher among recent arrivals, especially refugees. Manufacturing industry has declined and immigrant recruiters have sought higher skill levels. In contrast to previous practice, high levels of immigration went parallel with high levels of unemployment until 1989–90. The drop of 25 per cent in the intake in that year was probably caused by New Zealand recognition that employment prospects in both countries had become equally dismal.

Refugees

Australia has accepted over 400 000 refugees in the 45 years from 1945, most of them from communist states. Until 1975 these refugees found their way into employment without serious difficulty, although many had language difficulties. The main problem now faced by eastern European refugees is aging. Since 1975, however, refugees have come predominantly from outside Europe and have suffered much higher levels of unemployment. A significant proportion have also suffered trauma caused by warfare, genocide or torture, though this was also true of the post-war intake. While small programmes have been put in place to cope with this problem, they are marginal and poorly funded. Settlement policy does not recognize a refugee category after initial settlement. Refugees passing through the hostels were a major beneficiary of on-arrival services and English tuition. Once out in the community, though, they receive no special treatment. It is becoming increasingly clear that the main refugee groups—from Indo-China, Lebanon and Latin America—have serious adjustment problems. These are arguably even more severe for smaller groups from areas such as east Africa, Sri Lanka or Fiji.

Qualifications and Skills

Since the early 1950s it has been acknowledged that foreign skill qualifications are inadequately accepted in Australia. Trades and professions are strictly regulated as to entry. Historic traditions have meant that while British and other English-language qualifications are usually recognized, those from other backgrounds are not. The majority of post-war arrivals until the 1970s were poorly skilled and educated and this issue did not seem of major importance. Problems with the placement of Czechoslovak refugees in 1968, however, led to the creation of the Committee (later the Council) on Overseas Professional Qualifications (COPQ) in 1969. This was located within the Department of Immigration, was poorly resourced, and felt itself to be inadequate to the task of validating qualifications which varied between jurisdictions within the federal system. The Council in submissions to ROMAMPAS (1986) and CAAIP (1988) highlighted the inadequacies of COPQ. Prime ministerial interest in the latter year prompted the abolition of COPQ and the creation of a stronger agency, the National Office of Overseas Skills Recognition, within the Department of Employment, Education and Training (Castles 1989).

Discrimination

Virtually all immigrants before 1975 came from European backgrounds, including those born in Asia or Africa. While settlement policy included efforts to 'sell' non-British immigrants to a suspicious public, it was assumed that in the long run European descendants would assimilate to the majority culture, as they had largely done in the past. Since 1975 not only has assimilation been abandoned as a stated goal, but the sources of intake have moved towards Asia, the Middle East and other non-European areas. Normally between 30 per cent and 40 per cent have been broadly 'Asian', even while Britain and New Zealand remain as the major source countries. This has raised the issue of discrimination as relevant to settlement policy and to social harmony in general. All settlement policy for a century has had a stated or assumed objective of preventing or avoiding racial or ethnic conflict. The White Australia Policy was, of course, the clearest example of this. Discrimination in employment, housing and access to public services has been progressively illegalized since the first legislation was passed in South Australia in 1966. Most analysis of discrimination has found that Aborigines are the major victims. Commonwealth adoption of a community relations strategy in 1989 marks a recognition of the potential for racist discrimination against immigrants (OMA 1989).

Attitudes and Practices

Given the relatively benign state of ethnic relationships and immigrant settlement in Australia, there has been much less debate in the political arena about immigrant settlement than has been common, for example, in Britain or France (Freeman 1979). The parties have normally agreed to a consensual approach, much to the frustration of those who want more radical policies and those who are more conservative or racist. The immigrant constituency, which is subsidized from public funds, has not been very radical and has also deliberately avoided being identified with either side of politics. Ethnic radicalism in Australia stems from the Aborigines or from nativist or racist groups and individuals. These latter have been much less influential than might be supposed from Australia's recent history. While opinion polls regularly show large proportions who are against multiculturalism or Asian immigration, they also show similar proportions against all immigration. Australia has no recent history of race riots, other than fights outside hotels in remote country towns with large Aboriginal populations. In this century only two riots leading to deaths have been recorded—in Kalgoorlie in 1934 and between Australian and American servicemen in Brisbane in 1942.

This relatively peaceful history of community relations and of immigrant settlement obscures two very widespread (if often not measurable) influences on public policy. One is the fear that diversity will lead to lack of cohesion, social disharmony and eventual violence. The other is that all Australians should be treated equally, even if their circumstances are quite different. Both are aspects of the underlying egalitarianism and xenophobia which historians have seen as constituting part of the national identity developed between the 1880s and the 1940s. The effects of these two attitudes are mostly to inhibit the development of any special services for those of non-English-speaking or non-European background. Distinct refugee services have been inhibited by the widespread and quite erroneous belief that refugees already receive generous benefits not available to others. This myth seems to have its origins in the United States and is certainly untrue, though widely held, in Australia. Special tuition in English has been inhibited by the argument by trade unions that it is a privilege not available to others. This has been an important factor in limiting trade union support for English teaching in working time. The targeting of immigrants in equal employment opportunity programmes has been less effectively implemented, and is more widely resented and misunderstood, than targeting of women or Aborigines (Niland and Champion 1990). Subsidies for ethnic-specific welfare agencies have been severely criticized, even though subsidized welfare provision has been normal in Australia for over a century through religious denominations and other charities. Very small subsidies for mother tongue maintenance are attacked and eroded, while massive subsidies for denominational education continue.

DEFENDING THE STATUS QUO

All settlement and multicultural policy has to be made within an ideological framework and a set of political assumptions which often contradict the ethnic-specific, immigrant focused and multicultural approaches to which all governments have been committed since the early 1970s. As nearly all politicians and policymaking bureaucrats are native born or British, this contradiction frequently works to the disadvantage of non-English-speaking immigrants. Settlement policy is always under review. While such review gives opportunities for immigrant pressure to be exerted, it also provides opportunities to cut services or simply to erode them. In the early 1990s atmosphere of economic and budgetary stringency, contraction and erosion often look more attractive than expansion and improvement. The overall success of immigrant settlement since 1947 has blunted the edge of radical critiques, which have, in any case, not been very common or persuasive in recent years. Most argument about settlement services has been defensive rather than innovatory.

The defence of existing provision rests on several bases. There is an official recognition that as long as Australia has a planned programme of mass immigration on a universalist basis, it will need settlement programmes at least as generous as those currently existing. A commitment to refugee intake strengthens this argument. It is countered by those who believe that as skills increase and refugee numbers decline, the need for settlement programmes will diminish. This view was especially influential on the 1988 FitzGerald Report, but seems utopian. A vocal and well-educated ethnic lobby also exists, consisting of persons employed in settlement services who are often second generation Australians. This lobby is potentially more important than the often elderly, first generation immigrants dealt with by government through the Federation of Ethnic Communities' Councils and the Ethnic Communities' Councils. As with state-supported services for women and Aborigines, public funding has created the lobby which will pursue further funding. Some bureaucratic interests are also likely to defend settlement services, most notably a section of the Department of Immigration (though not all of it), the Office of Multicultural Affairs and the state ethnic affairs commissions. Finally, many politicians believe in the 'powerful ethnic lobby' or the 'ethnic vote' (Betts 1988). In the final analysis these beliefs will determine the extent to which settlement services are improved or modified in the future.

THE RATIONALE FOR SETTLEMENT POLICY

After the FitzGerald Report of 1988 there was a period of concentration on administrative and regulatory change, which diverted attention away from settlement issues. No major review of settlement policy was made between 1986 and 1991. In the latter year, however, the Commonwealth began to reassess some of its activities, including those still influenced by the Galbally Report of more than a dozen years before. The underlying rationale of settlement policies remained the same and was reasserted by FitzGerald, by the Office of Multicultural Affairs and by politicians of both major parties at both levels of government. This rationale had four major components (outlined in the following paragraphs), with the emphasis varying from time to time and aspect to aspect.

The first component was a desire to maintain and improve social harmony by avoiding ethnic conflict and the growth of disadvantaged ethnic minorities. Advocates of multiculturalism believed that this was best done by tolerating diversity and by modifying official practices and policies to take account of such diversity. Australian society has, in fact, remained quite harmonious, despite entrenched unemployment and growing long-term economic problems. The situation of the Aboriginal, rather than the immigrant, population is most clearly characterized by ethnic disadvantage.

The second component was the need to retain settlers, a higher priority in the 1970s than in the 1990s when advocacy of steady population growth has become less fashionable. Nevertheless, the tendency of skilled settlers from more prosperous countries to leave Australia has led to a diminution of net settlement in recent years and is of some concern to advocates of steady population development.

The third component was recognition of the economic inefficiencies inherent in attracting skilled migrants who cannot find work or cannot practise their skills because of language difficulties or unrecognized qualifications. The creation of a National Office of Overseas Skills Recognition, the reorientation of the National Policy on Language towards 'commercial languages', and a new emphasis on the economic benefits of having a multicultural, entrepreneurial and internationally oriented workforce are all evidence of this recognition that settlement is not simply a welfare issue but can produce positive economic outcomes if properly managed.

The fourth component was an emphasis on social justice as the basis of immigrant settlement, which implies a strengthening of the strategy of equitable access to, and enjoyment of, government services. This strategy was being evaluated during 1992, as were the officially subsidized grant-in-aid ethnic welfare workers and the Migrant Resource Centres set up following the Galbally Report of 1978.

Settlement policy in Australia is not predictable in the long term because of political and economic uncertainty and probable changes of government. It may be that the opponents of multiculturalism, a high level of immigrant intake and proponents of a 'lean' state will combine politically in such a way as to greatly reduce what many criticize as the 'social engineering' inherent in current policies. It may be that long-term economic recession will endanger social harmony and the immigration programme regardless of what public policies are in place. What has remained, so far, is the acceptance that immigrant settlement is a state responsibility requiring public provision and supervision.

9

SETTLEMENT POLICIES IN THE UNITED STATES

Robert L. Bach

In the last decade the United States has engaged in the largest review of immigration policy since the Dillingham Commission of 1911, passed a major law responding to undocumented immigration, and concluded the most significant 'legal reform' since the *McCarran–Walter Act* of 1952. Congressional leaders also plan soon to revise the *Refugee Act* of 1980.

This intense period of reform poses an unparalleled opportunity to examine historical and comparative dimensions of the formation and consequence of immigration policies. Although this chapter focuses solely on the United States, the current challenge raised by immigration to political reform is global. In Europe, for instance, politicization of immigration practices has already become a stumbling block to the formation of a European community (Messina 1990; Bovenker et al. 1990).

The purpose of this chapter is to identify several themes from the US immigration experience that may be of value for this historical and comparative task. The focus is on settlement policies, that is, state intervention into post-entry experiences of immigrants, refugees, and the communities into which they move. Settlement policies consist of both the content of legislative changes and the relationship of government activities to social, economic, political and cultural change of which immigration is part.

SETTLEMENT POLICIES

Settlement is a large social process that takes on more the character of social movements than discrete actions. It involves the organization of people, mobilization of resources, articulation of goals and interests, and political actions in a variety of arenas. Broader changes within the political economy, of course, provide structural limits to these settlement activities. Yet, mobilizing strategies of settlement aim to influence public decisions over the production and distribution of resources. They have the capacity to involve and to change established residents as much as they do newcomers.

Settlement policies involve institutional responses to broad-based social movements organized by and on behalf of both newcomer and established resident groups. They are different from, but connected to, admissions policies. The latter involve regulating the volume, characteristics and conditions under which newcomers enter the United States. Settlement policies are distinctly more encompassing than what is meant by the current use of 'immigrant policy'. The latter refers primarily to the needs and experiences of immigrants themselves. Its narrower focus reproduces one of the most potent biases in studies of immigration—the expectation that change occurs exclusively among newcomers.

Settlement policies involve actions taken by families, communities, churches, schools and organized interest groups, to name a few. For current purposes, this chapter focuses on state-sponsored activities. The state serves in this capacity as the locus of political organization and competition, and as an institution with structures, practices and resources.

Most discussions of US immigration reform focus almost exclusively on admissions policies. State intervention in post-entry activities of immigrants is largely ignored or even dismissed as inconsequential in shaping future economic and political progress. This analytical silence misrepresents the character of the state and creates a false impression about the apolitical nature of the settlement process.

Failure to examine the organization of the state in immigration reform leaves too much opportunity to become enthralled with the 'horse-trading' that always accompanies final compromises before legislation is passed. For example, although a serious reduction in the number of immigrants was never an issue in the latest legislative reforms, debates on admission policies fostered an artificial polarization of perspectives into 'restrictionism' and 'admissionism'. This polarization characterized, even demonized, arguments and analyses from both sides. The effect was to obscure significant, underlying shifts in political alliances that have consequences both for understanding the outcomes of legislative debate and for future social reforms.

The historical–comparative task taken up in this chapter requires examination of the 'mainsprings' of policy formation (Charlton et al. 1988). Although immigration and refugee issues often appear to be only episodic and secondary, they are deeply rooted in changes in the political economy and culture of receiving and sending states. Immigration reforms need to be understood as part of the pressures for change, organized within and against state structures and institutions (Bach 1978; 1985; 1990). Policies are not free-standing responses to new circumstances. Rather, they are historically conditioned actions linked to broader political and economic commitments. Their timing, content and structure result from direct and indirect pressures from outside the government and from organized interests and groups within the government.

This analysis focuses on the following dimensions of state involvement—linkage, intervention, institutionalization, and differentiation. Linkage involves the connections generated by local-level social and political mobilization to public issues, problems and programmes. Local activities draw the attention of government officials, and prompt (and often provoke) subsequent intervention. The state intervenes through design and implementation of services and programmes that both reflect the needs of the local community and express its own historical and institutional rules, organization, politics and ideologies. Paramount among these are efforts to establish and to protect the social conditions upon which market economies and democratic legitimacy rely (Bach 1978).

Throughout US history, much of the impetus for settlement reform has begun with local community action. Local residents, organizing across group and class lines, construct links between immigration and other public issues. As discussed subsequently, community movements organized a round of settlement policies at the turn of the century. The civil rights movement crafted a second major period of reform in the 1960s and 1970s (Bach 1990).

Institutionalization involves the state taking up local initiatives, establishing control, and becoming the organizer and provider of resources. Institutionalization is built upon 'patterns of prior government intervention', policy legacies which establish and condition responses to contemporary pressures (Evans et al. 1985, p. 42). For example, the US state is noted for its relative weakness, decentralization and fragmentation (Skocpol 1985, p. 27). National settlement policies reflect this pattern. They foster voluntary participation of community, ethnic and church groups to participate in a programmatically decentralized, but financially concentrated, national response to settlement. This structure is perhaps the hallmark of US settlement policy.

Settlement policies also contain strong contradictory pressures between the diversity and decentralized character of local initiatives and the standardized services, programmes and practices that are embedded in government-established rules. These pressures become a source of competition, a target of political contest, both among newcomers and the groups working on their behalf and by established residents pursuing policies directed specifically at immigrants and at broader, unrelated political and economic reforms.

State-sponsored settlement programmes aggregate these diverse constituencies. Once together, however, the unequal political strength of groups involved in lobbying over the distribution of economic and social resources differentiates among programmes, locations and beneficiaries. Institutionalization transforms the settlement movement. Groups come to share a common arena of competition, but no longer the common ground that may have existed within local communities.

TWO PERIODS OF SETTLEMENT

This section briefly explores two periods of settlement policy formation during the last century. Its purpose is not to provide a detailed historical narrative of these periods. Rather, the goal is to highlight the sequence of linkage, intervention, institutionalization and differentiation through which settlement policies are formulated and transformed.

Progressive Era Reforms

Several lessons can be learned from settlement experiences and policies developed from the 1880s to World War II. The Progressive Era serves as a beginning point for this discussion because it highlights in stark ways the connection of local community action to the state. Early American settlement policy emerged directly from social reform movements within urban communities where the interests, needs and problems of immigrants were combined with those of established residents.

From the 1880s to World War I, common ground for a loose array of reform activities involved mobilization against a pervasive, overarching conservative social ideology, Spencerian Social Darwinism. Reformers rejected its central tenets—unfettered industrial growth at the expense of social standards, and expanding social inequalities considered necessary consequences of competitive free enterprise.

The Progressive Era's settlement movement organized against the impact of this political economy on both newcomers and established residents. Immigrants participated in the movement both as primary objects of settlement programmes and services and as subjects involved in reform activities. Reformers borrowed ideas from the Social Gospel movement and developed their own ideological oppositions to Social Darwinism. In particular they focused activities on the causes of poverty rather than on the character and abilities of individuals. Reformers attacked community poverty for newcomers and established residents alike through experimental programmes designed to deliver immediate services. They sought to reshape the physical and social environment of local neighbourhoods by providing gyms, libraries and recreation rooms through local settlement 'houses' and schools. Local innovations also included building capacities to mobilize effectively, to organize leadership and to increase youth involvement.

Americanization programmes formed the vanguard of many of these local services. Settlement workers sought not only to assimilate newcomers from rich and diverse national backgrounds, but to transform the character of local communities. They offered English and citizenship classes alongside housing, improvements in local factories and opportunities for political representation. Some reformers pushed local initiatives further. Chicago-based reformers, for example, struggled to include 'advocacy of labor legislation, public welfare, better housing . . . improved education, and democratic reforms' (Trolander 1975, p. 19).

Many of these local reforms preceded governmental attempts to establish public programmes. Playgrounds, educational innovations, including curriculum changes, housing and health programmes were all established in settlements before being adopted by Boards of Education and other local authorities. Hiram House in Cleveland, for instance, introduced kindergarten, manual training, and domestic education classes. Later, the school board adopted similar programmes and expanded services to help immigrants learn English (Trolander 1969, p. 23). Even the larger goals of economic reform were initially articulated within neighbourhood reform groups. Settlement workers, for example, advocated for a state minimum wage law, stopping only when the *Fair Labor Standards Act* was finally passed (Trolander 1975, p. 111).

The settlement movement struggled to forge coalitions among groups with very different objectives and interests. For example, in Chicago Jane Addams worked against the local political machine. She sought greater democracy for local established residents both to empower native-born citizens and to incorporate immigrants in a way that would increase their civic participation (Trolander 1975, p. 14). Her battle for political reform at the municipal and ward level, however, brought her into conflict with the interests of some immigrant groups. Alliances with ward bosses, not opposition and reform, represented for some newcomers a quicker avenue of access to power and economic mobility.

Mobilization through ethnic solidarity often divided reformers as much as enhanced community organization. Group strategies especially created tensions between class and nationality-based alliances. These remained in the settlement movement until its demise in the 1930s. That demise, however, did not result primarily from the problems and tensions endemic to community coalitions. Rather, state intervention and institutionalization transformed the settlement movement.

Throughout the Progressive Era, settlement programmes were primarily self-financed. They raised their own funds from local sources and from programme participants, and depended fundamentally on volunteers. Financial control provided flexibility and freedom to design and pursue a local reform agenda.

Efforts to provide services, build institutions to bring people together physically and socially, and create neighbourhood stability required resources. Volunteerism reached its limits both in terms of the ability of settlement managers to recruit new staff and to ensure longer-term programmes and services. Staffing needs and capital investments in infrastructure alone created an overpowering requirement to solicit funds from groups and institutions who until then had remained outside the neighbourhood reform effort. Pressed by financial need, the settlement movement turned to charitable organizations, larger donors and philanthropists.

Financial links to larger organizations exposed the movement to new interests and goals and sacrificed decisionmaking power to centralized institutions. For example, the rise of the Community Chest system rationalized fund-raising for settlement house activities, but it also shifted control of decisions to pursue particular programmes to those who managed the Chests. The source of funding for settlement programmes became particularly important when those activities involved labour issues. Private companies used their financial resources to exert influence. Manufacturers' associations, for instance, used their representatives on philanthropic boards to oppose labour advocacy and attempts to improve civil and labour standards (Trolander 1975, pp. 20–1).

This shift of financial control had a profound effect on social action programmes. By the 1930s settlement groups in certain cities where local Boards were particularly conservative had largely abandoned reform programmes. The New Deal also fundamentally altered the role of the settlement. Large national programmes overwhelmed local reform activities, centralizing both programmatic design and financial control.

As the state absorbed management of settlement activities, local interests, with their unique combinations of nationality groups working together, were transformed into simply one of many recipients of federal aid. Government policies became the place of contest and competition both among these various aid recipients and their constituencies, and between immigration and broader economic and political issues. Competition caused many involved in settlement activities to pursue new issues and strategies.

Government-sponsored competition for resources was only one reason settlements faltered before reaching their goals. As the settlement movement progressed, innovation and experimentation declined.

This may have resulted from normal maturation. Some claimed, however, that reformers had lost their 'pioneering spirit'.

The professionalization of social work also drew attention away from social reform and focused on individuals' problems, especially their psychological dilemmas. Newly professionalized workers developed programmatic and personal agendas that competed with the interests of neighbourhood groups. The target of these agendas, the immigrant generation, had also matured, passing social reform onto its children. Already Americanized, many rejected the clubs, playgrounds and programmes built by and for their mothers and fathers. Others had already moved out of the neighbourhoods to seek economic and political gains in new arenas.

The key to the decline of the reform movement was the increased control of large contributors. More extensive programmes not only took sizeable portions of budget and staff time, they also created a dependence on funders. Settlement groups became just one of many competing for resources from a central authority. Local experimentation and coalitions among newcomers and established residents virtually disappeared as the nation turned to national social welfare policies.

Settlement movements also lost their reform orientation by failing to incorporate two critical issues—race and labour. This failure left a legacy of division between immigration issues and race and labour reforms which still reverberates through contemporary coalitions.

The response of settlement reforms to Black migration from the South varied among cities. Some settlements, notably in Boston, incorporated members of various groups into neighbourhood-based planning committees. Yet, race relations were never fully recognized as a problem during much of this early period. Many settlement reformers thought of their movement primarily in terms of White middle-class workers, especially volunteers, whose goals were to deliver assistance in poor ethnic neighbourhoods. Their greatest successes had been in helping immigrants assimilate (Trolander 1975, p. 148). These reformers often moved in separate circles. Some settlement houses preferred to close rather than include Blacks in their activities; others emerged that specialized in serving only Black immigrants.

Private enterprise helped to split settlement reforms into two camps. Business representatives who served on boards of community organizations often obstructed programmes aimed at helping workers. They selected goals and interests that were based on private profits rather than social need, and were generally antagonistic to labour issues.

When business joined reform coalitions, the outcome typically reflected private industry's superior financial and political strength. An example is cross-class alliances involving housing. Business groups supported housing programmes as part of urban renewal efforts that projected profitability, but they opposed public housing because it infringed on their private activities. Agreement was reached with reformers that allowed business to shape available programmes. This created opportunities for moderate social programmes to service local communities. Such programmes, though, split immigration-related settlement policies from broader agendas of community reform.

Civil Rights Reforms

During the 1950s and early 1960s, the foreign-born share of the US population dropped to near historical lows, and community reformers shifted their attention to other concerns. The two sources of political reform that continued to involve immigration included recurring battles to terminate the Mexican contract labour programme and the incremental expansion of refugee programmes. Although the government was involved directly in negotiating the Mexican contract labour programme, employment help, housing and, when needed, cash assistance were left to employers, their agents and local social service groups. Private organizations, especially church groups, assisted immigrants in times of trouble, even helping them return to Mexico when local aid and jobs were unavailable (Reisler 1976).

In a sense the Mexican contract labour programme represented an admissions policy with a punitive settlement plan. The lack of settlement aid to Mexican braceros, of course, was due to expectations that these were temporary workers who would eventually return home. These policies, though, also fit with a general approach to immigrants. These were years in which US immigration policy focused primarily on control of admissions. Settlement policies that followed from protectionist concerns focused on punitive practices, including detention and deportation, designed to protect and prevent established residents from encountering and interacting with unwanted newcomers. Fears of criminal aliens were particularly pronounced (Charlton et al. 1988; Plender 1988; Scanlan and Loescher 1983).

The Civil Rights Movement in the late 1950s and 1960s launched a new reform struggle that incorporated immigration issues. Coalitions formed among civil rights and labour groups and established links between local community activities and government programmes. Labour, religious and community groups organized to protest work and living conditions of Mexican braceros during their residence in the United States. The AFL–CIO once labelled those conditions 'imported colonialism', and linked them directly to the way other 'non-White' workers were being treated throughout the United States.

Linkages were also more formal, if unanticipated. Federal laws governing the treatment of Mexican bracero workers in South Texas became unexpected precedents for changes in national civil rights legislation. The first enforcement of anti-discrimination federal laws in housing and public accommodations occurred in response to violations against Mexican temporary workers. Southern legislators were caught in a quandary. They opposed civil rights legislation and especially the principle of federal intervention in state and local affairs. Yet, they had agreed previously to anti-discrimination clauses in the Mexican contract labour agreement as a condition for obtaining Mexican workers for local growers. The contradictory connection helped swing the congressional debate in favour of supporting anti-discrimination enforcement measures.

The Civil Rights Movement provided a framework of reform of immigration policies for the late 1960s. These were critical years in the institutionalization of settlement policies. On the political strength of the Civil Rights Movement, Congress terminated the Mexican contract labour programme and amended the *Immigration and Nationality Act* to eliminate national origins quotas. These reforms opened immigration to all regions of the world and made possible the volume and diversity of immigrants that came to the United States during the 1970s and 1980s. This diversity began to recreate the conditions for a renewed settlement coalition, initially organized at the community level but, eventually, prompting and provoking federal intervention.

Refugee programmes provided the clearest stimulus behind the transformation of settlement policy in the post–World War II era. The distinctive legal status of refugees—which highlighted the importance of the relationship of newcomers to the state—made possible programmes of special assistance after entry to the United States. It linked admissions to settlement policies and forged a more formal, institutional relationship between local groups and state and federal governments.

Following World War II, US policies treated refugees as an exception to the general framework of controlled admissions (Seller 1982). Refugees were individuals or small groups who escaped from behind the Iron Curtain to the West. The McCarran–Walter Act of 1952 formally incorporated into law the practice of using emergency authority and programmes to respond to these sporadic refugee outflows. Most refugees were admitted in limited numbers only through executive discretion of the Attorney-General's parole powers. Resettlement involved little state action. The *ad hoc*, irregular character of refugee admissions was reflected in small-scale, voluntary efforts. Church groups and others responded to crisis situations. They provided assistance directly to the families and individuals they resettled in their local communities and congregations.

The Hungarian uprising of 1956 and the exodus of large numbers of refugees was a turning point for refugee admissions and settlement policies (Charlton et al. 1988). It completely overwhelmed normal screening and entry controls and contradicted the image of refugees as exceptional. It also testified to the increasingly systemic character of refugee-like migrations. It alerted the nation to a future of larger, recurring refugee outflows and to the clearly inadequate policy instruments available to regulate refugee admissions and to manage settlement programmes.

The first major steps towards institutionalization began with the Federal Government's response to the Cuban refugee outflow in 1960. The Cuban Refugee Programme initiated a model of settlement which eventually led to a national domestic assistance programme. The Cuban Refugee Programme was forged out of both foreign policy interests and the rapidly changing role of the Federal Government in civil rights reforms and national public assistance programmes. These would culminate with the War on Poverty and Great Society programmes of the late 1960s. The Cuban programmes anticipated the orientation of many Great Society programmes which emphasized community action. In many instances programmes bypassed existing government agencies to create new connections with the groups and activities desired by federal authorities.

Cuban refugee settlement programmes began in the last years of the Eisenhower Administration. They continue still, 30 years later. The programmes began with steps similar to the assistance provided to earlier Hungarian refugees. As the numbers grew, however, and reception in Miami soured, programmes expanded to include a wide range of services and programmes. The federal effort sought to work through both existing voluntary agencies and directly through expansion of government programmes. Federal assistance included transportation costs and aid to local public agencies, schools and universities. In about a decade the Federal Government provided $130 million to Dade County schools, of which $117 million went to bilingual education and $12 million to vocational and adult programmes (Pedraza-Bailey 1985, p. 41).

The class composition of the Cuban flow was important in shaping the character of the resettlement effort. This was an immigrant élite. Resettlement was not a poverty programme, but a short-term reskilling and adjustment effort. The goal was to recreate an organic connection between the immigrants' class backgrounds and their place in the US economy. It involved professional retraining, especially among doctors and teachers, to reproduce a middle-level educational élite. The programme also sought to assist in maintaining both language and culture. It provided bilingual services and aid to schools that set precedents for other non-immigrant programmes. As Pedraza-Bailey has noted, the 'judicial mandate for bilingual education programmes in the public schools did not come about until the 1974 Lau vs. Nichols case . . . But bilingual education was in fact born in the school year of 1960 . . . [when] the federal government funded bilingual education programs for Cuban refugees ...' (Pedraza-Bailey 1985, p. 44).

These resettlement programmes established a state-federal relationship that continued well into the 1980s. The Federal Government conceived of its new role as intervening directly to provide financial aid to the refugees in South Florida where virtually no assistance system of its own existed. The link established the principle of direct federal assistance to a locality and a particular group.

The *Cuban Adjustment Act* of 1966 subsequently facilitated a direct relationship between Cuban refugees, South Florida and the Federal Government. It swept aside legal status as a bar to many activities, allowing Cubans who arrived in the United States the unique advantage of adjusting their status after only one year of residence. Florida, notoriously inflexible on social reform, also waived citizenship requirements for many skilled workers.

The preferential relationship developed between South Florida, the Cuban resettlement effort and the Federal Government established another policy precedent. It provided aid to local communities on the basis of perceived impact to a locality, rather than assistance to individuals. This set the stage for subsequent, larger funding. In 1980 Congress enacted special legislation to provide assistance to South Florida because of the arrival of Cubans and Haitians who were not covered by the *Refugee Act*. Popularly referred to as the Fascell–Stone amendment, after the legislators from South Florida who sponsored the bill, the law set aside federal funds targeted specifically to one locality. In fiscal year 1990 the Federal Government included an additional \$5 million for impact assistance to South Florida health and educational services. These funds were designed to compensate South Florida for services delivered to refugees even after they had resided in the United States for 10 years (Vialet 1990, p. 8). Refugee assistance to other localities has typically been limited to only a few years.

The Southeast Asian refugee crisis rekindled waning interest in resettlement policies. At first, the response repeated earlier strategies of *ad hoc*, temporary programmes targeted at small groups. There were special programmes and legislative authorities for those who fled Saigon in April 1975, others in 1976–77, and still more in 1978. These were quickly replaced by widespread recognition of the need for a comprehensive domestic resettlement programme. By 1979, when the admission rate to the United States increased to 14 000 a month, Congress and the Administration moved to stabilize and then to institutionalize settlement.

The *Refugee Act* of 1980 established a definition for admission that embraced international law, clearly separating refugee and immigrant admissions. Passage of the Act also fully institutionalized resettlement (Vialet 1990; Bach and Meissner 1991). The Act established a wide-ranging refugee assistance programme. It involved the Department of State in administering overseas processing and transition programmes, including English language training and cultural orientation. The State Department increased reception and placement grants to voluntary agencies to help support refugees' transition into local communities (Tillema 1981).

The *Refugee Act* of 1980 also redefined the relationship between federal, state and local governments. According to a 1980 Senate report, federal authority over immigration admissions carried with it a responsibility to assist states and local communities in adjusting to the consequences of immigration (McHugh 1990). The Act established the Office of Refugee Resettlement (ORR) and mandated a set of domestic programmes to help refugees achieve economic self-sufficiency. Domestic programmes included a full range of employment training and placement, English language training and cash assistance (Bach and Argiros 1991). Federal financial support reimbursed states for up to three years for cash and medical benefits paid to refugees. Assistance also included a broad range of social services. Ten years after the law went into effect, this domestic portion of the vast resettlement effort cost roughly $451 million a year.

Institutionalization of settlement policies reached its peak during the 1980s. Despite strong congressional support for the refugee programme, federal budget deficits led authorities to react to the size and cost of the national assistance programme and, especially, refugees' high public assistance rates. They began to reduce reimbursement for resettlement costs and to pass some of the costs to states where refugees settled. In 1986 ORR decreased the reimbursement period from 36 to 31 months, shifting $18.3 million in resettlement costs to states for the fiscal year 1986 and $30.6 million for the fiscal year 1987. In 1988 ORR reduced the period again to 24 months. By 1990 reimbursement covered only the first four months of refugees' residence in the United States.

Decreased support for post-entry policies also resulted from increasing overseas need and declining ability to pay. For example, in 1989 the President increased the refugee ceiling by 22 500 to allow the admission of additional Soviet Jews, Pentecostals and Armenians. Nearly $85 million was added to support admissions and overseas processing. None was added for domestic resettlement (Vialet 1990).

These changes were part of the restructuring of the federal-state relationship, the 'New Federalism' promoted during the Reagan presidency. The Federal Government withdrew from local programmes and turned over to state and local officials the obligations of community activities, including settlement activities (Morse 1990). This restructuring had several consequences. One was to turn state and local governments into interest groups that now had to compete for settlement resources. It also reinforced the concept that recipients of this federal assistance were other levels of government rather than the individual newcomers or communities.

This restructuring of settlement policies provided a framework for the legalization of undocumented immigrants under the *Immigration Reform and Control Act* (IRCA) of 1986. The legalization programme provided financial aid to states to cover increased costs to public treasuries as undocumented newcomers adjusted their status. Many of these settlement programmes were modelled after refugee resettlement activities. The State Legalization Impact Assistance Grants (SLIAG) represented a form of 'refugee-ization' of settlement policies for labour immigrants (Jacob 1980). It reimbursed states and local governments while temporarily disqualifying newly legalized workers and their families from federal programmes.

Settlement policies in the 1990s involve group competition for resources within a structure that is financially concentrated in the Federal Government and programmatically decentralized among states and localities. This structured competition maximizes the pressures that lead to inequality among groups and regions. State and local governments compete over claims to represent newcomers. Political power and influence increasingly determine funding patterns.

In such an atmosphere a curious paradox has emerged. The more interest groups focus on the needs of immigrants, the more their top-down approach to service delivery becomes self-defeating. Demands to extend new services and to create new programmes for immigrants after they settle in the United States conflicts with arguments that justify newcomer admissions on the grounds of their low cost and economic advantage. The cornerstone of this view is that the state is not involved. Yet, increasingly, competition for settlement resources promotes greater state involvement and funding. The result is that this type of settlement movement is making immigration more costly and, eventually, may undermine support for sustained levels of admissions.

Competition for federal resources at a time of budgetary problems strains community coalitions trying to serve both newcomers and established residents. A decade of increased privatization and greater dependence on federal aid has divided the interests of groups and localities and intensified the pressures working against coalitions. Divided and competing interests have shifted the terms of support for immigration reforms.

THE 1990s

The last decade has witnessed a deep polarization of the US political economy, with repercussions for immigrant admissions and settlement policies. Recalling the era dominated by Social Darwinist ideologies, modern social thought has embraced the central concerns of unfettered, aggregate economic growth, with its emphasis on innovation, new technologies, lower taxes, increased flexibility and entrepreneurship (Dahrendorf 1988). Market competition, not plans and public value, has become the ideological mantra of the 1990s.

This new interest in aggregate growth has resurrected the classic antinomy of growth and distribution. The emphasis on growth has politically devalued issues such as inequality, persistent poverty, widely perceived decline, marginalization, and excessive privatization that undermines civic participation. This neglect has made many problems seem even more intractable.

Polarization has also restructured political alliances. New alliances have been forged out of regional politics, a revised 'Cowboy against Yankee' syndrome, pitting the growing Sunbelt against a stagnating Northeast. Others have played upon differences in bureaucratic and community politics. Still others have focused on inherent problems in interest group politics to explain a growing fragmentation of public interest.

One of the primary political realignments involves the breakup of the civil rights–immigration coalition. Problems confronting this coalition may be due to pressures similar to those that ended the progressive settlement movement. For instance, the embourgeoisement of ethnic organizations has accompanied a narrowing of interests among a professionalized advocacy community. Some of these groups have turned their considerable organizing talents to specific concerns related to immigration rather than to wider objectives of social reform.

Another source of change is the maturation of the civil rights–immigration movement. Like its predecessors in the Progressive Era, the effect of years of organizing and programme development transformed reformers into lobby groups and service providers whose job became to compete for increased shares of public or private resources. Established interest groups now have entrenched programmes devoted to immigration and refugee settlement that require considerable financial resources to keep alive. Political goals have narrowed to defence of positions that win greater resources for particular constituencies.

Breakup of the civil rights–immigration coalition also involves shifts in the composition and ideological goals of the various reform groups. Increasing ethnic diversity in the United States has produced several civil rights movements with distinct agendas. Vast differences in wealth and power among these groups have made holding the established coalition together much more difficult.

The most important source of change involves political–economic restructuring in the 1980s. It has created the grounds for a very different coalition of interests. In place of the civil rights–immigration ranks, an immigration–business coalition has emerged that uses civil rights rhetoric to legitimize conservative business positions. In the name of promoting immigration, business groups pursue unregulated growth, without standards, protections or increases in quality of employment or living conditions.

The split in the civil rights–immigration coalition is widest on race and labour issues. Just as the Progressive Era settlement movement excluded and then faltered on economic and racial issues, current immigration politics lead to sharp divisions within the civil rights ranks. Once again, settlement strategies have failed to confront the fundamental issues of race and labour in America.

The most dramatic political split involves disagreement over the 1986 IRCA. The debate became so acrimonious at times that it virtually broke up the Civil Rights Leadership Conference, a traditional alliance between Hispanic, Black and labour groups. The law set out to overcome the anomaly of previous immigration law, to hold employers, not just workers, responsible for the legal status of their workforce. One outcome of the legislation could have been to make legal status an employment standard for the nation's business, to stand alongside health and civil rights protections. But the law failed to hold employers to that task. It shifted the burden of working and social protections to immigrants and local communities.

The Administration had to agree with the business lobby's insistence not to push strongly for enforcement to forge an alliance to pass this legislation. Employers and their organizations successfully resisted the transfer of responsibility to them. They won on the first round, the law's design, by weakening effective enforcement. This included enforcement of anti-discrimination measures as well as regulations against hiring undocumented workers.

The business lobby won a second round during implementation. According to many reports, employers simply did not change their behaviour. Most complied with the letter of the law but not its spirit (Bach and Brill 1991). The law failed, with government support, to turn legal status into a defensible employment standard. Employers' resistance to the law joined a decade or more of rollbacks in other employment standards and protections.

This business-led opposition to IRCA could have faced a different political challenge. Unexpectedly, the business lobby found an ally in several immigrant and ethnic lobby groups whose primary concern was the discrimination that could result if employers implemented the law incorrectly. Those fears, which were reasonably held after a decade of reduced anti-discrimination enforcement, merely aided the business lobby's interest in protecting employers from sharing responsibility for workplace conditions. Employers discriminate; they also hire undocumented workers. Yet, because of the coalition with immigrant advocacy groups, the business lobby was able to avoid blame for non-compliance with anti-discrimination legislation. They resisted enforcing employer sanctions, as they have with other publicly mandated protections (Bach and Meissner 1990).

The debate over IRCA was an important but indecisive episode in the emergence of the immigration–business coalition. A more decisive occasion involved passage of the *Immigration Act* of 1990. Some commentators have described the immigration–business coalition as opposed to discrimination caused by employer sanctions and to restrictionist attempts to limit family reunification. The record reveals something different. A deep split existed in the interests of coalition members which highlights the weakness of the alliance.

To illustrate the complexities of political reforms and shifting sands of coalition-building, the following table compares the votes of leading congressional figures on both immigration and civil rights issues. Table 9.1 describes the votes cast by four key senators on the 1986 *Immigration Reform and Control Act* and on the 1990 *Civil Rights Act.*

Table 9.1 Contrasting electoral positions on immigration and civil rights

Senator	*IRCA 1986*	*Civil Rights Act of 1990*
Orrin Hatch (R-Utah)	opposed	opposed
Alan Simpson (R-Wyoming)	favoured	opposed
Kennedy (D-Massachusetts)	opposed	favoured
Hatfield (R-Oregon)	favoured	favoured

Source: Congressional Quarterly, Senate Votes, 21 July 1990.

The voting records of Senators Simpson and Kennedy reflect well-established positions. Senator Simpson's support of IRCA focused on control of undocumented immigrants coming to the United States. He wanted to change the 'magnet of employment' to illegal immigration by penalizing employers who hired them. But he opposed charges that penalties led employers to discriminate against US citizens who looked 'foreign'. His vote against the *Civil Rights Act* of 1990 represented a consistent conservative view on discrimination issues. In contrast Senator Kennedy's voting record represented the liberal alternative on admissions and discrimination. He opposed IRCA out of concern for increased discrimination. These sentiments were echoed in his strong support for the *Civil Rights Act.*

The most revealing voting pattern is that of Senator Hatch. Senator Hatch has been one of the key figures in the business–immigration coalition. He has been active in both the 'family coalition' that supported the *Immigration Act* of 1990 and has sponsored repeal of IRCA's employer sanctions. Senator Hatch's voting record highlights the deeply contradictory views of the immigration–business coalition.

Senator Hatch opposed both the IRCA and the *Civil Rights Act* because each, he believed, burdened employers. The IRCA introduced a new employment regulation that required employers to accept responsibility for hiring undocumented workers. The *Civil Rights Act* held employers accountable for employment discrimination. His opposition struck the same chord, sounding an alarm to the business community's interests in unprotected labour conditions and civil protections.

Senator Hatch's votes on the *Immigration Act* of 1990 underscore the themes of the immigration–business coalition. The Senator joined several immigrant lobby groups to ensure that family visas were protected in the new law. He sponsored an amendment to prevent family preference visas from falling below the current level of 216 000. He also opposed new limits on visas for adult brothers and sisters of US citizens.

Senator Hatch, however, opposed each amendment that provided more than guaranteed numbers of admissions and, especially, those which attempted to improve protections and standards available to immigrants and their families. He voted to prohibit illegal aliens from receiving direct federal benefits, including social security, health care and housing benefits. He opposed a provision that would give the Attorney-General limited authority to allow benefits in hardship cases. He voted against a stay of deportation and work authorization to the spouse and minor children of aliens whose status was legalized under IRCA. He also voted to disallow undocumented immigrants from being counted in Census figures for reapportionment use. Finally, he joined Senator Helms in support of an amendment to increase job-related visas for professional and skilled workers and to cut family-preference and independent immigrants' visas.

As a leading figure in the immigration–business coalition, Senator Hatch's record clearly represents the interests contained in the alliance. Ironically, his support for immigration was a quota argument—precisely the logic he used to oppose the *Civil Rights Act*. He agreed to a minimal guarantee in the number of family preference visas, while opposing all measures that had anything to do with benefits, employment standards or protections. Clearly, the business lobby partner in the immigration coalition sought only unfettered, unregulated growth, including in this case larger absolute numbers of new arrivals. An accommodation of interests was achieved in which the primary point of agreement was simply larger numbers of admissions. The effect was to exclude from legislative reforms protections of employment and social standards, whether contained in immigration or civil rights legislation.

CONCLUSIONS

Recent scholarly debate on immigration contains a peculiar paradox that has been exploited in legislative debates. At a time when the US Government is more involved in settlement policies than at any time in history, some scholars have argued that immigration is virtually cost-free. This occurs also at a time when congressional, state and local authorities complain about the budgetary impacts of immigration and, increasingly, immigrant advocacy groups mobilize to compete for more federal aid to assist newcomers.

This paradox results from the emergence of a new anti-state intellectual paradigm. It is constructed by the coincidence of ideology among conservative economists and orthodox liberal thinkers. Within this anti-state paradigm, observers from both left and right have reasserted the core American myth that immigrants adjust quickly and easily without significant costs. The power of the myth, of course, stems from its partial truth. It also results, though, from the capacity to shape debate in a way that limits an understanding of the actual experiences. For example, current debates ignore that Cuban resettlement, one of the most successful experiences in US history, is also the one with the longest and most extensive history of direct governmental involvement. Rather than opening discussion on this correlation, the myth focuses attention on ideological tenets. If these issues are broached, both right- and left-wing scholars attack with charges of being anti-immigrant, anti-American, anti-myth.

New perspectives on immigration offer two broadly contrasting visions of the future of immigration and the US political economy. Both have direct and significant consequences for the development of settlement policies in the next decade. The first perspective has strongly influenced the immigrant–business lobby.

The first vision reasserts the central concerns of economic nationalism. Under pressure to understand how the United States can remain competitive in the world economy, a surprisingly coherent vision of the future has emerged based on three principles: unfettered growth, including not only unrestricted population increase, but also stimulated expansion through immigration; ideologies of social meritocracies reminiscent of Social Darwinism; and a collective morality tied to national destiny (Simon 1990; Borjas 1990; Wattenberg 1991).

Although these arguments emerged during debates on admissions policies, they rely on assumptions about the post-entry activities and experiences of immigrants, and about the character of the native-born workforce. For example, although most research shows that immigration rates alone have very little effect on overall national aggregate growth, the argument is that restrictions on employers' access to these labour supplies will undermine competitiveness and are, therefore, somehow unpatriotic. The ideal is to admit as many highly skilled immigrants to fill jobs at lower wages without the benefits of social and employment protections. This will bolster US competitiveness globally.

The perspective has also revived historically outmoded concerns for the 'quality' of new immigrants, and called for a shift in policy to select the 'right ones'. Little attention is given to the need to train and educate both newcomers and established residents to meet the demands of the new economy. Concerns about discrimination and other social and employment standards are simply excluded.

This perspective has generated interest in the destiny of the American nation (Wattenberg 1991). Making the nation great again, fulfilling an alleged historical mission to be the world's bearer of freedom, economic affluence and cultural achievement has reconstructed historical themes long abandoned. From this view, immigration has become a form of reverse manifest destiny, saving others and ourselves by allowing them to become like us.

A second broad view is less well articulated and is slowly developing within communities and reform movements throughout the nation. In contrast to economic nationalism, its focus is on the realities of the internationalized economy. The argument is not about restrictionism, either in terms of numbers or quality, because the option of closing or opening borders is not realistically available. In an already internationalized economy, selection of immigrants takes place primarily by the immigrants themselves—whether legal, illegal or temporary. The connection to the market is already achieved. Admissions regulations are merely means to gaining legal status and recognition.

This view strives to refocus discussion on employment and social conditions and the mechanisms to protect them. This emerging perspective focuses on three overarching principles: human rights principles embedded in legal status, employment standards, and civil rights. In place of unfettered growth is improvement in employment standards and productivity; rather than quality of immigrants, the focus should be on quality of job opportunities and employers. In place of manifest destiny, the collective morality and legal framework is a commitment to human rights.

This emerging perspective is particularly important for the 1990s as political–economic discussion focuses on a North American common market, free trade zones and increased labour mobility. The purpose of these initiatives, of course, is to accelerate aggregate economic growth by providing unfettered access to resources, markets, consumption and labour. In many cases such agreements represent a formal recognition of what already exists—transborder labour markets. A circulation of unregulated, unprotected use of labor, though, also creates another form of expansion, the deepening of inequality, labour abuse, and civil and human rights violations.

The state is a primary, but not unique, institution that is presently involved in creating, defending and blocking the pursuit of these rights and conditions. Change in state policies to take up the new social reforms are unlikely to emerge from within the Government or the temporary coalitions formed around particular legislative changes. Rather, changes begin with realignments of demographic, political and economic forces within local communities. The 1990s could spark a new round of settlement movements that are as likely to work against established institutional policies as they are to compete for financial and programmatic assistance from the Government.

10

SETTLEMENT CHARACTERISTICS OF IMMIGRANTS IN AUSTRALIA

Michael J. Webber

The fundamental social processes in western societies are class, ethnicity and gender. Social processes are social relations between groups, influencing relations between individuals in the different groups. Class describes relations derived from different levels of access to and control over social resources. Ethnicity refers to relations derived from differences of 'race' or birthplace. Gender identifies relations derived from sexual differences. These processes of class, ethnicity and gender are defined over space. Spatial structures are relations derived from differences in access to the environment that society has constructed.

Societies exist in space. Society and social processes cannot exist without material environmental support. Social life is embodied in its historical geography, as spatial organization concretely expresses social processes (Gregory 1978; Soja 1989): the nature of class, ethnic and gender groups is reflected on Australian ground. Our numbers and our social relations are revealed in tree cover, land quality, ownership patterns, service facilities, freeways and construction of suburbs, a fact that has been belatedly recognized in the debate about immigration numbers (Clarke et al. 1990; Murphy et al. 1990). Therefore spaces are constructed differently where class, ethnic and gender divisions are different. However, as well as reflecting or embodying social relations, space also forms their basis. Australian spaces maintain or modify social relations: our land area, resource endowments, patterns of light and dark spaces in cities, and suburban form all guide relations between classes, ethnic groups and genders. The characteristics of class, ethnic and gender groups reflect spatial structures and therefore evolve differently in societies that have different spatial organizations.

These ideas amount to several claims. People's experience of social life depends in large measure on their class, ethnic, gender and spatial background. Clearly, people's experience of one process depends on their position with respect to the others. Also, the social meaning of ethnicity, class and gender evolves differently in Melbourne than in a city with different geography. These claims, though, do not specify the relative significance of different processes or the mechanisms that generate them, much less the manner in which they interact. These are matters for empirical research. One important aspect of that research concerns the degree to which ethnicity has a direct influence on Australian life rather than an indirect influence through class and gender. Another concerns the interrelationships between social processes and Australian spaces.

ETHNICITY

Ethnicity refers to relations derived from differences of 'race' or birthplace (Gordon 1964) and has several bases. 'Racial' distinctions are frequently made in Australia. The most serious of these distinctions have been between immigrant (post 1788) and Aborigine, perhaps the deepest divide in Australian society. Other 'racial' distinctions have been between Asian or Black immigrants and the bulk of the population, which is White: Australians may be prejudiced (de Lepervanche 1984a), but whether this translates into effective discrimination is unclear (Wooden 1990). People are also distinguished by birthplace. Conventionally, Australians distinguish people born in Australia from people born overseas and differentiate further those born in the main English-speaking countries from those born in non-English-speaking countries (Wooden 1990). Northern Europeans are sometimes distinguished from southern and eastern Europeans (Collins 1988). A third set of distinctions is related to 'heritage' or 'culture', comprising language and social mores. For example, Italian immigrants and some of their children and grandchildren comprise Italian-Australians, united by a capacity to speak Italian, a tendency to identify with Italy's successes, and an inclination (or need) to interact with other Italian-Australians.

Evidently, the category of ethnicity is chaotic. It refers to phenomena that range from the deepest divide in Australian society to a preference for soccer teams. Furthermore, the public discourse about ethnicity has changed through time, from the racism of post-war immigration policies to current official support for multiracialism and multiculturalism (de Lepervanche 1980). The enormous range of empirical referents is matched by a similar range of theoretical interpretations of ethnicity (Barth 1969; Cox 1948; Kakakios and van der Velden 1984; Morrissey 1984; van den Berghe 1981).

This chapter focuses on distinctions associated with birthplace. Aboriginality is excluded, as are the characteristics of second generation Australians. Three main groups of attribute are differentiated by birthplace in Australia. One is demographic (Hugo 1990): patterns of morbidity, mortality, fertility and other demographic measures (Holton 1990). The second is cultural (Kalantzis 1988): languages, foods, clothes, dances and child-rearing practices. The third is socio-economic status, on which this chapter will focus. Since ethnicity is cross-cut by class and gender, the implications of birthplace for social and economic position depend on class and gender position too. In addition, immigration introduces to a society people acculturated to different forms of class and gender relations. Immigration alters the relative sizes of class and gender groups, changes their form and may divide them. Ethnicity is therefore significant not only directly, but also by its interrelations with class and gender formation within Australia.

Four features of post-war immigration to Australia provide important background. First, immigration has been primarily about settlement (Martin 1984). The intention of immigration policy, not simply its effect, has been permanent settlement. High proportions of migrants have been in households and have been women (see Hugo 1990, pp. 56–8 on gender selectivity in migration).

Second, immigration has been dominated by people from English-speaking backgrounds (ESB) and countries. ESB immigrants are defined as comprising people from the UK, Ireland, New Zealand, the USA, Canada and South Africa. In 1945–85, 48.7 per cent of immigrants came from these six countries (DIEA 1986), and in only one decade—the 1950s—did such persons form less than 40 per cent of the immigrant intake.

Third, immigration has occurred in waves. Years of high immigration from one region have been succeeded by years of high immigration from other regions, though the largest inflow has always come from English-speaking countries. In the 1940s non-English-speaking background (NESB) immigrants came predominantly from eastern Europe; in the 1950s from northern and southern Europe; in the early 1960s from southern Europe; and in the 1970s and 1980s from Asia (Storer 1985). Therefore, to compare the occupational status of birthplace groups is to compare groups that have on average lived in Australia for different lengths of time and that have arrived during different economic circumstances: the labour market has been much tighter since the mid-1970s than in the 1950s and 1960s and the spatial distribution of housing opportunities has changed over time (Hugo 1990). Different birthplace groups have therefore faced different obstacles in settling.

Fourth, the birthplace groups have entered Australia in different settler categories. In 1988–89, 46 per cent of settlers from Central and South America, 20 per cent of those from northern Europe, and 18 per cent of those from Southeast Asia entered as refugees or under other humanitarian programmes (compared to 7.5 per cent of all settlers); 62 per cent of those from northeast Asia, 52 per cent of those from the UK and Ireland, but only 22 per cent of those from Southeast Asia entered as skilled migrants, a category that included 30 per cent of all settlers (BIR 1990). People from different birthplaces have brought on average different levels of resources, contact with workplaces, and psychological trauma.

CLASS, GENDER AND SPACE

Class and gender processes correspond to some well-known aspects of our daily lives. There are wide distinctions between people in terms of occupational status and income (Table 10.1), distinctions that correlate with various indicators of quality of life (Broom and Jones 1976). The occupation and income of parents and their offspring are correlated (Broom et al. 1980) to a higher degree in Australia than in the USA (Jones 1981). On average, the occupational status and income of women is lower than that of men (Power 1975): whereas most men are employed as managers, professionals, paraprofessionals or tradespersons, most women are employed as clerks or salespersons (Table 10.1). The differences in occupation and income between individuals and between men on average and women on average are to a large degree not explained by differences in measurable skill or experience (Stromback and Williams 1985). These distinctions are supported by spatial structures and in turn affect those structures, links that provide a framework for the relations between ethnicity and space.

Different parts of the city offer distinct physical, infrastructural environments and different levels of provision of child care and community facilities (Fincher 1990). Nevertheless, these distinctions are dominantly male ones. Spatial variations in the class position of women are less wide than those of men (Pratt and Hanson 1988). So the class position of women in their home (depending partly on a spouse's class position) may differ from that in their place of work; by contrast men experience more homogeneous perceptions of class and tend to have the same class position at work and at home. The experience of class is gender specific.

The process of reproducing gender roles is constrained by the spatial structure of cities. Modern gender roles, which have translated a biological capacity to reproduce into other aspects of social reproduction (MacKenzie 1988), may have originated in the privatization of family life and the spatial separation of production and reproduction in nineteenth-century cities (McDowell 1983). The division of urban space reflects and influences the gender division of labour, women's role in the family and the separation of home and work (McDowell

1983). Women's lives are constricted by housing forms that demand upkeep time and suburban locations that isolate them from work, facts that were associated with their post-war withdrawal from the labour market (for alternatives, see Hayden 1986). Women's lives are also constricted by lack of mobility arising from their role as child carers, restricting their opportunities for employment and increasing the time required to travel to and from paid work (Little et al. 1988). Ironically, the cost of suburban housing is one of the forces that has now prompted women to return to paid work. Because of their domestic roles, however, many women are limited to part-time employment, and commonly experience career interruptions (Martin 1984; Jamieson 1989).

Thus, the creation of suburbs, associated initially with the separation of home and work, single family dwellings and the separation of classes, was predicated on a particular form of gender relations. Spatial structure, however, has also influenced the evolution of gender practices. The existing spatial structure is a force conserving the gender and class practices of the past. Even so, the demand for commodities and housing implicit in suburbanization has created a demand for increasing income and required some change in gender and class roles as more and more women are forced into the labour market.

CLASS, GENDER AND ETHNICITY

Immigration displaces people to a place with existing (different) class and gender processes. These processes, operating through household divisions of labour and labour markets, have produced distinct strata. Many institutions act to reorganize and reproduce the stratification—organizations, unions, state, service delivery systems, the voluntary sector—and to slot immigrant men and women into it. To some degree, then, the relations between ethnicity and space are mediated by class and gender.

Migration generally causes people to lose occupational status, if not income. Campbell et al. (1990), in a study of over 270 immigrants in Melbourne, illustrate this fact. Prior to arrival in Australia, fewer women were employed than men: 33 per cent of females as compared to 72 per cent of males were employed. The first job in Australia for both males and females (but especially females) was overwhelmingly in manufacturing in the semi- and low-skilled occupations of operators and labourers. Indeed, there was a highly significant difference between the occupations of the people before and after migration. Males and females were much more highly concentrated in clerical, sales, operating and labouring occupations than they had been in their home country. For individuals, migration prompted downward occupational mobility and women lost status to a greater extent than men (see Table 10.1).

Table 10.1 Occupation by birthplace 1986

Occupation group	*Australian born*		*Immigrants (ESB)*		*Immigrants (NESB)*	
	% *male*	% *female*	% *male*	% *female*	% *male*	% *female*
Managers and professionals	26.5	18.9	27.7	18.3	22.6	15.8
Para-professionals and tradespersons	29.7	10.6	32.6	11.8	32.0	10.3
Clerks and salespersons	16.6	57.4	15.2	53.8	12.1	38.6
Operators and labourers	27.3	13.5	24.5	16.0	33.4	35.3
Total	100.0	100.0	100.0	100.0	100.0	100.0

Note: ESB refers to immigrants from the main-English-speaking countries—UK, Ireland, NZ, US, Canada, South Africa; NESB refers to immigrants from non-English-speaking countries, that is, all other countries.

Source: Collins 1988, p. 84.

The sources of these patterns of disadvantage have been extensively studied (Holton 1990; Wooden 1990). There are two potential disadvantages: migrants may arrive with fewer of the skills and experiences that are rewarded in the Australian labour market or they may be differently rewarded for those skills and experiences. Studies in the human capital tradition have observed that the relative wage levels and occupational status of immigrants improve with length of residence in Australia, length of schooling and English language skill (Stromback 1984; Beggs and Chapman 1988; Evans and Kelley 1986). However, Australian-born persons earn more than comparable immigrants, and females do relatively worse than males (Stromback 1984). Also, the returns to education are lower for immigrants than for Australian-born persons (Beggs and Chapman 1988 and Evans and Kelley 1986 say that this is due to differences in the quality of education). Apparently, both sources of disadvantage operate.

To some extent such studies miss the point. By definition a non-English-speaking migrant is not a native speaker of English. In addition, recent immigrants are severely constrained in acquiring formal English language skills: there are financial demands to earn enough to set up house in Australia; long waiting lists for courses (especially full-time ones); courses that are inappropriate for people from widely different backgrounds (educated or illiterate, old or young); and the difficulties of learning English while in a full time job. Most migrants, by policy, have few English language skills; equally, many of their children are disadvantaged at school by poor English skills (Kalantzis and Cope 1984; Williams 1987; but see Bullivant 1988).

In any event, Campbell et al. (1991) question the view that migrants' occupational status improves over time. The migrants in Campbell's sample did experience some improvement in their occupational status after their first job, so some retrieved the lost status during their careers in Australia. But most of the upward mobility of migrants that is apparent in cross-sectional studies of employed people arises because (1) those in operating and labouring occupations have a high propensity to leave the labour force and (2) a high proportion of managers are small shopkeepers (Castles et al. 1989). Most migrants (especially women) never retrieve the occupational status they lost on arrival (see Table 10.2).

Table 10.2 Occupational distributions of birthplace and gender groups

High status groups
Above average (for the gender) managers and professionals; less than 30 per cent for labourers.
Males—Australia, Czechoslovakia, Germany, Hungary, The Netherlands, Malaysia, Egypt, Canada, United States.
Females—Canada, United States.

Medium status groups
Males—United Kingdom and Ireland, Italy, Poland, Spain, USSR, China, Cyprus, India, Sri Lanka, New Zealand, Australia.
Females—United States and Ireland, Austria, Czechoslovakia, Germany, Hungary, The Netherlands, Poland, USSR, India, Malaysia, Sri Lanka, Egypt, New Zealand, Australia.

Low status groups
Over 60 per cent of employment as labourers.
Males—Greece, Malta, Yugoslavia, Lebanon, Turkey, Vietnam.
Females—Greece, Italy, Malta, Spain, Yugoslavia, Lebanon, Turkey, China, Cyprus, Vietnam.

Note: The occupational groups are: managers and administrators; professionals, paraprofessionals; tradespersons; clerks, salespersons; plant and machinery operators and drivers, labourers.

Source: Australian Bureau of Statistics, Census of the Commonwealth of Australia, 30 June 1986, unpublished tabulation.

So there is a process of settlement in the labour market, but it is limited. Most immigrants, especially NESB ones, enter lower-status occupations than Australian-born people and most are more poorly rewarded for their skills and experiences. Immigrant women are at a greater occupational disadvantage compared to their Australian-born counterparts than are immigrant men. The change in occupational status associated with migration is especially acute for females. Also, the failure to attain higher status occupations is more marked for women than for men. Migration has a class character, which is gender specific.

Such conclusions have been interpreted as evidence that the labour market in Australia is segmented (Collins 1988). The theory of segmented labour markets refers to two processes: first, creating different kinds of jobs with clearly demarcated, non-overlapping labour markets; and second, allocating each person to one of those labour markets (Peck 1989). Once allocated to a labour market it is difficult to escape to another market in which jobs are better paid, more interesting or more secure. Operating through such characteristics as education, experience, language and ability to work for the hours required, these allocations reproduce both gender and ethnic segregation within the labour market. The usual classification of ethnic and gender groups into segments, however, is not borne out by formal statistical procedures and differs in different cities (Webber et al. 1989); the evidence about the creation of segmented labour markets in Australia is not compelling.

Immigration has also influenced the evolution of class and gender relations within Australia. Immigration is predominantly by persons who enter the working class as employees, working for private corporations without decisionmaking responsibility. It is mainly by people who enter the occupations of least status within Australian society. Some immigrants escape these limitations to set themselves up in small businesses (Castles et al. 1989). Also, partially because of their relatively low income and their need for consumer durables with which to establish their new life, immigrant women are more likely to be employed—and to be employed in low status occupations—than are their Australian-born counterparts. Thus immigration has had quantitative effects on class and gender in Australia, but it has had qualitative effects too.

Immigration has, it is said, altered the characteristics of jobs in Australia. The introduction of low-skilled, non-English-speaking persons into the manufacturing labour force has prompted employers to modify jobs to fit the characteristics of immigrants by deskilling jobs and reducing the amount of training provided to employees (de Lepervanche 1984b). This has increased the need for more unskilled immigrants (Birrell and Birrell 1981), whose presence in turn reduces the incentive to improve working conditions within firms. According to such arguments, immigration has diminished the quality of working life in

Australia and prompted manufacturing firms to focus on the low skill, low quality end of markets. However, those Australian industries in which migrants form a relatively large proportion of the workforce also exhibit relatively high productivity growth (Fitzpatrick 1982) and evidence exists that since the mid-1970s immigration has tended to raise Australian living standards (Nevile 1990). Other arguments have claimed that immigration has tended to fragment the working class (Collins 1984; Morrisey 1984; but see Lever-Tracy 1984).

Similarly, gender and ethnicity interact (Bottomley 1984). Australian expectations in the 1950s and 1960s about the social role of married women were contradicted by the financial need of immigrant mothers to work (Martin 1984). The employment of immigrant mothers contrasted with stereotypical sex roles: working mothers lacked child care and after-school programmes and were made to feel guilty about leaving their children. Fincher et al. (1991) have documented the extent to which working NESB parents have had to rely on relatives or split shifts in order to care for pre-school children. Little wonder that the employment experience of NESB immigrant women has proved so marginal.

Several distinctions in the labour market sustain ethnicity. These derive from the class and gender of migrants to Australia, their language competence, their length of settlement and the fact of their being immigrants. Whether they derive also from discrimination is difficult to decide. Some (Wooden 1990) dismiss the possibility of effective discrimination on theoretical grounds. Yet Evans et al. (1988) report that 20 per cent of NESB immigrants claim to have experienced discrimination and that 30–40 per cent of employers prefer to hire an Australian born to an equivalent immigrant; the possibility of discrimination exists. Recent immigrants also report behaviour that may hide discrimination: demands for 'Australian accent' or for 'Australian experience' may be attempts to discriminate, though they may also be real requirements for particular jobs. Immigration has also affected class and gender relations within Australia by altering the quality of working life, providing the basis for ethnicity, and giving rise to a group of highly exploited women.

CLASS, GENDER, ETHNICITY AND SPATIAL STRUCTURE WITHIN CITIES

Immigration can interact with spatial structure in two ways. There may be a direct interaction between ethnicity and spatial structure unmediated by class and gender. Ethnicity can also interact indirectly with spatial structure through its relationship with class and gender. An important task is to determine the relative significance of the two interactions. We begin by examining the residential structure of immigrant groups within cities.

A common procedure for examining the spatial structure of cities as residences is factorial ecology. In this procedure the social and economic characteristics of residents are collapsed into a few major dimensions or groups of attributes. Commonly, between three and six dimensions are identified. In Australia such ecologies have been identified for the metropolitan areas of Adelaide (Stimson 1974), Melbourne (Jones 1969; Maher and Whitelaw 1975), Sydney (Badcock 1973), and for all six state capitals (Logan et al. 1975). These studies have consistently identified the three groups of attributes familiar in North America: familism/urbanism, socio-economic status and ethnicity. Sometimes other dimensions have been identified as well. Socio-economic status is an empirical outcome of class processes, though it measures the class position of males rather than of the population as a whole. Equally, measures of ethnicity derive from ethnic processes. There is more difficulty in interpreting the dimension of familism/urbanism in the terms of this chapter.

Factorial ecologies identify class, ethnicity and gender as fundamental attributes that distinguish urban residential areas. Socio-economic status (class) is high in particular sectors of cities. In Sydney, for example, high scores are recorded in areas of the north shore (Badcock 1973). Familism, a measure of gender practices, distinguishes middle and outer suburbs from the inner city. This is true in Sydney (Badcock 1973) and other cities. Ethnicity also exhibits a particular spatial pattern. Generally, high proportions of immigrants are found in clusters within the metropolitan areas. In Melbourne in 1961 measures of ethnicity varied more over the city than did either class or urbanism/familism, and low status immigrants were more highly clustered than high status immigrants (Burnley 1980, pp. 197–8).

Soon after Australia's post-war immigration programme had begun, spatial concentrations of immigrants appeared within cities. In the 1950s immigrants from the UK and NZ exhibited the least segregation from the Australian pattern; those from The Netherlands were largely concentrated in the (then) outer suburbs; southern Europeans resided mainly in inner-city areas, though some were market gardeners in outer-suburban areas; immigrants from central and eastern Europe were heavily concentrated in industrial zones on the outer fringes of metropolitan areas (Zubrzycki 1960, pp. 80–3). Later, in the mid-1960s, Badcock discovered a small group of inner-city areas in Sydney in which more than a quarter of the population was born overseas—and over half of those were born in southern Europe. By contrast, immigrants from English-speaking countries and northern Europe had tended to settle in the outer suburbs.

Table 10.3 Indices of residential segregation

Country of birth	*Sydney 1966*	*Melbourne 1954*	*Melbourne 1961*	*Melbourne 1981*
UK and Ireland	19.12	9.63	10.97	22.20
Germany	23.88	25.93	23.70	27.70
Netherlands	27.93	37.46	37.87	–
Poland	37.17	35.22	34.93	–
Italy	30.08	44.81	41.51	44.70
Yugoslavia	32.36	35.78	35.49	48.10
Malta	48.10	53.07	52.17	60.70
Greece	53.78	41.54	50.35	45.30

Source: Sydney data from Badcock (1973, p. 11); Melbourne data for 1954 and 1961 from Stimson (1974); Melbourne data for 1981 from Division of National Mapping (1984, p. 41).

One effect of this clustering is that within Australia's metropolitan areas immigrant and Australian-born populations are spatially separated (Table 10.3). These indices show the percentage of each subpopulation that would have to change residence for its population distribution to match that of all persons. Most of the birthplace groups are highly segregated, apart from the UK and Ireland; but southern Europeans were and remain extremely segregated from the population as a whole. The most highly segregated of the newly arrived groups are the Vietnamese.

In the 1970s and 1980s new immigrants located somewhat differently. The inner local government areas (LGAs) of Sydney and Melbourne received about one-third of all immigrants who settled in Sydney and Melbourne between 1976 and 1986 (though they contained only 20 per cent of the population of those metropolitan areas). But more than one-third of the immigrants went to the new fringe LGAs of Sydney and Melbourne. There has been a greater tendency in the 1970s and 1980s than in the 1950s and 1960s for recent immigrants to locate in the far outer suburbs.

Despite this tendency, areas of residential concentration of immigrants can still be identified (Collins 1988, p. 41). In 1981 three LGAs in Sydney had at least 30 per cent of their population born overseas (Botany, Fairfield and Marrickville), forming a zone to the south and west of the central city. In Melbourne there were nine such LGAS; they included inner-city LGAs adjacent to the central city (Brunswick, Collingwood, Fitzroy and Richmond), some middle distance industrial suburbs (Footscray, Sunshine) and some outer-suburban areas (Keilor, Oakleigh, Whittlesea). In Adelaide there was only one such LGA, and in other capital cities, none. Even in these areas, though, more than 60 per cent of the population was born in Australia: Australian cities have not developed enclaves on the US scale (Birrell 1990).

These data provide little information about the manner in which class, gender and ethnicity interact in forming the spatial structure of cities. Across Australia as a whole, areas in which there is a high measure of ethnicity are also areas in which live few males who are in high prestige occupations, many males who are in blue-collar occupations, many women in the labour force, many males and females who are employed in manufacturing, and few self-employed persons (Sweetser 1982). In Melbourne in 1981, collection districts in which many NESB people lived were also areas in which few people earned a personal income of more than $15 000 per year; few were professional, technical and administrative workers and conversely many were tradespersons, process workers and labourers; few people had acquired trade certificates, many had no qualifications; few dwellings had at least two cars; and many dwellings were apartments (Division of National Mapping 1984, p. 41). Thus ethnicity does in fact correlate with variables that measure class and (to a lesser degree) with variables that measure gender practices.

In the 1970s and 1980s the supply of inner-city single family dwellings dried up for immigrants. The middle class rediscovered the inner-city residential areas—rent controls having been removed in the mid-1960s, industry having suburbanized (Horvath and Engels 1985) and increasing numbers of women having entered the labour force. Therefore, immigrants in the inner city are now those who rent from a state housing authority. Since they cannot compete with middle-class residents, immigrants in single family dwellings are being pushed to suburban areas. Similarly, recent state housing construction has focused on outer-suburban areas, which is also where the remaining hostels for new immigrants are located (see Whitelaw and Humphreys 1980 for the significance of hostels on the future location choices of immigrants). Thus, the Vietnamese in Melbourne are located either in inner-city areas where public housing is concentrated or in outer suburbs near the hostels (Birrell 1990).

Immigrants tended to buy housing rather than rent it (Burnley 1982, p. 95), partly because rental housing was being sold off, but also because of what Price (1963) and Burnley (1980, p. 205) have called a culture of land and home ownership among many southern European immigrants. In Australia ethnic differences in rates of home ownership still exist, even though class differences in home ownership do not (Burnley 1980, pp. 205–6); while the proportion of households who owned or were buying their home in 1981 was about 70 per cent for those born in Australia, UK and Ireland, it was 90 per cent for Italian born, 84 per cent for Greek born and 80 per cent for Yugoslav born (Badcock 1984, p. 185). (Of course, these data could also reflect the proportion of young adults who live at home.) This culture of home ownership has tended to produce stable concentrations of ethnic populations.

An additional element is significant, however: a high proportion of immigrant households contain two or more workers, and a high proportion travel to work by bus, train or tram. To such communities in the 1960s the inner city offered relatively easy access to nearby workplaces by a relatively dense network of public transport. Indeed, Burnley (1982, pp. 97–101) draws on an interview survey to show that proximity to work was important in the residential choice of immigrants—though less significant than nearness to relatives and to ethnic facilities. A preference for living near relatives, however, is not merely a matter of friendship; when social services are in short supply, expensive or linguistically inappropriate, relatives perform important economic functions for working mothers—especially child care and shopping; where households are socially more isolated than in a country of birth, relatives serve to reduce loneliness and offer support for women; where people lack adequate English language skills, relatives provide an accessible social group. By such reasoning, the spatial structure of ethnicity is mediated by class (occupation or income) and gender (females at work) practices.

This evidence suggests that ethnicity is one of the most salient dimensions along which places in Australian cities are differentiated. To some extent, this differentiation is directly associated with ethnicity. Ethnic concentration, though, is also a class process, as is indicated by the generally low proportion of NESB persons in any local government area and by the economic functions that spatial concentrations assist. To some degree, too, ethnic concentrations are associated with different gender practices, notably proportions of women in employment. To this extent, the structure of class and gender is reflected in the residential differentiation of Australian cities through ethnicity. However, the relative significance of ethnic, class and gender processes in the observed spatial structure is not clear, partially because the original research did not seek to collect or to interpret data in this fashion.

Once created, though, such a spatial pattern (of ethnic concentrations in inner-city residential areas) has also affected the evolution of class, gender and ethnic characteristics within Australia. Dense immigrant communities make it easier to form and maintain the ethnic culture and economy (Jones 1969): retail outlets and community organizations are an obvious manifestation of this on Melbourne's cultural landscape. If ethnicity works to maintain differentiated markets for professionals (Kakakios and van der Velden 1984), ethnic markets and consumers must be spatially concentrated. Equally, the presence of concentrations of relatively low status workers must have served to restrain some of the older inner-city manufacturing industries from suburbanizing and perhaps from mechanizing in response to labour shortages. While inner-city Fitzroy provides a low wage female labour force, Holeproof need not seek a supply of female labour in the suburbs. Spatial structure serves also to modify social processes.

UNITED STATES COMPARISONS

Immigration to the United States has differed from that to Australia in three major respects. First, relative to population, immigration to Australia has been an order of magnitude greater than that to the USA (up to one per cent per annum, as compared to 0.1–0.2 per cent). Even so, American immigration has been numerically over three times as large as that to Australia, and when that immigration has been spatially concentrated it has led to much larger communities than in Australia. Second, post-war immigration to the USA has been overwhelmingly from non-English-speaking countries (especially Latin America and Asia) whereas nearly a half of immigrants to Australia have come from English-speaking countries. Immigrants to the USA compare with NESB immigrants to Australia rather than with all immigrants to Australia. Third, post-war immigration to the USA has been accompanied by a migration of Blacks, primarily from southern rural areas to northern industrial cities. In many respects this internal migration of Blacks disguised until recently the impact of post-war immigration on US cities (except perhaps in the Southwest, where Hispanics have been more numerous than Blacks).

Many migrants in the USA perform less well than the native born. Fewer immigrants than native born are managers or administrators (though more are professionals); fewer are in technical, sales, clerical or skilled jobs (Papademetriou et al. 1989, pp. 25–37). The relative economic position of Mexican, Puerto Rican, Cuban and recent Asian immigrants to the USA is similar to that of NESB immigrants to Australia. In 1980 only 11 per cent of Mexican Americans and 14 per cent of Puerto Ricans were employed in professional, technical, managerial and administrative positions, compared to 26 per cent of the population as a whole (Feagin 1989, pp. 268, 292), and there is evidence that in the 1970s the household income of Hispanics declined relative to that of Anglos (Moore and Pachon 1985, p. 73). Equally, despite popular images of the economic success of Filipinos, Koreans and Vietnamese, there is evidence of downward occupational mobility upon migration (Montero 1979; Papademetriou et al. 1989, p. 40). Whereas Asian American households in 1980 earned slightly more than the White American average, they contained 30 per cent more workers; thus the average income of Asian American workers was only 80 per cent that of White Americans (Feagin 1989, p. 356). In many respects female immigrants perform relatively less well than their male counterparts (Rodriguez 1989; Moore and Pachon 1985).

The correlates of the labour market performance of immigrants have been widely studied (for reviews with different flavours, see Greenwood and McDowell 1990; Papademetriou et al. 1989). Cross-sectional evidence exists that the incomes of immigrants rise with the period of residence in the USA and are related more to post-migration work experience than to experience before migration (Chiswick 1978). The effects of education on the earnings of immigrants are debated, seeming to vary with ethnicity and the language in which that schooling is conducted (see, for example, Reimers 1984; Carlson and Swartz 1988; Feagin 1989, p. 356). Evidently, the class and gender characteristics of non-English-speaking immigrants are broadly similar in the USA and Australia (see also Barrera 1979). However, Papademetriou et al. (1989, pp. 158–9) argue that the labour market position of immigrants depends on the structure and needs of the local labour market rather than being nationally determined.

The absolute size of the immigration flows into some regions of the USA dwarfs those into Australia. In 1980 Los Angeles SMSA, with 9.9 per cent of the US population, had 26 per cent of all recent male immigrants and over 45 per cent of all recent Mexican male immigrants; Miami, with two per cent of the US population, contained 73 per cent of all recent Cuban male immigrants; New York, with 12 per cent of the US population, had 18.5 per cent of all recent male immigrants and 40 per cent of all of those from Central and South America (Papademetriou et al. 1989, p. 52). Correspondingly, the effect of immigrants on particular cities has been far larger than in Australia (sometimes creating Third World employment and housing conditions within First World cities (Soja 1989). By 1980, for example, a majority of the population of Miami was Hispanic, and Anglos formed a minority of the population of Los Angeles county (Soja 1989). By contrast, in 1991 no Australian local government area contained less than 55 per cent of Australian-born people.

Levels of ethnic segregation in American cities are high, particularly for Blacks. The level of Hispanic residential segregation varies from city to city (Moore and Pachon 1985, pp. 60–1): in the Southwest, the segregation of Mexicans from Anglos seems to be declining (though their segregation from Blacks is increasing) but there is an increasing separation of Puerto Ricans from both Blacks and Whites in Boston and New York. Spatial segregation, though, is not a simple measure (Massey and Denton 1987); the residential dissimilarity of Hispanics is tending to decline where there is little immigration (e.g. Columbus) but to remain stable (e.g. New York) or to increase (Los Angeles) where immigration remains high. It is too early to tell whether these newly immigrated groups will follow their European predecessors in being assimilated into American cities.

The origins of the residential concentration are varied. Foreign-born legal immigrants select destinations within the USA on the basis of established family and ethnic connections rather than on the basis of economic conditions (Papademetriou et al. 1989: 190). These connections enhance labour market performance. Within cities, Hispanic concentrations of population have derived from areas of inner-city slums (Puerto Ricans in New York); in the Southwest, though, barrios often derive from pre-Anglo Mexican residential locations or from early labour camps (Moore and Pachon 1986, pp. 59–61). Continued residential segregation is thought to reflect class (household income), discrimination in housing markets and a desire for ethnic cohesion that either reflects physical and psychological fear or mirrors the creation of cultural or economic enclaves (Eyles 1990).

The Cubans in Miami provide the best example of the formation of an economic enclave. As a group they have done relatively well economically, perhaps because they migrated (initially) as a group, having substantial resources, social networks and access to government support. (In general, being confined to an ethnic enclave does not seem to impose a wage penalty on immigrants (Ong 1987; Chiswick 1988).) They are sufficiently numerous to offer a market for Cuban entrepreneurs as well as to provide the labour to exploit in production (Wilson and Portes 1981; Portes and Bach 1985). Here is a clearer case of a (spatially limited) economic enclave than has been established in Australia. The construction of this ethnic group has an identifiable class basis that rests in space; Barrera (1979) has also described in detail how Hispanic ethnicity was constructed as a class process in the Southwest.

The class and gender characteristics of recent immigrants to the USA thus compare in many respects to those of NESB immigrants to Australia. However, published data do not permit a quantitative comparison of the relative position of immigrants in the two countries: both are disadvantaged with respect to income and occupation. That commonality does not carry over into the construction of similar urban forms: immigrants in US cities appear to be residentially more segregated than in Australian cities and their presence would appear to have effected greater changes on the economies of American cities than Australian cities. These differences may arise from the far greater numbers of immigrants in some US cities than in Australian ones; though relative levels of immigration are smaller in the USA than in Australia, immigrants comprise a greater proportion of the population of New York or Los Angeles than of Melbourne or Sydney.

CONCLUSIONS

Post-war immigration to Australia has led to the formation of distinct birthplace groups. Non-English-speaking immigrants are on average disadvantaged in the Australian labour market; females in such groups are even more disadvantaged. The degree of this disadvantage varies by birthplace as well as by gender. What is more, immigration affects the class and gender position of those who migrate. To this extent, immigrant settlement in Australia is a class and gender process.

Immigrant settlement, though, is also an ethnic process. Ethnic identity and organization provide social and psychological supports to their members as well as offering variety in Australian life. Even so, the ethnic process has been encouraged not only by the state, but also by particular class and gender processes; excluded from Australian social and workers' organizations and exploited by co-ethnic employers and professionals, immigrants have turned from participation in Australian class and gender organizations to ethnic organizations.

Settlement is at heart a spatial process. The class and gender characteristics of many immigrants have forced them to a small number of locations that offer access to cheap housing, available jobs and linguistically appropriate services. The locational characteristics of immigrants reflect ethnic processes (cultural and linguistic access), class processes (occupational and income characteristics) and gender processes (family kinds and household divisions of labour). The spatial structure of Australia's cities in turn reinforces class and gender practices by embedding them, and is central to the formation of ethnic groups—particularly among relatively immobile populations.

The characteristics of immigrant groups are not purely ethnic. Indeed, the construction of ethnic groups reflects in part class and gender processes. It follows that programmes to facilitate the adjustment of immigrants to Australian life cannot be purely multicultural; immigrants, particularly non-English-speaking and female immigrants, are not simply recently arrived Australians who like to meet in ethnic clubs. Australian life must change also, to recognize and to remedy the class and gender processes that are at work in forming and deforming the lives of immigrants.

PART IV

IMMIGRANT MINORITIES AND MULTICULTURAL POLICIES

11

AUSTRALIAN MULTICULTURALISM

SOCIAL POLICY AND IDENTITY IN A CHANGING SOCIETY

Stephen S. Castles

THE EMERGENCE OF MULTICULTURALISM

About five million persons from some 100 countries have come to Australia as settlers since 1945 (BIR 1990, p. 32). Today two-fifths of the Australian population are immigrants or children of immigrants. Since the inception of the immigration programme in 1947 public policies have gone through a number of stages: 'assimilationism' up to the mid-1960s, followed by 'integration' until the early 1970s, and then 'multiculturalism'. But multiculturalism has evolved as well, passing through three main stages. Each stage is concerned with both social policy and the definition of national identity, and is determined by a number of factors: the political agenda of the government in power, the changing economic and social context, patterns of migration and settlement, the need to secure public support for immigration policies, and the desire for good community relations.

ASSIMILATIONISM: 1947 TO THE MID-1960s

When the post-war immigration programme got under way, ALP Immigration Minister Calwell promised the Australian public that there would be 10 British immigrants for every 'foreigner'. It was widely believed that non-British immigration would threaten national identity and social cohesion. Once it had become clear, however, that British immigration would be insufficient to sustain demographic and economic growth, eastern and southern Europeans were recruited. This made it necessary for the Government to find a way of maintaining homogeneity and of allaying popular fears. The solution was found in assimilationism: the doctrine that immigrants could be culturally and socially absorbed and rapidly become indistinguishable from the existing Anglo-Australian population.

Government measures to encourage successful settlement and assimilation included provision of initial accommodation and basic English courses, as well as help in finding work. Social security benefits were at first available only to British Commonwealth immigrants, but were later extended to other groups. The Government subsidized voluntary efforts to assist the cultural assimilation of the newcomers, particularly through the 'Good Neighbour Councils' (Jakubowicz 1989). Once admitted, most migrants were treated as future citizens. Naturalization could be obtained after five years, and immigrants had the right to bring in family members. Migrants were to work and live among Australians to avoid the formation of ethnic enclaves. The school was to have a key role in making the children of migrants into Australians; there should therefore be no special courses for migrant children, and they were to be forced to speak English from the outset (Martin 1978; DIEA 1986; Wilton and Bosworth 1984; Vasta 1990).

INTEGRATION: THE MID-1960s TO 1972

By the 1960s the basic contradiction of assimilationism was becoming obvious: 'New Australians' were meant to speak English, live among Anglo-Australians and behave just like them, but at the same time, forces within the migratory process were leading to labour market segmentation and social segregation. Migrants whose passage was assisted by the Government had initially been directed into heavy industrial jobs (such as the iron and steel industry), or into infrastructure construction, such as the Snowy Mountains hydro-electric scheme. Other migrants, especially southern Europeans, took factory jobs on arrival because these were the only positions available to them. Because of lack of qualifications and poor knowledge of English, migrant workers were the main source of labour for the new factories of Sydney and Melbourne, which became 'southern European occupational ghettoes' (Lever-Tracy and Quinlan 1998). Migrants settled in the industrial suburbs and the inner-city areas close to their work, where housing was relatively cheap, while Anglos moved out to new suburbs. Moreover, many local people were suspicious of the newcomers and avoided contact with them.

It became obvious that many migrants were living in isolation and relative poverty—especially in the event of illness, accident or family breakdown (Martin 1978). Migrant children were failing at school, often due to lack of support in learning English. Departing numbers rates were increasing and it was becoming harder to attract new immigrants. The result was a series of policy changes which heralded the demise of both assimilationism and the White Australia Policy. Measures introduced between 1965 and 1972 included an Integration Branch within the Department of Immigration, immigrant welfare grants for community agencies, a Committee on Overseas Professional Qualifications, a special law providing for English courses for children and adults, English language courses on television and at the workplace, and the first steps towards a Telephone Interpreter Service (DIEA 1986, p. 31). The Minister for Immigration announced in 1966 that a few well-qualified immigrants from Asia would be admitted under stringent conditions (DIEA 1986, p. 23). This was the first crack in the racist immigration policy which had been zealously applied since 1945—to the point of denying entry to Asian wives of returning Australian soldiers.

MULTICULTURALISM PHASE 1: MIGRANT RIGHTS 1972–75

From about 1970, ALP leaders began to realize that non-English-speaking background (NESB) migrants formed a distinct part of Australian society with special needs. Moreover, they represented a significant proportion of working-class voters, and their votes could be decisive in some urban constituencies. The ALP set out to woo the 'migrant vote', setting up Greek and Italian sections, paying attention to migrants' educational and welfare needs, advertising in the ethnic press and selecting a few migrants as candidates (Collins 1988, pp. 135–7). The victory of the ALP in the 1972 election, after 23 years of conservative government, seems to have been partly attributable to this policy.

The Whitlam Government adopted non-discriminatory entry criteria, finally doing away with the White Australia Policy. It also abolished privileges for British settlers. At the same time, in line with traditional Labor views on the threat to jobs caused by immigration, the Government reduced immigration considerably. In 1973 Immigration Minister Al Grassby spoke of multiculturalism for the first time in a famous speech on 'the family of the nation' (Grassby 1973). Grassby explicitly rejected assimilation, seeing the increased diversity of society as a cultural and economic enrichment. It is often argued that this speech marks the beginning of Australian multiculturalism, but in fact the emphasis in ALP policies was not on cultural pluralism but on improving welfare and education systems (Castles et al. 1990, p. 59).

The Australian Assistance Plan—the centre-piece of social policy reform—put special emphasis on migrant disadvantage. A Migrant Task Force was set up to consult with migrant groups on their needs, and the best ways of implementing improvements. Specific measures included the right to invalid and widows pensions, migrant housing and low-interest loans, family health insurance, and work-based child-care programmes employing workers of appropriate ethnic backgrounds (Jakubowicz et al. 1984, pp. 60–1). Such policies were not based on an explicit ethnic group model, yet the involvement of migrant spokespersons and groups in planning and implementation did encourage the formal constitution of ethnic organizations. Bodies such as the Australian–Greek Welfare Society, the Italian welfare agencies COASIT and FILEF, and the Ecumenical Migration Centre began to play a part in defining issues and policies. A migrant rights movement developed, leading to the formation of Ethnic Communities Councils (ECCs) in all states (DIEA 1986, pp. 31–4).

MULTICULTURALISM PHASE 2: CULTURAL PLURALISM 1972 TO THE MID-1980s

When the Liberal–Country Party Coalition was re-elected in 1975, immigration intakes were increased, and the need to respond to the Indo-Chinese refugee crisis led, for the first time, to significant entries of Asians. Liberal leader and Prime Minister Malcolm Fraser had learnt the significance of the 'ethnic vote' from the 1972 election, and now went to considerable lengths to win the support of ethnic community leaders. The previous government's funding for migrant welfare programmes had drawn many members of the emerging migrant middle class into support for the ALP. Yet the Fraser Government's neo-liberal economic and social policies meant abandoning many of the welfare measures introduced between 1972 and 1975. The strategy adopted by Fraser was to redefine multiculturalism to emphasize cultural pluralism and the role of ethnic organizations in providing welfare services.

Fraser emphasized the value of multiculturalism as a way of achieving national identity (usually referred to as social cohesion) in an ethnically diverse society. This 1978 statement is typical: 'The Government accepts that it is now essential to give significant further encouragement to develop a multicultural attitude in Australian society' (quoted in Foster and Stockley 1988, p. 31). The bodies set up to produce and disseminate the appropriate ideas included the Australian Institute of Multicultural Affairs (AIMA) and the Special Broadcasting Service, which was to provide multicultural television and radio services. The Adult Migration Education Programme was expanded, and a Multicultural Education Programme was developed for schools.

Welfare policies towards migrants were reshaped in accordance with the Galbally Report (1978). This fitted into the neo-liberal agenda of cutting government expenditure, denying the role of class position in socio-economic disadvantage, and giving individuals, families and local communities more responsibility for dealing with social problems. The problems encountered by migrants were defined as individual deficiencies, resulting from poor English, lack of knowledge of Australian institutions, or failure to adapt to an industrial society. Migrant welfare was removed from the mainstream social system and delegated to the ethnic group through a system of grants to ethnic organizations. This provided welfare on the cheap, since pay, staffing levels and conditions could be lower than in government agencies (Jakubowicz et al. 1984, p. 81).

Thus by the late 1970s, multiculturalism based on an ethnic group model had emerged as a major government strategy concerned simultaneously with developing the ideological legitimation for an ethnically diverse society, cutting government expenditure and enhancing social control over minorities.

MULTICULTURALISM PHASE 3: ACCESS AND EQUITY SINCE 1983

The Hawke ALP Government, which was elected in 1983, initially cut immigration intakes, then increased them again from 1986, believing this would stimulate economic growth. Apart from a few minor changes, the multicultural policies of the previous government were at first continued. In the early 1980s initiatives for change came mainly from the state governments of New South Wales (NSW) and Victoria. These established Ethnic Affairs Commissions to ensure that government services were suitable for and accessible to people of all ethnic backgrounds. The slogans of 'participation' in NSW, and 'access and equity' in Victoria were meant to emphasize that it was up to government to remove structural barriers to migrants' economic, social and political opportunities.

Non-discriminatory entry policies and multiculturalism had developed in a period in which most people believed that immigration contributed to economic growth and improved living standards. As Australia's economic perspectives became more uncertain, people began to question the benefits of immigration and the level of expenditure on multicultural services. The 'Great Immigration Debate' started in 1984, when the prominent historian Geoffrey Blainey called for restrictions on immigration and warned against what he called the 'asianisation of Australia' (Blainey 1984; Markus and Ricklefs 1985; Castles et al. 1990, pp. 116–38). Blainey received a good deal of public support. Politicians of both left and right began to feel that there was a groundswell of opposition to multiculturalism, and that cuts in the area would meet little criticism. In the 1986 Budget the ALP Government abolished the Australian Institute of Multicultural Affairs, and cut funding for English as a Second Language teaching and for the Multicultural Education Programme. Plans were also made to merge the Special Broadcasting Service with the Australian Broadcasting Corporation.

The party strategists, however, had miscalculated: the cuts led to protests and demonstrations by migrant organizations. This ethnic mobilization threatened the ALP hold on marginal seats in Sydney and Melbourne. In an amazingly rapid about-turn, many of the measures of 1986 were reversed in early 1987. The new direction was signalled by: the establishment of an Office of Multicultural Affairs (OMA), with wide powers to monitor government policy; the appointment of an Advisory Council on Multicultural Affairs (ACMA) to advise the Prime Minister and to develop a 'National Agenda for a Multicultural Australia'; the dropping of the proposed SBS–ABC merger; and an administrative restructuring which created a Department of Immigration, Local Government and Ethnic Affairs, headed by a senior Cabinet minister.

Debates over immigration and multiculturalism have continued. In 1988 the FitzGerald Report of the Committee to Advise on Australia's Immigration Policies (CAAIP 1988) asserted that many Australians did not understand multiculturalism and were worried that it was leading to a division of the nation into separatist cultural minorities. It also implied that immigration policies were being strongly influenced by ethnic lobby groups, and no longer reflected the interests of Australia as a nation. The debate was taken up by then Opposition leader, John Howard, who attacked multiculturalism, and stated that a future Liberal–National Government would reserve the right to restrict Asian immigration to safeguard 'social cohesion'. Although Howard received considerable public support, especially in the letter-columns of popular papers and on talk-back radio, there was little élite support. Many employers emphasized the economic merits of immigration. The unions and the ALP attacked Howard's proposed 'One Australia' policy as a veiled return to the White Australia Policy. Liberal leaders in states with large migrant populations—Nick Greiner in NSW and Jeff Kennett in Victoria—refused to support their federal leader. Howard lost the leadership of his party soon afterwards, and it is widely believed that his policies on immigration and multiculturalism were a contributory factor. Subsequent Liberal leaders have expressed support for non-discriminatory entry policies and for multiculturalism.

The ALP Government has again attempted to reshape multiculturalism, emphasizing its economic benefits. New immigration policies since 1989 have been designed to increase the proportion of highly skilled immigrants. At the same time it is argued that a multicultural population is better placed to respond to the challenges of increased international trade and communication, and above all to provide the opening to Asia which is seen as crucial to Australia's future. The National Policy on Language, which was adopted in 1987 (Lo Bianco 1987), has the aim of encouraging bilingualism, including the learning of languages of economic and strategic significance, especially Asian languages, as well as maintaining the 'community languages' of migrant groups. In the social policy area, the Government has argued the need to move away from services for specific ethnic groups. The slogan of 'mainstreaming', introduced in the mid-1980s by the NSW Government, has been generally adopted as a principle for restructuring government services. All commonwealth government departments are now required to produce annual 'Access and Equity Statements' designed to ensure that their services are responsive to the needs of a diverse population.

The most significant statement of the new approach to multiculturalism is contained in the National Agenda for a Multicultural Australia (OMA 1989), launched by the Prime Minister with great fanfare in July 1989. The National Agenda identifies 'three dimensions of multicultural policy': (1) cultural identity—the right of all Australians, within carefully defined limits, to express and share their individual cultural heritage, including their language and religion; (2) social justice—the right of all Australians to equality of treatment and opportunity, and the removal of barriers of race, ethnicity, culture, religion, language, gender or place of birth; and (3) economic efficiency—the need to maintain, develop and utilize effectively the skills and talents of all Australians, regardless of background.

In the National Agenda multiculturalism is essentially seen as a system of rights and freedoms, which, however, are limited by an overriding commitment to the nation, a duty to accept the Constitution and the rule of law, and the acceptance of basic principles such as tolerance and equality, English as the national language and equality of the sexes. Multiculturalism is not defined in terms of cultural pluralism or minority rights, but in terms of the cultural, social and economic rights of all citizens in a democratic state. The programme contained in the document is based on the recognition that some groups are disadvantaged by lack of language proficiency and education, together with discrimination based on race, ethnicity, gender, and so on.

The measures announced in the National Agenda include: (1) improvements in procedures for recognition of overseas qualifications; (2) a campaign to improve community relations; (3) strengthening of the Government's Access and Equity strategy; (4) extension and improvement of multicultural broadcasting; (5) a number of initiatives to improve opportunities for learning English; (6) a commitment to support learning of other languages; and (7) reviews of Australian law and administrative decisionmaking to ensure that they are appropriate to people from different cultural backgrounds.

THE CHANGING CONTEXT OF MULTICULTURALISM

After this brief history of Australian multiculturalism, it is now possible to examine some of its essential features at the beginning of the 1990s. First, the societal context has changed dramatically since the policy was introduced. The early 1970s can be seen in retrospect as the end of a period characterized by (1) political, strategic and economic orientation towards Europe and the USA; (2) a eurocentric culture; (3) high economic growth rates and prosperity; (4) mass permanent immigration of migrant workers and their families, predominantly of southern European peasant background; (5) a match between the demand for low-skilled labour by manufacturing, construction and service industries and the relatively low levels of education and qualifications of most migrant workers; (6) the emergence of first-generation ethnic communities of European background.

All these factors have now shifted. The end of the cold war, the integration of western Europe, the rise of northeast Asia and the growing significance of transnational capital are all undermining the structures on which Australia's world view was based. By the end of the 1980s, trade and investment from Japan and other northeast Asian countries was decisive for Australia. The economy retained its essentially colonial character as an exporter of primary commodities and an importer of manufactured goods. Attempts to develop Australian manufacturing collapsed in the period of restructuring after 1973; the share of manufacturing in GDP declined from 28 per cent in 1965 to 17 per cent in 1985—a greater relative fall than in the USA or the UK (David and Wheelwright 1989, p. 7). This economic structure leads to extreme vulnerability, which makes itself felt through high unemployment, rising foreign debt and declining living standards.

The character of migration has also changed dramatically in the last two decades. Entries from Europe (with the exception of Britain) virtually ceased from about 1970. Immigration from non-European sources, including Lebanon and Turkey, Latin America, Asia and Oceania, grew especially from the late 1970s. The new immigration is far more heterogeneous than in the past—not only culturally, but also with regard to educational and occupational experience. Immigrants include entrepreneurs and highly skilled professionals, as well as unskilled migrant workers and refugees. In the 1950s and 1960s the main points of economic incorporation for NESB migrants were low-skilled factory or construction jobs. These provided reasonably secure work and income during initial settlement. Many immigrants were able to move into better jobs later and to accumulate savings to buy a house or to set up a small business. Today, a large proportion of these entry-level jobs have disappeared through economic restructuring. The process of incorporation is now more complex and is frequently marked by long periods of unemployment and insecurity, especially for low-skilled groups (Castles and Collins 1990).

Multiculturalism emerged in the 1970s as a 'first generation strategy' geared to the needs of European immigrants (Jayasuriya 1989). It was largely seen in terms of the cultural dynamics of rapid modernization experienced by people of peasant background entering an industrial society. This raises the question as to whether multicultural policies and institutions meet the current situation, which is characterized by the coexistence of an ageing European migrant generation, a second (and third) generation of European background raised and educated in Australia, and highly diverse immigrant groups (and emerging second generations) of Asian origin.

INSTITUTIONAL STRUCTURES

Unlike Canada, which has its *Multiculturalism Act*, Australia's legal basis for multicultural policies is provided through a variety of laws, such as the *Migration Act* of 1958, the *Migration Legislation Amendment Act* of 1989, the *Racial Discrimination Act* of 1975 and the *Sex Discrimination Act* of 1984. Compliance with these laws is monitored by the Human Rights and Equal Opportunity Commission. The states also have equal opportunity legislation and, in some cases, laws against racial vilification. As announced in the National Agenda, the Law Reform Commission is examining the need for changes in Australian law to make it appropriate to a multicultural society. Current deliberations within the Commission indicate little support for a 'Multiculturalism Act'. Nor are major legislative changes likely, although some modifications may be made in procedures and legal support services. It is generally felt that a unitary legal system based on democratic values does not permit special rules for different ethnic groups (Australian Law Reform Commission 1991). Australian multiculturalism is thus based more on government policies and special agencies than on specific laws.

At the central government level, multicultural policies are co-ordinated by the Office of Multicultural Affairs in the Department of Prime Minister and Cabinet. OMA has a wide-ranging brief, which includes monitoring bills and Cabinet submissions, vetting departmental Access and Equity Statements, and publicly promoting multicultural policies and good community relations. The Department of Immigration, Local Government and Ethnic Affairs (DILGEA) is responsible for a range of settlement services, including the Adult Migrant Education Programme (mainly responsible for English courses); the grant-in-aid system of support to migrant welfare organizations; and the Telephone Interpreter Service, which provides interpreters for all languages throughout Australia. DILGEA also funds a quasi-autonomous Bureau of Immigration Research.

Several other departments have special sections concerned with multicultural issues. For instance, the Department of Employment, Education and Training has a National Office for Overseas Skills Recognition, is involved in implementation of the National Policy on Language, and shares responsibility with the state education authorities for migrant and multicultural education. A variety of ministerial advisory bodies involve the wider community in the discussion of multicultural policies. Finally, the Federal Government finances the Special Broadcasting Service, which provides radio and television broadcasts in English and other languages to meet the needs of ethnic communities and to promote wider cultural understanding.

Most states have ethnic affairs commissions (EACs) or offices, which have a role similar to that of OMA: they advise the Government, vet new laws, try to make state government services more accessible to members of all ethnic groups, co-ordinate language services, and generally promote good community relations. The NSW EAC, for example, is responsible for a system of Ethnic Affairs Policy Statements, through which each government department sets out its plans for making its work appropriate to an ethnically diverse population. Local authorities are also supposed to prepare such statements. Most EACs have part-time commissioners, appointed to facilitate communication between government and community. State education, health and community services departments generally have multicultural units to provide interpreting and translation services and to plan service delivery. There are units to deal with specific problems affecting NESB people, such as recognition of overseas qualifications, aged care, occupational health, women's issues, and drug and alcohol dependency.

State education departments have the main responsibility for providing English courses and special learning support for immigrant children. They also provide multicultural education for all students, although the meaning of this varies considerably from state to state. It generally means influencing the curriculum of subjects such as social studies, Australian studies, geography, history and English. Recently, the National Policy on Language has led to increased emphasis on learning both community languages and those useful for economic reasons.

Multiculturalism is a major focus for a number of non-governmental bodies, such as the Ethnic Communities Councils and their federal body, the Federation of Ethnic Communities Councils of Australia (FECCA), which was established in 1979. The social and cultural organizations of the various ethnic communities frequently make statements on multicultural policies. There are multicultural or ethnic affairs units in bodies such as the Australian Council of Trade Unions. Special non-governmental agencies (generally subsidized from public funds) are concerned with provision of information and counselling, or improving services for particular groups, such as migrant women and youth. Representatives of unions, employers associations and ethnic organizations serve on multicultural consultative bodies. However, multiculturalism is above all a public policy issue, which has not played a major part in the private sector. The private bodies function essentially as pressure groups, calling on government to improve resources and services.

Although there is no space here for an analysis of government budgets, it may be said that direct expenditure on multicultural institutions and policies is small, compared with the large budgets in areas such as social security, health and education. This is consistent with the idea of 'mainstreaming': multiculturalism does not mean providing specific and different services for members of different ethnic groups, but rather making general services accessible to and suitable for everybody. Apart from initial settlement services (hostels, English courses and information) and language services, immigrants have the same basic needs as the rest of the population. They make far more use of public hospitals, schools, employment services, and so on, than of any special migrant or ethnic agencies.

The social policy aspect of multiculturalism does not consist mainly of specific institutions or services, but rather of a set of practices within virtually all institutions and services. The multicultural content of services, however, is hard to measure, and can easily be reduced to mere rhetoric. Mainstreaming at a time of severe fiscal constraint may simply mean cutting migrant services without providing adequate mainstream alternatives (Jakubowicz 1989). Government Access and Equity Statements or Ethnic Affairs Policy Statements may consist of well-meaning platitudes that are never implemented. In a study commissioned by the Federal Department of Community Services and Health, Meekosha and Jakubowicz found that a combination of structural racism, reduced resources, privatization of welfare functions and managerial corporatism within the Department were marginalizing the interests of NESB clients. The managerial emphasis on cost-effectiveness disadvantaged minority groups because it was more costly to respond to their needs than those of the Anglo-Australian majority (Meekosha and Jakubowicz 1989).

ETHNICITY, SOCIAL POLICY AND IDENTITY

Multiculturalism appears in retrospect as a necessary consequence of mass immigration and growing cultural diversity. The state was forced to work out new social policies and to address the consequences of diversity for community relations and national identity. In both areas the question of defining ethnicity and of the significance attached to the ethnic group are crucial.

The initial approach was to deny that immigrants had special group needs. For nearly 20 years, Australian authorities treated immigrants and their children as individuals who had to learn English, adapt to Australian customs and assimilate into Anglo-Australian society. Cultural difference was seen as a potential threat to the 'social cohesion' of the nation, which, however, could be readily countered through assimilationism. Total immersion was the paradigm: apart from on-arrival measures—such as reception camps, English courses and Good Neighbour Councils—there were no special social or cultural policies for immigrants. This corresponded to the overall residualist approach to welfare (Mishra 1990, pp. 79–91; Castles, F. G. 1985; Jakubowicz et al. 1984). In a situation of full employment it was believed that the labour market and rising living standards would automatically overcome barriers of both class and national origin. Australia was a 'lucky country', with an affluent, egalitarian and classless society, offering endless opportunity for those prepared to work hard (Horne 1964).

By the 1960s it could no longer be denied that certain migrant groups were concentrated in low-skilled working-class positions, and that they were susceptible to a range of social disabilities (Martin 1978; Jakubowicz et al. 1984). At the same time, processes of cultural maintenance and community formation were increasingly significant. The result was a shift to a model of integration, which recognized the continuing role of migrant groups and the need for special services for migrants. This paved the way for the initial stage of multiculturalism based on a model of migrant needs and rights. The ALP's approach to multiculturalism from 1972 to 1975 did not centre on a notion of ethnicity. Rather it fitted into an overall attempt to establish a welfare state based on the continuing salience of class as a determinant of life chances.

Recession and economic restructuring from the mid-1970s made it all the more obvious that the 'lucky country' dream of full employment, prosperity for all and a classless society was unattainable. Real wages and the employment security of blue-collar workers declined, while the prevalence of poverty and the gap between the rich and the poor grew. The second stage of multiculturalism, developed by the conservative government of 1975–83, was an attempt to manage increasing diversity, while moving away from general welfare rights for migrants (or indeed the population as a whole). The ethnic group model was based on the notion that the main determinant of social relations and identity was culture, defined in static terms as the language, customs, traditions and behavioural practices which migrants brought with them as 'cultural baggage'. This made it possible to speak of the 'Italian community', the 'Vietnamese community', and so on, and to assume that these had common needs and interests, expressed by community associations and their leaders. The ethnic group model homogenized migrant populations, ignoring the link between the migratory process and socio-economic position in favour of an interpretation of ethnic disadvantage based on cultural dissonance, language difficulties and failure to adapt. This allowed the privatization of social welfare provision for immigrants through subsidies to ethnic welfare and cultural associations.

The recognition of ethnic associations and their leaders as legitimate representatives of migrant group interests also provided a model for re-thinking national identity. Acceptance of cultural diversity did not threaten social cohesion if culture could be defined essentially as language plus folklore and relegated to the private sphere of the family, the ethnic association and the colourful festival. Cohesion in the public sphere could be safeguarded by insisting that ethnic groups must adhere to 'overarching Australian values' (Smolicz 1985), while the majority population was encouraged to develop a 'multicultural attitude'. Community relations were thus based on permitting a limited amount of difference, while calling on the Anglo-Australian majority to be tolerant.

The changes in multicultural policy described above are clearly linked to the Hawke Government's general approach to welfare. Access and Equity policies and mainstreaming mean a move away from the ethnic group model in providing services to immigrant groups. The emphasis now is on removing structural barriers (defined in the National Agenda as those based on race, ethnicity, culture, religion, language, gender or place of birth) to participation in Australian society. The role of the state is to guarantee rights of participation in all areas of society and to ensure equity in its own service provision. The National Agenda also addresses the issue of identity, stressing cultural and ethnic diversity and laying down the right to maintain cultural identity. Taken together, the Government's multicultural and social justice policies appear to provide a social-democratic concept of citizenship for an ethnically diverse nation. Citizenship is defined in terms of a set of civil rights to personal liberty including the right to cultural identity), of political rights to participation in the democratic institutions, and of social rights of access to income, health care, education and welfare (compare Jayasuriya 1990, p. 18). All these are seen as entitlements of 'all Australians'—they are not tied to ethnicity or culture, and there is no expectation of assimilation as a precondition to enjoyment of the rights. The blueprint, however, seems to contain a number of contradictions and unresolved issues, which will now be examined.

INCLUSION OR ETHNIC RIGHTS?

Defining citizenship in a multicultural society in inclusionary terms appears to leave no long-term role for specific social policies for ethnic minorities. In practice, though, there is still a wide range of specialized services and agencies, and ethnic organizations lobby for their continuation and improvement. There is a very real problem here: basing service delivery on ethnicity tends to segregate and marginalize migrants, but ignoring ethnicity and catering for migrants only within general services can mean neglecting special needs and perpetuating structural discrimination.

In any case a big gap exists between the ideology of equity and the real persistence of inequality and social marginalization. Even if ethnicity is not a cause of social disadvantage, it is surely a marker of it. People who belong to certain ethnic groups (particularly southern Europeans, Latin Americans, Lebanese, Turks and Indo-Chinese) tend to have lower occupational status, lower incomes, higher unemployment rates and a variety of special health and educational needs (DIEA 1986; ABS 1989). Ethnicity and class often correlate, and some groups of migrant background are likely to be structurally marginalized by mainstream services. So a social justice policy may have to include special measures to address the needs of particular groups.

There is clearly an unresolved tension between the inclusionist model of rights and the ethnic group model which developed in the 1970s and 1980s. The ethnic group model created expectations and institutions that cannot easily be ignored. Multiculturalism provided a socio-political role for ethnic associations which put a premium on the construction of culturally based definitions of needs. Indeed, it has been argued that pluralist models of welfare delivery actually helped to construct a special form of ethnicity and its associated organizations and leaderships (Castles et al. 1990, ch. 4; Jakubowicz et al. 1984). Thus despite the emphasis on rights of 'all Australians' in the National Agenda, OMA, DILGEA and other government bodies continue to subsidize ethnic organizations in a variety of ways.

The tension between inclusionary and ethnic group models is likely to increase. The ethnic group model which postulates common interests of a particular 'ethnic community' may have had some justification with regard to the first generation southern and eastern European migrant workers of the 1950s to the 1970s. Can it apply, though, to the much more disparate experience and needs of the second and third generations of these backgrounds, or to some of the Asian groups, which are highly differentiated from the outset? Indeed members of some groups now experience relatively little socio-economic disadvantage, but are still subject to exclusionary practices in terms of political and cultural rights. Above all racism against visible minorities (discussed below) may affect people who are economically assimilated.

MINORITIES AND POWER

The definition of citizenship provided by the National Agenda for a Multicultural Australia and the Social Justice Strategy appears in the final analysis as an ideology of inclusion supported by residualist social policies to deal with the most blatant forms of injustice. Officially: 'The central objective of the Government's social justice strategy is to develop a fairer, more prosperous and more just society for every Australian' (Hawke and Howe 1990, p. 1). Yet at the same time deregulation and fiscal constraint make general income support impossible, despite growing unemployment and poverty. The new social policy is thus about equality of access to government services, rather than about the quality of the services offered. Nor is it about equality of resource distribution or of economic condition. But since political power is linked to economic resources, it is doubtful whether the 'barriers to participation' can really be tackled by this approach. The real aim thus appears to be, as Jakubowicz (1989) has put it, to distinguish better between the 'deserving and the undeserving poor'.

In reality, major Australian institutions in both the public and private sectors are still based on British, US and—to a lesser extent—western European models. Their structure and organizational culture tend to exclude people who show differences in appearance, speech, behaviour or values from positions of power. The widespread preference for people with qualifications obtained in 'Anglo-Saxon countries' is an example (Castles et al. 1989; Mitchell et al. 1990). An examination of the Australian Public Service has shown that both first and second generation NESB people are under-represented at the higher levels, and that they have achieved lower positions than would be expected on the basis of their length of service and qualifications (Public Service Commission 1990, pp. 29–32). NESB people are rarely members of federal or state parliaments, or members of government advisory bodies concerned with areas of general importance, such as economic policy (Jupp et al. 1989). As Jupp (1984, p. 182) has pointed out, 'Power in the corporate sector, in the parties, in the bureaucracies, in the professions, in the media and in the unions—is still in varying degrees, in the hands of people of British or Irish origin'. Indeed, it might be added, it is in the hands of White, middle-class, middle-aged men.

This suggests that the political task of changing central institutions to truly reflect a multicultural society has yet to be undertaken. Jayasuriya (1990, p. 25) suggests that the likely agents of change are social movements demanding the expansion of citizenship rights. He therefore predicts the development of a new form of interest group politics based on ethnic criteria. Although this might appear to present new answers to the dilemma of inclusion versus ethnic rights, and to the disparity between formal political rights and real power, it is far from clear that this type of mobilization is taking place. The old model of ethnic mobilization based on a temporary nexus between ethnicity and class is losing its general appeal, but an identity-based model (perhaps similar to the 'ethnic revival' concept common in the USA in the 1960s) has yet to emerge.

IDENTITY AND RACISM

Political mobilization (of both minorities and the majority) based on ethnicity is most likely to emerge if the definition of identity central to multiculturalism fails to gain acceptance. This has two aspects: the promise of group identity based on cultural rights for minorities, and the concept of national identity based on diversity for the nation as a whole. The model could break down if minorities feel their group rights are mere tokenism, or if the majority feels threatened by a perceived watering down of their cultural dominance within the overall concept of national identity.

The National Agenda emphasizes cultural identity as a central aspect of multiculturalism, although it also places limits on the degree of cultural autonomy permitted. The right to maintenance of cultural heritage, including language and religion, leads to the concept of ethnic group interests and the protection of minority rights. Since such interests cannot find adequate expression through parliamentary democracy based on majority rule, the state has to take on the role of protector of minorities. But how are political and bureaucratic office-bearers to know what the minority interests are? Clearly, there is a need for processes of consultation with minorities outside the normal parliamentary system. These processes provide a continued legitimation for ethnic associations and leaderships. There are two problems here. The first is that cultural pluralism may be accompanied for some groups, as already outlined, by exclusion from real power and by socio-economic disadvantage. In that case, minorities may regard the multicultural definition of identity as a sham which merely veils their continuing marginalization.

The second problem is that members of the Anglo-Australian majority may see these pluralist structures as special privileges that unfairly claim public resources. Indeed, this criticism has wide currency through media reports (for instance Barnett 1986), political speeches (for example the speeches of Opposition leader Howard referred to above) and even official reports (CAAIP 1988). This leads on to the question of the extent to which multiculturalism provides a satisfactory resolution of the issue of national identity for the majority. If being Australian can no longer be derived from common British heritage and traditions, what is its basis? Many of the debates during the 1988 bicentenary addressed this issue. Official efforts moved uneasily between pageants on the history of British colonization, attempts to placate Aboriginal protests on their continuing marginalizations, and calls to celebrate the successes of immigration and diversity (Castles et al. 1990, p. Postscript). No satisfactory recipe was found for linking cultural diversity and national unity in a state of growing economic insecurity.

In this situation, racist definitions of identity, which seemed to be declining up to the mid-1970s, have made something of a comeback. Mention has already been made of the 'Blainey Debate' of 1984 and its sequels. Public opposition to immigration (particularly of Asians) and to multiculturalism appears to have been strongest among working-class people, who are particularly threatened by current processes of economic and social change. Some spokespersons of the Returned Services League (RSL), which has a large working-class and lower middle-class membership, have been particularly virulent in their anti-Asian statements. Such attitudes are often translated into racial vilification or violence. Evidence presented to the National Inquiry into Racist Violence of the Human Rights and Equal Opportunity Commissions in 1989–90 shows that most Asian immigrants and many southern Europeans have experienced abuse, harassment or even assault. The Gulf War was accompanied by widespread harassment of and discrimination against Arabs and Muslims. The strength of the potential for racism and ethnocentrism is hardly surprising since racism against non-Europeans was official policy until about 25 years ago.

CONCLUSIONS

Australia has become a society of great cultural and ethnic diversity in a very short period. Multiculturalism has emerged as the only possible formula for managing both social policy and identity in this situation, and has played a central part in the successful model for immigrant settlement and community relations. Multiculturalism, nevertheless, has not gained acceptance among some sections of the Anglo-Australian population, who feel threatened by processes of rapid economic, social and cultural change.

Multiculturalism itself has changed considerably in recent years. In the late 1970s its language was of 'enrichment' through diversity and 'dignity' through cultural maintenance. The focus on cultural pluralism matched both the social policy priorities of the conservative government and the interests of mainly middle-class leaderships seeking to articulate the demands of first generation European immigrant workers. The experience which transcended class difference was the cultural isolation and social marginalization resulting from assimilationism; multiculturalism set out above all to redress this. Today, cultural pluralism has lost its central role as a minority demand, partly through changes in the economic and political context, partly through changes in the make-up of the NESB population, and partly because multiculturalism itself has demonstrated that formal acceptance of diversity does not in itself necessarily improve the position of minorities.

The first generation southern and eastern European cultural brokers are therefore losing their leadership role, although ethnic organizations remain significant and governments continue to stress cultural rights. The new leaders are of Asian as well as European origin, and belong mainly to the second generation, that is, those of NESB migrant parentage. They have been educated in Australia, understand the system well, and are often employed within the bureaucracy. They articulate the needs of ethnic minorities not in cultural but in bureaucratic terms, as expressed in the catch-words of Access and Equity. These new leaderships still make use of cultural markers in order to maintain links with their constituency. The concept of the ethnic community as a social category which transcends both class and generation is crucial to their position.

The location of this new NESB leadership group is contradictory: leaders belong both to the ethnic communities (which they construct and mobilize) and to the state (for which they work in one way or another). This contradiction reflects the tensions within multiculturalism, which is both a public policy designed to manage diversity and a way of articulating minority interests. Similarly, the current form of multiculturalism embodies the potential conflict between an inclusionary declaration of civil, political and social citizenship for all and a pluralist model based on ethnic groups as interest groups. A further tension exists between the guarantee of the right of minorities to be culturally and linguistically different and their exclusion from positions of real power if they exercise that right.

Multiculturalism is likely to be a central element of Australian public policy for the foreseeable future, but it has yet to reach a stable and coherent form. Further controversy and change are therefore likely. Considerable work is still needed before multiculturalism can provide a satisfactory framework for social policy and for national identity in a period when Australia needs both to reshape its internal economic and social structures and to re-orient its international relations.

12

MAKING THEM US

THE POLITICAL INCORPORATION OF CULTURALLY DISTINCT IMMIGRANT AND NON-IMMIGRANT MINORITIES IN THE UNITED STATES

Louis DeSipio and Rodolfo O. de la Garza

The United States and Australia are multicultural countries. Indeed, the United States has for most of its history been more diverse than is Australia today. Yet, unlike Australia (see Castles, ch. 11 in this book), the United States has had few, if any, national public policies or programmes that are designed to recognize, legitimize and encourage the maintenance of diverse cultures and languages. Instead, the US approach to the management of diversity has been two-pronged: to celebrate, but not legally enshrine, diversity in the culture (Fuchs 1990); and to seek the political incorporation of both immigrants and indigenous minorities into the liberal polity as equal individuals. As it extended from White European to 'culturally distinct' non-European immigrants and to non-White indigenous populations, the effectiveness of the incorporative stance has progressively dissipated.

It is not easy, then, to develop a discussion of multicultural policies in the United States that neatly parallels events in Australia because the two societies have responded so differently to their culturally distinct populations. This chapter proceeds from an appreciation of two fundamental differences between the Australian and American cases. The first is that there is in the United States a long history of concern regarding culturally distinct groups that is not always connected empirically or politically to immigration as it is necessarily in Australia. The reasons are obvious. The United States contains large indigenous culturally distinct populations: Indians, Mexican Americans and African Americans. Mexican Americans include Mexicans who lived in that part of northern Mexico that the United States acquired as part of the Treaty of Guadalupe Hidalgo in the US–Mexican war and those who settled in this area between 1848 and the 1920s. During these years, there were no border controls and American institutions did not effectively penetrate much of this area. Thus, in effect, the region retained its Mexican character throughout this period, and even the Mexican origin settlers in the area are most accurately described as natives. The United States also contains a large population of African origin brought to the United States as slaves as early as the seventeenth century. Their descendants are also natives. The presence of these three groups has long generated concern about how the nation should respond to culturally distinct populations. Given that these are native groups, this debate has been much less fundamentally linked to the immigration–acculturation process than it is in Australia.

The second important distinction between the two cases is that there has been no question in Australia of the denial of basic political rights to persons, of whatever national origin (other than Aborigines), who have attained Australian citizenship. However serious racial and ethnic discrimination may be in various parts of Australian life, access to the ballot has been non-controversial. Sadly, this has not been the case in the United States. Some groups never had access to US citizenship. African American slaves and, eventually, freedmen had no citizenship rights until the ratification of the Fourteenth Amendment. From 1882 to 1952 Congress denied Asian immigrants the right to become US citizens through naturalization. At other times, formal citizenship rights did not include the rights associated with citizenship, such as the vote. From the end of Reconstruction to the 1960s, for example, most Blacks did not have the franchise. Similarly, from 1848 to the 1970s, most Mexican Americans and, later, Puerto Ricans and other Latinos were denied free access to the ballot box. This deliberate and legal exclusion of citizens, whether native or foreign born, from the electoral process is one of the major themes of American history. The legacy of this exclusion remains a critical political issue today.

The issues raised by these elemental facts are far too broad to be addressed in a short essay. We therefore propose to focus on the processes of political incorporation of foreign-born naturalized citizens and of the native born who experienced political exclusion. We assert that their incorporation on the basis of individualist liberal principles is a defensible alternative to a policy of explicit multiculturalism. However, our analysis will show that in some respects this approach has fallen far short of its stated ideals. On the other hand, in its approach to illegal residents (herein referred to as the undocumented) and to long-term non-citizen residents, national policy has been surprisingly inclusive.

The political incorporation policy of the United States addresses three issues. First is whether the institutions of the Government are meant to represent those persons legally resident but not citizens and those persons resident without formal legal status. American policy, we will show, driven largely by the courts, provides at least indirect representation and, in some cases, rights of participation for non-US citizens.

The second issue concerns access to citizenship. Formally generous, citizenship law has been only partially successful in its implementation. Our discussion will consider not only the basic naturalization law, but also statutory techniques (registry and legalization) that have been devised to distribute eligibility for US citizenship to undocumented residents. Finally, we address the question of the rights of political participation that accrue to persons who acquire citizenship. The principles enshrined in the Constitution and the Bill of Rights guarantee every citizen full and equal access to the political process. All levels of government, however, have denied these rights to particular groups and individuals on a broad scale and have only recently stimulated national policies to eliminate obstacles to the enfranchisement of non-Anglo segments of the population.

We conclude with a cautionary note. While the United States has consciously avoided multicultural policies at the federal and, for the most part, at the state level, many people censure as divisive governments that promote the political incorporation of culturally distinct groups. For example, critics of bilingual ballots assert that they are a strategy designed by Latinos to prevent incorporation and, eventually, to Balkanize the United States. Instead, we demonstrate that bilingual election materials are an attempted remedy for past discrimination against native-born Mexican Americans and are well within the individualist liberal principles that otherwise characterize political incorporation in the United States. We raise this cautionary note because attacks on these programmes may have the unintended effect of generating demands among excluded groups for federal multicultural policies in the United States. We assert that to be successful, liberal incorporative strategies must be open to everyone regardless of nativity, ethnicity or race.

THE BASIS FOR REPRESENTATION: THE DECENNIAL CENSUS AND REAPPORTIONMENT

Representatives and direct taxes shall be apportioned among the several States which may be included within this Union, according to their respective Numbers, which shall be determined by adding *the whole number of free persons*, including those bound to Service for a Term of Years, and excluding Indians, not taxed, three fifths of all other persons ...

Article One, Section 2 of the Constitution (emphasis added)

Representatives shall be apportioned among the several States according to their respective numbers, counting *the whole number of persons in each State*, excluding Indians not taxed ...

Fourteenth Amendment, Section 2 (emphasis added)

Reapportionment—the reallocation of congressional seats among the states according to changes in population—and redistricting—the redrawing of congressional and other elective districts within each state—attained enhanced political significance in the 1960s for two reasons. First, after 1962 states were required to create population-based congressional and legislative seats of equal size, according to the principle of one person one vote (*Baker* v. *Carr* 1962). Second, the federal government created new state and local level programmes which were funded according to population-based formulas. Thus today population growth may require the creation of new congressional and state legislative districts, population loss (whether absolute or relative, that is, less growth compared to other jurisdictions) may eliminate districts, and either result may allow politicians to redraw jurisdictional boundaries so as to enhance their political base. Federal transfer payments also rise and fall with shifts in population.

Officials, therefore, are extremely attentive to the results of the decennial Census. Most critics are concerned with undercounts and seek post-enumeration adjustments. Others are concerned about 'overcounts' in districts other than their own resulting from the inclusion of undocumented immigrants in the Census. These conflicts often require zero-sum solutions, and self-interested politicians cannot be expected to resolve them. The federal courts, then, have become the arena to debate the accuracy and completeness of the Census count. In a series of rulings over the past decade concerning who should be counted and whether the results should be adjusted, the courts have come to interpret the phrase 'whole number of persons' to include both the undocumented and those missed in the Census.

Counting the Undocumented

As the 1980 and 1990 Censuses approached, individuals and groups challenged the decision to count undocumented immigrants for the purposes of apportionment (and by implication for redistricting). In 1980 the Federation for American Immigration Reform (FAIR) brought suit in the federal court to prevent the Census Bureau from counting the undocumented for the purposes of apportionment. In 1990 Congressman Thomas Ridge brought a revised version of this suit. In both instances the courts refused to hear the case. In the process, however, the courts noted in non-binding *dicta* that the founding fathers wanted everybody counted.

The 1980 case *FAIR* v. *Klutznik* (1980) sought to enjoin the Census Bureau not to include the undocumented in the population count provided to Congress for the purposes of apportionment. While dismissing the case on a technical point—FAIR's lack of standing—the Circuit Court held that the Constitution was not ambiguous: the undocumented are 'persons' within the meaning of Article One, Section 2, Clause 3 of the Constitution (Bean and de la Garza 1988).

In anticipation of the 1990 Census, FAIR attempted to remedy two of the weaknesses in its 1980 litigation. First, it sought to gain standing by filing suit in the name of Pennsylvania Congressman Thomas Ridge and 40 other Congress members who could show potential personal loss in representing states likely to lose seats after the 1990 Census. Second, FAIR filed the suit during the Census's planning stages so it could not be argued that the collection of information was too far along to be interrupted. Despite these modifications, the court again refused to require that the Census change its enumeration plans. The District Court, citing the 1980 case, dismissed the suit for lack of standing (*Ridge* v. *Verity* 1989).

Adjusting the Census

The constitutional mandate to count the whole number of persons raises a second problem. As survey research and statistical techniques have become more refined, the inability of the Bureau to count all people (regardless of legal status) has become more evident (Bailar 1988). This undercount is not evenly distributed across the population. In 1980 African Americans and Latinos were six to eight times more likely to be missed by Census enumerators than were Whites, and poor people were more likely to be missed than the affluent. As a result, poor urban and rural areas faced more serious undercounts than affluent and suburban areas.

Preliminary analysis of the 1990 Census finds that the undercount problem worsened. For the population as a whole the Bureau estimates that it counted between 97.5 per cent and 98.3 per cent of the national population. For Blacks, the range of those counted was 93.8 per cent to 95.6 per cent. The estimated Latino undercount was greater. The Bureau counted just 92.7 per cent to 95.8 per cent of Latinos (US Bureau of the Census 1991).

The deleterious impact of the decline in the accuracy of the Census has been mitigated by the federal courts. After the 1980 Census at least 36 jurisdictions filed suit to require an adjustment. Like FAIR's suit, this litigation failed because the plaintiffs lacked standing. As well, like FAIR, the cities facing an anticipated undercount in 1990 changed their strategy. First, they filed suit well before the count began. Second, most joined in a single suit, captioned as *City of New York* v. *US Department of Commerce* (1990). These plaintiffs were granted standing.

For its part, the Census Bureau made the best of a bad situation. Instead of continuing with the litigation or appealing the adverse ruling granting standing to the jurisdictions facing an undercount, the parties entered an agreement under which a post-Census sample of households would be taken to evaluate the accuracy of the enumeration. Based on this sample, the Secretary of Commerce would decide by 15 July 1991 whether to undertake an adjustment. The Bureau would label all Census results provided to jurisdictions for reapportionment before this date as preliminary, and users would be advised that the data were subject to statistical adjustment.

On 15 July the Secretary of Commerce, against the advice of the Director of the Census Bureau, announced that the Census would not be adjusted. As this essay was written soon after this decision, it was too early to analyse its effect. It is safe to predict, however, that areas with undercounts will return to court to seek judicial redress. It is also possible that some jurisdictions will attempt to redistrict based on unofficial adjusted numbers, causing litigation by jurisdictions with relative overcounts (Barringer 1991). Thus, the adverse determination by the Secretary of Commerce may put this controversy back in the courts. While the effect of judicial recognition of the jurisdiction's standing to challenge the accuracy of Census counts and of the potential validity of statistical adjustments may be limited for the 1990 Census and redistricting that follows, the precedent is important for future Censuses.

The partial resolution of these twin debates over counting the undocumented and adjusting the Census to remedy undercounts promotes an inclusive use of the Census as a tool for representation. The courts interpreted the Constitution's mandate to count the whole number of persons to include the undocumented and potentially to include those who cannot be counted through traditional means. Thus, the courts have assured indirect representation to all residents of the United States regardless of legal status or national origin.

The newly assured indirect representation has political value for the undocumented and recently legal immigrant communities. In addition to the higher levels of funding it brings to their communities through federal transfer payments, it increases the number of elected officials in areas with large immigrant populations. Although the elected officials do not rely on the votes of these residents, many recognize that their presence assures that officials can keep their seats through the next cycle of redistricting. As one Texas legislator noted, his district 'would not have been created if not for the undocumented' (de la Garza 1989). In some jurisdictions the undocumented are assured not simply indirect representation, but also political access. In New York and Chicago, for example, all residents may vote in school board elections, regardless of legal status. Thus, judicial interpretations of the mandate to count the 'whole number of persons' have implications well beyond simple enumeration.

FROM REPRESENTATION TO CITIZENSHIP: NATURALIZATION, REGISTRY AND LEGALIZATION

The terms of access of immigrants to participation in the American political system have been a regular feature of the national political debate. With few and notable exceptions, federal policy has encouraged incorporation of immigrants through relatively liberal access to citizenship.

The initial debate over incorporation focused on naturalization. Among the first acts of Congress was the passage of a naturalization law (*1 Stat. Law 103*, enacted 26 March 1790). The debate over access to formal political incorporation of immigrants residing in the United States has taken on an added dimension in the twentieth century. As Congress began to establish standards for immigration in the 1870s, it made possible a new class of immigrant—the undocumented immigrant. People continued to immigrate despite the steady increase in immigration restrictions, so the number of those without legal sanction grew. By the 1970s some, including the then director of the Immigration and Naturalization Service (INS), claimed (without empirical grounding) that as many as 12 million undocumented immigrants resided in the United States (Chapman 1976).

Thus, two kinds of policy to integrate immigrants have evolved. The first is the formal, constitutionally-mandated process of naturalization open to legal immigrants. The second process is legalization, which has developed to recognize long-term undocumented residents as permanent and to grant them status as legal resident aliens. Both of these policies offer long-term non-citizen residents voluntary access to citizenship.

Naturalization

Congress established the basic structure of US naturalization law in the 1790s. Designed to encourage immigration and population growth, it mandated a two-year residency period (extended to five years in 1795 and briefly to 14 years from 1798 to 1801, then returning to the current five years) and demonstration of 'good moral character'. In the twentieth century Congress added English language speaking and writing and civics requirements. Despite these changes, United States naturalization requirements are lax compared to those of western European states and comparable to those of Australia in terms of formal requirements (though with a longer period of residency) (Brubaker 1989).

The relative simplicity of the formal naturalization process is borne out by INS data. In the 82 years for which naturalization data are available (1907–89), just 532 338 of the 13 076 535 applications have resulted in judicial denials, a rate of 4.1 per cent (US Immigration and Naturalization Service 1990). In the past decade this denial rate has fallen to 1.9 per cent. Besides these formal judicial denials, the INS uses its administrative authority to review applications and applicants before judicial action. Though historical data does not exist on administrative denials, the recent past has seen 20 per cent to 25 per cent of applicants encouraged to withdraw their applications voluntarily in the face of advice that the courts will formally deny the application upon INS's recommendation (Pachon and DeSipio 1991). Denial, whether judicial or administrative, does not result in deportation or any sanction except for having to begin the application process anew.

Despite the high level of discretionary administrative denials, naturalization applicants perceive the process itself as being relatively easy. Ninety-two per cent of applicants who took the naturalization exam in a recent national study of Latino naturalization patterns passed on their first try. Of these respondents, 48.0 per cent reported it to be very easy and 27.2 per cent found it to be somewhat easy. Just 22.6 per cent of respondents found the exam to be very hard or somewhat hard (National Association of Latino Elected Officials Educational Fund 1989, hereafter NALEO, and unpublished data from the NALEO National Latino Immigrant Survey).

Nonetheless, many immigrants do not become naturalized. In 1980 approximately two-thirds of immigrants resident in the US for more than five years had become citizens. However, slightly more than one-third of Mexican, Colombian and Dominican immigrants had been naturalized compared with nearly 80 per cent of European immigrants (US Bureau of the Census 1983). Survey data suggest that the reason for non-naturalization is not lingering commitment to the home country, but instead confusion about how to become naturalized and doubts about its benefits (NALEO 1989, pp. 16–20). The INS does little to remove this confusion; although the pattern may be changing, the service has traditionally denied that it has any role in promoting citizenship (NALEO 1985, pp. 16–17). Instead, it relies on promotion through voluntary organizations that do not receive government funding for citizenship promotion.

Registry

By the 1920s Congress was concerned about the presence of large numbers of long-term residents who lacked clear status, either as legal immigrants or as citizens. This pool of individuals included immigrants who evaded (often unintentionally) the weak immigration controls in place before World War I, immigrants who were naturalized before control over naturalization was centralized in 1907 but who could not prove their naturalized status, and married women (who could not be naturalized in their own right before 1922) who had clouded legal status based on the actions of their spouses.

Congress resolved the problems created by these immigrants in 1929 with the mechanism of registry which allowed undocumented immigrants who could demonstrate that they had been in the United States since 30 June 1921 to register with the INS and legalize their status (*Public Law* 962, enacted 2 March 1929). As the problem of unclear immigration status is a continuing one, Congress has updated the Act several times. Most recently, in a section quite separate from its legalization provisions, the *Immigration Reform and Control Act* (IRCA) granted eligibility to register to any immigrant who could demonstrate residence since 1 January 1972 (*Immigration Reform and Control Act* of 1986, Section 203). Between 1986 and 1989 this most recent update of registry resulted in nearly 60 000 long-term undocumented residents being registered, converting their status from undocumented to legal resident alien (Davidson 1991).

Little controversy or public awareness surrounded the extension of registry contained in IRCA. The ease with which Congress was able to extend the benefit of immediate legal status to persons resident since 1971 contrasted sharply with the controversy over the legalization provisions in IRCA for those resident only since 1981 (Espenshade 1989).

Legalization(s) Under IRCA

As the number of undocumented residents grew in the 1960s and 1970s and public concern intensified, Congress developed a legalization programme that was only available for a specified time. As a result of IRCA, nearly 1.8 million formerly undocumented residents achieved a temporary legal status by early 1990. An additional 1.2 million agricultural workers, frequently with little previous residence in the United States, also received legal status through the legislation's Seasonal Agricultural Worker (SAW) provisions (US Immigration and Naturalization Service 1990, pp. XXIV–XXV).

The legislative history of IRCA is long and tortuous and the law itself is complex, involving legalization, agricultural labour guarantees and employer sanctions. These are described in greater detail in Miller's chapter in this book. Here we need only draw out the implications of IRCA for our argument about incorporation policy.

Legalization assured a path to legal status and potential citizenship for undocumented residents who could prove six or more years of continuous residence in the United States (Gonzalez-Baker 1990). The standards of proof and the definition of 'continuous' were far more rigorous than for registry. Yet, despite the hurdles, two million applicants successfully met the initial requirements. This number is larger than the total resulting from three years of legal immigration even at the high rates of the late 1980s.

Congress added another component to the bill to ensure sufficient support for passage. Agricultural interests who had long been major users of undocumented labour demanded that their need for seasonal manual labour should not be overlooked in the effort to 'control' the border. The result was a unique compromise that has been characterized by one analyst of IRCA as the most 'inclusive' of the bill's provisions (Gonzalez-Baker 1990, p. 40). Agricultural workers who could prove just 90 days of seasonal agricultural labour between 1 May 1985 and 1 May 1986 were eligible for a two-year temporary visa. After these two years the transition to permanent residence was almost automatic.

A further element in the compromise over agricultural labour offered a less liberal possibility of legalization for some future immigrants. The Replenishment Agricultural Worker (RAW) provisions of IRCA established an as yet unused category of immigration specifically for agricultural labour. Unlike the Bracero Programme or European guest worker programmes (Brubaker 1989), RAW offers permanent residence after three years of agricultural labour.

The final component of IRCA important to this discussion are the employer sanction provisions. By imposing fines on employers who knowingly hire undocumented immigrants, this programme seeks to reduce the demand for the labour of undocumented immigrants and, therefore, 'regain' control of the borders. Advocates of employer sanctions assumed that if demand for labour declined, then undocumented migration would halt, and that short-term undocumented immigrants already in the US would return to their countries of origin. The enforcement and, as a result, the effect of employer sanctions has been minimal to date. Nevertheless, the theory behind the programme indirectly protects both the citizen and the legal permanent resident from being undermined by a business decision to undercut wages by hiring the undocumented.

The picture of IRCA painted here is selective and, as a result, rosy: We have focused on the components of the bill that help individual immigrants. The bill was, however, a compromise between varied interests and contains provisions that limit the civil rights of its undocumented beneficiaries as well as the native born (de la Garza 1991). In addition, administrative rule-making needlessly excluded many eligible applicants. INS's failure to grant legal status to ineligible family members of persons eligible for legalization caused distress and may well have prevented some applications from eligible applicants. Despite these failings, the bill accomplished a great deal. More than three million undocumented residents of the United States came out of the shadows and started on the road to full citizenship.

Although they have had little effect so far, two other provisions of the bill will shape the future debate over immigration. The employer sanctions provisions establish a structure for limiting future undocumented immigration, should there be the political and economic desire to accomplish this end. Second, some agricultural labourers received guarantees of future political incorporation.

The United States has developed a series of structures to incorporate immigrants into the larger political system. Naturalization policy has long allowed legal immigrants to become citizens with few formal requirements and relatively short residence. The 1986 legalization programmes (and registry on which it was based) similarly offer a path to permanent residence and citizenship that many have followed. In each of these programmes bureaucratic obstacles are often greater impediments than statutory requirements. What is striking is that repeated efforts have been made to incorporate those who have entered the country illegally, despite restrictive immigration statutes. The United States has recognized a continuing obligation to extend rights to the undocumented.

FULL CITIZENSHIP WITHOUT REGARD TO NATIONAL ORIGIN

Since the nation's founding, the eligibility rules for political participation have become progressively less restrictive. Initially a privilege of the landholding, formal political participation became the right of White men regardless of class by the 1820s, male former slaves after 1865, and women in 1919. Late in the nineteenth and early in the twentieth centuries this right expanded in many states to include non-citizen immigrants who had stated their intention to naturalize (Rosberg 1977).

Although these formal expansions of group access continued both at the state and national levels into the 1900s, the percentage of eligible voters who went to the polls began to decline around the turn of the century. Scholars disagree over the causes of this trend (Burnham 1981), but one generally recognized factor is the steady enactment beginning in the late nineteenth century of laws and practices restricting ballot access of southern Blacks and, increasingly, of the poor of all races (Key 1949, particularly chapter 25). By the 1960s few southern Blacks voted, and those who tried were subject to harassment and violence.

By the mid-1960s a national consensus spurred by the Civil Rights Movement demanded redress of this situation. The 1965 *Voting Rights Act* (VRA) and its extensions seek to assure equal electoral access to all. This legislation, however, does not give extra rights to any group or individual. Instead, it seeks to assure that all individuals will be treated equally before the law and that state and local jurisdictions will not abridge any individual's rights.

The passage of the 1965 Act prohibited southern jurisdictions from activities that limited the Black vote. It eliminated literacy tests and empowered the US Attorney-General to review all new voting laws ('pre-clearance') and to appoint registrars and monitor elections. The 1970 extension began a process of liberalization that extended the narrow focus of the 1965 law. For the first time, federal voting protection was extended to areas with Latino populations. However, there was no debate in Congress about whether the protections designed to guarantee Blacks' voting rights in 1965 should be extended to Latinos or other language minorities.

The absence of concern about Latino voter participation changed with the *Voting Rights Act* of 1975 which granted basic protection to language minorities. In addition, it required that jurisdictions with more than five per cent of a single covered language minority, and an illiteracy rate among the language minority higher than the national English illiteracy rate, provide bilingual election materials.

The Latino community first became involved in the debate over the VRA with the 1975 Act. Mexican Americans and Puerto Ricans testified in support of extending the law's coverage to the 'Spanish heritage' community. Two patterns emerged in this testimony. First, the situation described was similar to that experienced by African Americans in the South before 1965. Second, the most serious problem for Latinos were efforts in Texas to restrict Mexican American voting (de la Garza and DeSipio 1990).

Vilma Martinez of the Mexican American Legal Defense and Education Fund (MALDEF), for example, testified that the 'pattern of abuse in Uvalde County [Texas] is strikingly reminiscent of the Deep South in the early 1960s' (US Senate 1975, pp. 756–70). Among the practices she found were the refusal to place registered Mexican American voters on voting lists, election judges invalidating ballots cast by minority group members, the refusal to name minority group members as deputy registrars, and election judges refusing to aid minority voters illiterate in English. Martinez went on to note the techniques used in Texas and other states of the Southwest to exclude or dilute Mexican American electoral participation: educational segregation, at-large elections, anti-minority gerrymanders, and stringent third-party ballot access requirements.

MALDEF's testimony is representative of that offered in support of extension of the VRA to Latinos. Considerations such as the need for bilingual voting materials and the problems of at-large elections and malapportionment were alluded to, but were not the focus of testimony. Witnesses offered qualitative judgements with minimal quantitative evidence. From the committees' perspectives, perhaps, little more than generalizations were required. Perceived overt discrimination, particularly in Texas, earned Latinos nationwide the special protections and rights extended to Blacks a decade before with the added benefit of bilingual election materials (Thernstrom 1987).

INDIRECT REPRESENTATION AND FORMAL INCLUSION OR MULTICULTURALISM IN DISGUISE?

We have endeavoured in this discussion to explicate the immigrant incorporation policy of the United States and to relate it to the formal electoral access available to citizens. As indicated, US policy does not privilege groups. Although political rights vary by status, all residents are assured indirect representation and long-term immigrants, regardless of legal status, have access to US citizenship. For the citizen, the *Voting Rights Act* assures that all individuals have equal access to formal participation, regardless of nativity.

Despite the individual focus of these policies, critics contend that the United States is, in fact, moving towards multicultural policies. Led by such organizations as US English and FAIR, the representation and inclusion that underlie the programmes discussed here are attacked as special interest programmes. Implicit in these charges is that the programmes challenge fundamental American values, particularly the centrality of the English language, the Eurocentric national stock, and a shared national identity (rather than multiple partially integrated group identities) (Fuchs 1990).

Each of the three kinds of policy discussed has been criticized as fomenting divisiveness. The indirect representation provided by a complete Census count for non-citizens and non-permanent residents raises the criticism that citizens have more relative influence and, as a result, are either more represented or the elected officials are less representative in districts with large non-citizen populations (Skerry 1989). Similarly, efforts to legalize the undocumented population appeared to some to reward lawlessness. Finally, the VRA requirement that bilingual election materials be provided has been described as condoning separatism among immigrants (Nelson 1984).

Instead of examining each of these charges individually, we discuss only the final one. We present it as an example of how the implicit immigrant policy and formal electoral access guarantees of the United States are distinct and not a covert multicultural package.

Congress's failure to investigate the reasons for Latino non-voting and its provision of bilingual ballots without extensive hearings raises a significant point overlooked by advocates of English language ballots. Congress provided bilingual election materials, like the rest of the VRA, as a strategy to remedy past discrimination. In this case the past discrimination was the dual nature of society (Montejano 1987), and particularly of schools in Texas and the Southwest (Carter 1970). If they were able to attend school, native-born US citizens of Mexican origin received a second-rate education that denied many functional literacy in English. Thus, just as literacy tests and intimidation had to be removed to enfranchise Blacks, bilingual ballots had to be provided for many native-born Spanish speakers, especially Mexican Americans and Puerto Ricans, so that they could vote.

The inadequacy of the public education offered to Mexican Americans and, by extension, to other Latinos was on the public policy agenda in 1975. In the previous year the Supreme Court had ruled (*Lau* v. *Nichols* 1974) that federally funded school districts had to 'take affirmative steps to rectify language deficiency [of national-origin minority students] in order to open its instructional program to these students' (quoted in San Miguel Jr 1987, p. 183). In this ruling the court recognized that remedies for past discrimination included not just desegregation, but also the dedication of special funds, in effect the creation of a special entitlement. The justification for this right was past discrimination, not cultural maintenance.

Congress approached the 1975 extension of the VRA in a similar manner. The fierce debates over the original passage of the Act in 1965 were replaced in 1975 with a general acceptance of the remedial nature of the bill's provisions. Congress did not search for reasons that Latinos vote at lower levels than the population as a whole (which would include cultural and class-related factors). Instead, it looked for kinds of state discrimination that had restricted Latino electoral participation and sought to remedy these. Presumably, by the logic of their application, these remedies should be eliminated after the legacy of the discrimination disappears.

CONCLUSIONS

The philosophical and functional foundations of US incorporation policy are different from those of Australia. While US policy gradually emerged to assure individual representation, incorporation and electoral access to all residents, the multicultural programme in Australia reached out to specific groups to give them unique and continuing access to state resources.

In part the dilemma for the United States emerges oddly from the pressures placed on existing policies by their critics. It is possible that continued high levels of immigration and lack of economic advance among second and third generation immigrants in the United States will create demands for state cultural support. The present system, however, steadily moves immigrants' political loyalties away from their national origin bonds and towards a series of other class, regional and partisan political coalitions. If the critics of the current policies succeed in marginalizing immigrants from representation or if they successfully deny ethnic groups full political participation, they will only serve to increase the pressures for multicultural policies.

CONCLUSION

James Jupp and Gary P. Freeman

Australia and the United States have much in common. The continental US and Australia are of the same geographical size, but they are quite different in terms of population density and distribution, ethnic and racial composition and orientations towards the past and the future. The optimistic belief that nineteenth-century Australia was 'the America of the future' soon gave way before the reality of an arid interior and distance from acceptable sources of new populations. Australia settled into a long-term pattern of supplying the United Kingdom with raw materials, food and profits and acting as a safety valve for what many in Britain regarded as 'surplus population'. The impact of major depressions in 1891 and 1929 and of two world wars left many Australians very conscious of their vulnerability to world events. The United States, in contrast, increasingly came to shape world events. If Americans were at all conscious of Australia, it was as the 'lost paradise' of a thinly inhabited frontier society without urban or racial problems, which some idealized as America's forsaken past.

One immediate contrast is between American optimism about immigration and Australian pessimism and concern. Yet this overlooks ambivalences in both societies. From the United States Dillingham commission of 1911, through the legislation of the 1920s and 1930s, American policy became restrictive and almost fearful of mass immigration. Its racial exclusions, while not as explicitly stated as Australia's, had the same effect of preserving White European supremacy. Its national quota system, while not as consciously directed towards British intake as the Australian assisted passage schemes, had the same effect of limiting entry from less 'assimilable' or 'acceptable' sources. Australia, in contrast, became more welcoming to non-British migrants after 1947 and began the very process which United States policy had been trying to slow down, the creation of a multicultural society. But the maintenance of White Australia, the absence of a large indigenous non-European population, and distance from the source countries always allowed Australia a degree of caution which the United States could not, or would not, exercise. Australia did not feel the same obligations towards its Asian and Pacific neighbours as did the United States towards Latin America and, especially, Mexico. Nor did it have massive seasonal demand for agricultural labour or a large Black rural population seeking relocation in industrial cities.

CONTROL

In the nineteenth century there was little effective control of immigration, nor was such control regarded as desirable by the English-speaking democracies. Australia pioneered strict entry limitations under the White Australia Policy. This gave discretion to officials through the operation of a dictation test and was designed to allow the exclusion of anyone, including British subjects, thought undesirable. The United States followed suit and erected elaborate barriers against a range of people, including polygamists and communists. By the 1920s both countries were operating national quota systems, although these were regarded as temporary expedients in Australia where non-British pressures to enter were limited. Immigration control has had several objectives: to exclude ethnic, racial or social groups felt to be undesirable or threatening; to limit numbers in times of economic depression; to influence the ethnic composition of the overall population; to select desired occupations and educational attainments; and to respond to domestic public opinion. Since the 1930s both nations have acknowledged an obligation to admit refugees from disturbed situations, predominantly from communist or fascist political systems.

Australia has found it easier than the United States to exercise entry control, but has also been more openly anxious to do so. Without land borders and relatively remote from main transport links, Australia needs to establish entry controls at fewer than twenty points, all of which have to be reached by plane or ship. The vast coastline gives access mainly to uninhabited desert land, as several boatloads of people from Asia have recently discovered. It is impossible to walk or drive into Australia, as many millions do every week into the United States. The closest point to another country is across the Torres Strait, and there is some slight seepage down through the islands and into Queensland. However, until recently this area, too, was inaccessible by regular passenger transport. Entry from New Zealand is restricted by the need to provide evidence of New Zealand citizenship, comparable to the requirements for Canadian entry into the United States. There are only three million New Zealanders and no-one commutes internationally to work, as do many between southern Ontario and Michigan.

The challenge of entry control is thus quite different in the two societies. Australia has all the mechanisms in place to restrict unauthorized entry, but lacks an effective follow-up system for those who overstay temporary visas. All arrivals other than New Zealanders require a visa, which makes Australia unique among developed societies, especially for tourist entry. Unlike most such societies, though, Australia has resisted national identification systems, other than the requirement of a taxation number. Illegal entrants must necessarily be caught by accident, or through sporadic raids inspired by informants. It is probable that such methods are targeted on 'visible' immigrants who are either racially or linguistically different from the majority. The largest number of overstayers are from Britain, but the highest proportions come from sources such as Tonga, Poland, Pakistan or Fiji. Proposals to impose severe visa restrictions on arrivals from such societies were recently resisted and defeated in parliament.

The United States, as chapters in this book clearly indicate, is less effectively restrictive. Faced with mass pressures from Mexico and the demands of agribusiness for temporary labour, the United States has been unable to exclude large numbers of illegal entrants. It is more effective in limiting those seeking skilled or professional employment. One consequence is that larger proportions of less skilled immigrants have entered the United States than is the case for Australia in recent years. They are absorbed into an economic system in which labour conditions and wages are much less rigorously regulated than in Australia and in which normal levels of unemployment have, until recently, been higher.

THE SOCIAL CHARACTER OF IMMIGRANTS

The United States prides itself on turning the poor and needy into prosperous and even rich citizens. Part of the national myth is that individual and group progress is on a scale and at a speed possible 'only in America'. To eastern European Jews before 1914 the magnet was 'little Golden America'. Subsequent waves of immigrants have accepted this myth and have often sustained it by business and professional success. In doing so they have frequently surpassed the achievements of Black, Hispanic and Native Americans, not to mention many southern Whites. Immigrant poverty does not characterize the United States to the same extent as native-born poverty, which often takes forms much more severe than anything recently experienced in Australia. However, much of the Australian debate about immigration proceeds as though the social problems associated with race in the United States will be reproduced by mass immigration, which has so far failed to be the case. Australian intake and settlement policy seeks to avoid the creation of social or geographical ghettoes and is influenced by the fear that ethnic variety must create social disharmony. A concern with 'social cohesion' has marked the Australian public policy debate for over 40 years. In the United States there is also such concern in the face of a much higher level of crime and violence. It is rarely directly related to immigration policy, although it certainly was in the early years of this century.

The social character of immigrants has concerned domestic opinion in both societies, but at different times and for different reasons. In the nineteenth century the Protestant majority feared Catholic influence, especially from Ireland. Echoes of this continued in Australia into the 1950s, especially as most continental European migration at that time was also Catholic, the Irish stream having dried up after 1920. In both societies Catholics now form about one-quarter of the population but their integration into mainstream society is such that undue attention is no longer paid to their influence. The Australian assisted passage schemes allowed selectors to limit the proportions of Irish migrants to Australia in a way not open to the United States, to which the great majority of Irish immigrants went in the last century. The United States was effective in limiting national quotas. This was scarcely a problem in Australia except in the 1920s, when migrants were redirected from southern Europe in response to US restrictions. Both were able to exclude Chinese under specific legislation, although the United States did not impose the restrictions on Filipinos under American rule that Australia applied to Indians within the British Empire. Queensland did not develop as a multiracial society, whereas Hawaii did. Many Americans see Asian immigrants today as model citizens, while Australians remain more ambivalent.

CITIZENSHIP, RIGHTS AND DUTIES

Australia and the United States are among the oldest democracies in the world, with elected institutions based on mass suffrage for over 150 years, with concepts of individual rights and freedoms written into their laws and practices, and with strong political parties which have passed through several generations of supporters. Apart from the initial suppression of the Aborigines, the domestic history of Australia has been more peaceful than that of the United States, lacking revolution, civil war or territorial conflict. Most importantly, Australia had a dual system of national loyalty until 1949, when Australian citizenship was finally created, whereas the United States from its foundation has stressed a single loyalty to the state and nation which overrides all other differences. The struggle for universal franchise, embracing Blacks and women, was longer and more difficult in the United States, though the granting of full civil rights to the indigenous peoples has proved equally difficult in both countries.

The concept of citizenship in both countries includes full exercise of individual and civil rights by all who have qualified and the protection of many rights even for those who are still non-citizens but legally resident. In the United States many non-citizens were entitled to vote in the past, allowing the early creation of ethnic voting blocs in some of the major cities based on recent immigrants. In Australia the concept of citizenship was limited to British subjects, and many privileges, such as land ownership, were denied to others. Under the White Australia Policy the ability to acquire citizenship was limited on racial grounds, just as the effective exercise of citizenship was denied to many Black Americans until the 1960s. The basic difference has lain in the American emphasis on individual rights, guaranteed by the Constitution and defended in the courts. The Australian Constitution guarantees almost no individual rights, other than freedom from religious tests for public appointments under Section 116. In many respects the immigrant or the alien has less legal protection in Australia, although this does not necessarily mean that their lot is any less secure than it might be in America.

The importance of citizen rights becomes greater as ethnic diversity increases. The possibility of discrimination, disadvantage and even violence is always present in multicultural societies, though not necessarily more so than in more uniform nations. The maintenance of national solidarity and political consensus is, at least in theory, more problematic when ethnic, religious or cultural loyalties break up the uniformity of the citizenry. Australia has always been more ethnically homogeneous than the United States. Its insecurity about cultural diversity is probably greater though scarcely manifest in nativist or racist politics.

NEW NATIONS OF IMMIGRANTS

The United States consciously describes itself as 'the first new nation', with the national motto *E Pluribus Unum* (or unity from diversity). For most of its history, many Australians saw their country as closely related to another, namely the United Kingdom. There is no suggestion of diversity in the national motto *Advance Australia*, rather the notion of uniform advance towards common goals. Yet both have committed themselves to building democratic and prosperous societies through immigration, with equal rights for all whether born locally or elsewhere. Many American influences have shaped recent Australian practice, especially in the areas of equal rights and protection for women and ethnic minorities, including the indigenous Aborigines. Older

Australian traditions based on working-class solidarity look increasingly old-fashioned because they assumed ethnic homogeneity and male domination.

One question often asked in Australian debates about immigration is whether 'Australia will become like America'. The general implication is that this would be undesirable, with racial violence, ghettoes and a 'confused national identity'. However, the United States does not have a confused national identity, having put a great deal of educational and propaganda effort into creating a sense of 'Americanism'. Riots and ghettoes have not been caused by immigration but by economic forces impacting on unskilled native-born Americans of ethnic minority origins. If Australia is confused about its own identity this is because social, economic and intellectual change has been very rapid, with immigration being only one factor although a very important one. It is at least arguable that a multicultural Australia with a large and varied immigrant intake is better able to cope with all these changes than the small, narrow and provincial society which previously existed. Many Australians resent this analysis, but it is at least as probable as its opposite. Certainly the United States has become a major world power, given exceptionally great economic and social opportunities to most of its people, and opened its doors to many millions, all on the basis of sustaining a multicultural society with a significant level of immigration. The task for Australia is rather to avoid the problems which America has faced. Some of these at least, like the persistence of underprivileged Black and Hispanic minorities, are never likely to arise elsewhere.

Australians also have to come to grips with the issue of how many more people their delicate environment can support. Despite the strength of environmentalism in the United States, Americans have been less concerned than Australians about the impact of their civilization on its natural surroundings. It may be that Australia cannot increase its population indefinitely on the basis of mass immigration at current levels. If this can be scientifically established then Australian governments must take the necessary steps to control intake more rigorously. Equally, many Americans are realizing that their profligate use of natural resources presents serious national and international problems. It would be most unfortunate if both societies saw immigration restriction as a panacea for economic and social problems which have other causes. Nor, of course, would it be sensible to see immigration as in some way a solution for comparable problems without other factors being taken into account.

BIBLIOGRAPHY

AUSTRALIA

Administrative Review Council (1986), Report to the Attorney-General, *Review of Migration Decisions*, Report No. 25, AGPS, Canberra.

Arthur, E. (1991), The Impact of Administrative Law on Humanitarian Decision Making, DILGEA, unpublished, Canberra.

Australian Bureau of Statistics (1989), *Overseas Born Australians 1988—A Statistical Profile*, AGPS, Canberra.

Australian Bureau of Statistics (1990), *The Economic Status of Migrants in Australia*, AGPS, Canberra.

Australian Institute of Multicultural Affairs (1982), *Evaluation of Post-Arrival Programs and Services*, AIMA, Melbourne.

Australian Law Reform Commission (1991), *Multiculturalism: Family Law*, Australian Law Reform Commission, Discussion Paper 46.

Babcock, B. A. (1973), 'The residential structure of metropolitan Sydney', *Australian Geographic Studies*, 11, pp. 1–27.

Barnett, D. (1986), 'How the bloated ethnic industry is dividing Australia', *Bulletin*, 18 February.

Beggs, J. J. & Chapman, B. J. (1988), 'The international transferability of human capital: immigrant market outcomes in Australia', in L. Baker & P. Miller (eds), *The Economics of Immigration*, AGPS, Canberra.

Bennett, S. (1989), *Aborigines and Political Power*, Allen & Unwin, Sydney.

Betts, K. (1988), *Ideology and Immigration: Australia 1976 to 1987*, Melbourne University Press, Melbourne.

Birrell, R. (1984), 'A new era in Australia's immigration policy', *International Migration Review*, vol. 18, pp. 65–84.

—— (1990), *The Chains That Bind: Family Reunion Migration to Australia in the 1980s*, AGPS, Canberra.

Birrell, R. & Betts, K. (1988), 'The FitzGerald report on immigration policy: origins and implications', *Australian Quarterly*, vol. 60 (3), pp. 261–74.

Birrell, R. & Birrell, T. (1978), 'The dynamics of immigration policy in Australia', in R. Birrell & C. Hay (eds), *The Immigration Issue in Australia*, Department of Sociology, La Trobe University, Bundoora, Vic.

—— (1987), *An Issue of People: Population and Australian Society*, Longman Cheshire, Melbourne.

Blainey, G. (1984), *All for Australia*, Methuen Haynes, Sydney.

Borrie, W. D. (1975), *First Report of the National Population Inquiry*, AGPS, Canberra.

—— (1988), 'Changes in immigration patterns since 1972', in J. Jupp (ed.), *The Australian People*, Angus & Robertson, Sydney.

Borrie, W. D. et al. (eds) (1947), *A White Australia—Australia's Population Problem*, Australasian Publishing Company, Sydney.

Bottomley, G. (1979), *After the Odyssey: A Study of Greek Australians*, University of Queensland Press, St Lucia, Qld.

—— (1984), 'Women on the move: migration and feminism', in G. Bottomley & M. de Lepervanche, *Ethnicity, Class and Gender in Australia*, Allen & Unwin, Sydney, pp. 98–108.

Bottomley, G. & de Lepervanche, M. (1984), *Ethnicity, Class and Gender in Australia*, Allen & Unwin, Sydney.

Brooks, C. & Volker, P. A. (1985), 'Labour market success and failure: an analysis of the factors leading to the workplace destinations of the Australian population', in P. A. Volker (ed.), *The Structure and Duration of Unemployment in Australia*, BLMR Monograph, AGPS, Canberra.

Broom, L. & Jones, F. L. (1976), *Opportunity and Attainment in Australia*, ANU, Canberra.

Broom, L., Jones, F. L., McDonnell, P. & Williams, T. (1980), *The Inheritance of Inequality*, Routledge & Kegan Paul, London.

Bull, H. (1975), 'The Whitlam Government's perception of our role in the world', in B. Beddie (ed.), *Advance Australia—Where?*, Oxford University Press, Melbourne.

Bullivant, B. (1988), 'Missing the empirical forest for the ideological trees', *Journal of Intercultural Studies*, 9, pp. 58–69.

Bureau of Immigration Research (1989), *Australian Immigration, Consolidated Statistics No. 15, 1988*, AGPS, Canberra.

—— (1990), *Australia's Population Trends and Prospects 1989*, AGPS, Canberra.

—— (1990), *Settler Arrivals 1988–89*, AGPS, Canberra.

Bureau of Labour Market Research (1986), *Migrants in the Australian Labour Market*, AGPS, Canberra.

Burnley, I. H. (1980), *The Australian Urban System*, Longman Cheshire, Melbourne.

—— (1982), *Population, Society and Environment in Australia*, Shillington House, Melbourne.

—— (1989), 'Settlement dimensions of the Vietnam-born population in metropolitan Sydney', *Australian Geographical Studies*, 27, pp. 129–54.

Campbell, I., Fincher, R. & Webber, M. J. (1991), 'Occupational mobility in segmented labour markets: the experience of immigrant workers in Melbourne', *Australian and New Zealand Journal of Sociology* (in press).

Castles, F. (1988), *Australian Public Policy and Economic Vulnerability: A Comparative and Historical Perspective*, Allen & Unwin, Sydney.

—— (1989a), 'Social protection by other means: Australia's strategy of coping with external vulnerability', in Francis Castles (ed.), *The Comparative History of Public Policy*, Polity Press, New York, pp. 17–55.

—— (1989b), 'Welfare and equality in capitalist societies: how and why Australia was different', in Richard Kennedy (ed.), *Australian Welfare: Historical*

Sociology, Macmillan, Melbourne, pp. 55–73.

Castles, S. & Collins, J. (1990), 'Restructuring, migrant labour markets and small business', *Migration*, no. 8.

Castles, S., Cope, B., Kalantzis, M. & Morrissey, M. (1990), *Mistaken Identity: Multiculturalism and the Demise of Nationalism in Australia*, 2nd ed., Pluto Press, Sydney.

Castles, S., Mitchell, C., Morrissey, M. & Alcorso, C. (1989), *The Recognition of Overseas Trade Qualifications*, AGPS, Canberra.

Castles, S., Collins, J., Gibson, K., Tait, D. & Alcorso, C. (1989), *The Global Milkbar and the Local Sweatshop: Ethnic Small Business and the Restructuring of Sydney*, OMA, Canberra.

Clarke, H. R., Chisholm, A. H., Edwards, G. W. & Kennedy, J. O. (1990), *Immigration, Population Growth and the Environment*, AGPS, Canberra.

Collins, J. (1984), 'Immigration and class: the Australian experience', in G. Bottomley & M. de Lepervanche, *Ethnicity, Class and Gender in Australia*, Allen & Unwin, Sydney, pp. 1–27.

—— (1988), *Migrant Hands in a Distant Land: Australia's Post-War Immigration*, Pluto Press, Sydney.

Committee of Review of the Adult Migrant Education Programme (1985), *Towards Active Voice* (Campbell Report), AGPS, Canberra.

Committee to Advise on Australia's Immigration Policies (1988), *Immigration: A Commitment to Australia* (FitzGerald Report), AGPS, Canberra.

Cowlishaw, G. (1988), *Black, White or Brindle: Race Relations in Rural Australia*, Cambridge University Press, Melbourne.

David, A. & Wheelwright, T. (1989), *The Third Wave: Australia and Asian Capitalism*, Left Book Club, Sydney.

de Lepervanche, M. (1975), 'Australian immigrants 1788–1940: desired and unwanted', in E. L. Wheelwright & K. Buckley (eds), *Essays in the Political Economy of Australian Capitalism*, vol. 1, ANZ Publishing Company, Sydney.

—— (1980), 'From race to ethnicity', *Australian and New Zealand Journal of Sociology*, 16, pp. 24–37.

—— (1984a), 'The "naturalness" of inequality', in G. Bottomley & M. de Lepervanche, *Ethnicity, Class and Gender in Australia*, Allen & Unwin, Sydney, pp. 49–71.

—— (1984b), 'Immigrants and ethnic groups', in S. Encel & L. Bryson, *Australian Society*, Longman Cheshire, Melbourne, pp. 170–228.

Department of Immigration and Ethnic Affairs (1982), *Review '82: Review of Activities to 30 June 1982*, AGPS, Canberra.

—— (1986a), *Don't Settle for Less: Report of the Committee for Stage 1 of the Review of Migrant and Multicultural Programs and Services* (Chairman, James Jupp), AGPS, Canberra.

—— (1986b), *Review of Activities to 30 June 1986*, AGPS, Canberra.

Department of Immigration, Local Government and Ethnic Affairs (1988a), *Access and Equity Initiatives: Three-Year Plan 1987–90*, AGPS, Canberra.

—— (1988b), *Australia's Population Trends and Prospects 1988*, AGPS, Canberra.

—— (1990), *Review '90: Annual Report 1989/90*, AGPS, Canberra.

Division of National Mapping, Australian Bureau of Statistics & Maher, C. A. (1984), *Melbourne . . . A Social Atlas*, Division of National Mapping and Australian Bureau of Statistics, Canberra.

Dwellings, Australia, Catalogue no. 2498.0, Australian Bureau of Statistics, Canberra.

Dyster, B. & Meredith, D. (1990), *Australia in the International Economy in the Twentieth Century,* Cambridge University Press, Cambridge & Melbourne.

Emy, H. & Hughes, O. (1988), *Australian Politics: Realities in Conflict,* Macmillan, Melbourne.

Ethnic Affairs Commission of New South Wales (1978), *Participation: Report to the Premier,* NSW Government Printer, Sydney.

Evans, M. D. R. (1989), 'Immigrant entrepreneurship: effects of market size and isolated labour pool', *American Sociological Review,* 54: 950–62.

Evans, M. D. R. & Kelley, J. (1986), 'Immigrants' work: equality and discrimination in the Australian labour market', *Australian and New Zealand Journal of Sociology,* 22, pp. 187–207.

Evans, M. D. R., Jones, F. L. & Kelley, J. (1988), 'Job discrimination against immigrants?', in J. Kelley & C. Bean (eds), *Australian Attitudes,* Allen & Unwin, Sydney.

Federation of Ethnic Communities' Councils of Australia (1988), *Annual Report 1987–88,* Sydney.

Fincher R., Webber, M. J. & Campbell, I. (1991a), *Immigrant Women in Manufacturing Work,* OMA, Canberra (forthcoming).

Fincher, R. (1991b), 'Caring for workers' dependents: class, gender and local state practice', *Melbourne Political Geography Quarterly* (in press).

—— (1991c), *Immigration, Urban Infrastructure and the Environment,* AGPS, Canberra.

FitzGerald, S. (chairman) (1988), *Immigration: A Commitment to Australia, The Report of the Committee to Advise on Australia's Immigration Policies,* AGPS, Canberra.

Fitzpatrick, M. D. (1982), 'Migrant employment: implications for industry performance', in D. Douglas (ed.), *The Economics of Australian Immigration,* University of Sydney Press, Sydney.

Foster, L. & Stockley, D. (1988), *Australian Multiculturalism: A Documentary History and Critique,* Multilingual Matters, Clevedon and Philadelphia.

Foster W. & Baker, L. (1991), *Immigration and the Australian Economy,* AGPS, Canberra.

Galbally, F. (1978), *Review of Migrant Services and Programs,* AGPS, Canberra.

Garnaut, R. (1989), *Australia and the North-East Asian Ascendancy—Report to the Prime Minister and the Minister for Foreign Affairs and Trade,* AGPS, Canberra.

Gibbons, W. (1990), 'Migration Act reform; a window into decision making', National Immigration Outlook Conference, Bureau of Immigration Research, November.

Grassby, A. (1973), *A Multi-Cultural Society for the Future,* Department of Immigration Reference Paper, AGPS, Canberra.

Hage, G. (1990), The Crisis of Multiculturalism, unpublished paper, Sydney.

Hawke, R. J. L. & Howe, B. (1990), *Towards a Fairer Australia: Social Justice Strategy Statement 1990–91,* AGPS, Canberra.

Heath, I. (1990), 'Immigration law and the changes of 19 December 1989', seminar paper delivered 27 April to the Centre for Migrant Studies, Monash University, Melbourne.

Holton, R. (1990), 'Social aspects of immigration', in M. Wooden, R. Holton,

G. Hugo & J. Sloan (eds), *Australian Immigration: A Survey of the Issues*, AGPS, Canberra, pp. 158–226.

Holton, R. & Sloan, J. (1990), 'Immigration policy—intake and settlement issues', in Wooden et al., (eds), *Australian Immigration: A Survey of the Issues*, AGPS, Canberra, pp. 293–348.

Horne, D. (1964), *The Lucky Country*, Penguin, Ringwood, Vic.

Horvath, R.J. & Engels, B. (1985), 'The residential restructuring of inner Sydney', in I. H. Burnley & J. Forrest (eds), *Living in Cities*, Allen & Unwin, Sydney, pp. 143–59.

Hughes, H. (1985), *Australia in a Developing World*, 1985 Boyer Lectures, ABC, Sydney.

Hughes, R. (1987), *The Fatal Shore*, Collins Harvill, London.

Hugo, G. (1990), 'Demographic and spatial aspects of immigration to Australia', in M. Wooden, R. Holton, G. Hugo & J. Sloan (eds), *Australian Immigration: A Survey of the Issues*, AGPS, Canberra.

Human Rights Commission (1985), *Human Rights and the Migration Act 1958*, Report No. 13, AGPS, Canberra.

Immigration Reform Group (1962), *Immigration Control or Colour Bar?*, Melbourne University Press, Melbourne.

Jakubowicz, A. (1984), 'Ethnicity, multiculturalism and neo-conservatism', in G. Bottomley & M. de Lepervanche, *Ethnicity, Class and Gender in Australia*, Allen & Unwin, Sydney.

—— (1988), 'Welfare provision', in J. Jupp (ed.), *The Australian People*, Angus & Robertson, Sydney.

—— (1989), 'The state and the welfare of immigrants in Australia', *Ethnic and Racial Studies*, vol. 12, no. 1.

Jakubowicz, A., Morrissey, M. & Palser, J. (eds), (1984), *Ethnicity, Class and Social Welfare in Australia*, Social Welfare Research Centre, University of New South Wales, Sydney.

Jamieson, N. (1989), *Part Time Work of Women in Melbourne*, Department of Geography, BA Honours thesis, University of Melbourne, Melbourne.

Jayasuriya, L. (1989), 'Australian multiculturalism adrift: the search for a new paradigm', paper presented at National Conference on Images of Multiculturalism in the Media, Ethnic Communities Council of NSW, Sydney.

—— (1990), 'Multiculturalism, citizenship and welfare: new directions for the 1990s', Department of Social Work and Social Policy 50th Anniversary Lecture Series, University of Sydney, Sydney.

Jenkins, D. (1990), 'The tricky task of cutting immigration', *Sydney Morning Herald*, 14 May, p. 17.

Joint Standing Committee on Migration Regulations (1990), *Illegal Entrants in Australia—Balancing Control and Comparison*, First Report, AGPS, Canberra.

Jones, F. L. (1969), *Dimensions of Urban Social Structure*, University of Toronto Press, Toronto.

—— (1981), 'Social stratification in Australia', in P. Hiller (ed.), *Class and Inequality in Australia*, Harcourt Brace Jovanovich, Sydney, pp. 40–55.

Jupp, J. (1984), 'Power in ethnic Australia', in J. Jupp (ed.), *Ethnic Politics in Australia*, Allen & Unwin, Sydney.

—— (1991), *Immigration*, Sydney University Press, Sydney.

Jupp, J. (ed.) (1989), *The Challenge of Diversity*, AGPS, Canberra.

Jupp, J., McRobbie, A. & York, B. (1989), *The Political Participation of Ethnic Minorities in Australia*, AGPS, Canberra.

—— (1991), *Settlement Needs of Small Newly Arrived Ethnic Groups*, AGPS, Canberra.

Kakakios, M. & van der Velden, J. (eds), (1984), 'Migrant communities and class politics: the Greek community in Australia', G. Bottomley and M. de Lepervanche, *Ethnicity, Class and Gender in Australia*, Allen & Unwin, Sydney, pp. 144–64.

Kalantzis, M. (1988), *Ethnicity Meets Gender Meets Class in Australia*, Centre for Multicultural Studies, University of Wollongong, Wollongong.

Kalantzis, M. & Cope, B. (1984), 'Multiculturalism and education policy', in G. Bottomley and M. de Lepervanche (eds), *Ethnicity, Class and Gender in Australia*, Allen & Unwin, Sydney, pp. 82–97.

Kunz, E. F. (1988), *Displaced Persons*, ANU Press/Pergamon, Sydney.

Lever-Tracy, C. (1984), 'A new Australian working class leadership: the case of Ford Broadmeadows', in G. Bottomley and M. de Lepervanche, *Ethnicity, Class and Gender in Australia*, Allen & Unwin, Sydney, pp. 123–43.

Lever-Tracy, C. & Quinlan, M. (eds), (1988), *A Divided Working Class*, Routledge, London.

Lewins, F. & Ly, J. (1985), *The First Wave: The Settlement of Australia's First Vietnamese Refugees*, Allen & Unwin, Sydney.

Lipski, S. (1990), 'The media—in whose image', paper presented to the Bureau of Immigration Research, National Outlook Conference, 14–19 November, Melbourne.

Lo Bianco, J. (1987), *National Policy on Languages*, AGPS, Canberra.

Logan, M. I., Maher, C. A., McKay, J. & Humphreys, J. S. (1975), *Urban and Regional Australia*, Sorrett Publishing, Malvern, Vic.

Maddock, K. (1983), *This Land is Our Land: Aboriginal Land Rights*, Penguin, Ringwood, Vic.

Maher, C. A. & Whitelaw, J. S. (1975), *Structure and Change in Inner Melbourne 1961–1971*, Department of Geography, Monash University, Melbourne.

Markus, A. & Ricklefs, M. C. (eds) (1985), *Surrender Australia? Essays in the Study and Uses of History: Geoffrey Blainey and Asian Immigration*, Allen & Unwin, Sydney.

Martin, Jean (1978), *The Migrant Presence*, Allen & Unwin, Sydney.

—— (1984), 'Non English-speaking women: production and social reproduction', in G. Bottomley and M. de Lepervanche (eds), *Ethnicity, Class and Gender in Australia*, Allen & Unwin, Sydney, pp. 109–22.

Matwijiw, P. (1988), 'Public policy on immigrants', in J. Jupp (ed.), *The Australian People*, Angus & Robertson, Sydney.

Meekosha, H. & Jakubowicz, A. (1989), 'Increasing opportunity or deepening disappointment? Access and equity in the Department of Community Services and Health', *Migration Action*, vol. XI, no. 1.

Mitchell, C., Castles, S. & Tait, D. (1990), *The Recognition of Overseas Professional Qualifications*, AGPS, Canberra.

Morrissey, M. (1984), 'Migrantness, culture and ideology', in G. Bottomley and M. de Lepervanche, *Ethnicity, Class and Gender in Australia*, Allen & Unwin, Sydney, pp. 72–81.

Mulvey, C. (1986), 'Wage levels: do unions make a difference?', in J. Niland (ed.), *Wage Fixation in Australia*, Allen & Unwin, Sydney.

Murphy, P. A., Burnley, I. H., Harding, H. R., Wiesner, D. & Young, V. (1990), *Impact of Immigration on Urban Infrastructure*, AGPS, Canberra.

National Population Council (1985), *Access and Equity*, AGPS, Canberra.

—— (1990), *Grant of Resident Status on Spouse/De Facto Spouse Grounds to Visitors*, A Report by a Working Party of the NPC, DILGEA, Canberra.

Nevile, J. (1990), *The Effect of Immigration on Australian Living Standards*, AGPS, Canberra.

Niland, C. & Champion, R. (1990), *EEO Programs for Immigrants*, AGPS, Canberra.

O'Reilly, D. (1990), 'Putting the recovery before the race', *Bulletin*, 29 May, p. 34.

Office of Multicultural Affairs (1989), *The National Agenda for a Multicultural Australia*, AGPS, Canberra.

—— (1991), *Making It Happen: Access and Equity at Work Around Australia*, AGPS, Canberra.

Page, B. & Painter, M. (1989), 'The public service', in R. Smith & L. Watson (eds), *Politics in Australia*, Allen & Unwin, Sydney.

Palfreeman, A. (1967), *The Administration of the White Australia Policy*, Melbourne University Press, Melbourne.

—— (1975), 'Non-European immigration into Australia', *Australian Outlook*, vol. 29, no. 3, pp. 349–54.

Parkin, A. (1984), 'Ethnic groups, social change and public policy in Australia', *Current Affairs Bulletin*, vol. 61, no. 3, pp. 15–26.

Pollard, D. (1988), *Give and Take—The Losing Partnership in Aboriginal Poverty*, Hale & Iremonger, Sydney.

Price, C. A. (1963), *Southern Europeans in Australia*, Oxford University Press, Melbourne.

—— (1979), 'Immigration and ethnic affairs', in A. Patience and B. Head (eds), *From Whitlam to Fraser: Reform and Reaction in Australian Politics*, Oxford University Press, Melbourne.

Pryles, M. & Bravender-Coyle, P. (1988), 'Legal status of non-citizens', in J. Jupp (ed.), *The Australian People*, Angus & Robertson, Sydney.

Public Service Commission (1990), *Maximising Diversity: A Report on the Employment of People of Non-English Speaking Background in the Australian Public Service*, AGPS, Canberra.

Ray, R. (Senator) (1990), Second Reading Speech by the Minister for Immigration, Local Government and Ethnic Affairs on the Migration Legislation Amendment Bill 1989, Parliament House, Canberra.

Reid, G. & Forrest, M. (1989), *Australia's Commonwealth Parliament: 1901–1988*, Melbourne University Press, Melbourne.

Review Group to the Victorian Minister for Immigration and Ethnic Affairs (1983), *Access and Equity: The Development of Victorian Ethnic Affairs Policies*, Government Printer, Melbourne.

Review of Migrant and Multicultural Programs and Services (1986), *Don't Settle for Less* (Jupp Report), AGPS, Canberra.

Review of Post-arrival Programs and Services for Migrants (1978), *Migrant Services and Programs* (Galbally Report), AGPS, Canberra.

Reynolds, H. (1987), *Frontier*, Allen & Unwin, Sydney.

Rosecrance, R. (1964), 'The radical culture of Australia', in Louis Hartz (ed.), *The Founding of New Societies*, Harcourt Brace Jovanovich, New York.

Sheridan, G. (1990), 'Hawke's ethnic time bomb', *Australian*, 21–2 April, p. 15.

Singer, S. & Liffman, M. (eds) (1984), *The Blainey Debate in the Press 1984*, The Clearing House on Migration Issues, Melbourne.

Smolicz, J. J. (1985), 'Multiculturalism and an overarching framework of values', in M. Poole, P. de Lacy and B. Randawa (eds), *Australia in Transition*, Harcourt Brace Jovanovich, Sydney.

Stimson, R. J. (1974), 'The social structure of large cities', in I. H. Burnley (ed.), *Urbanisation in Australia: The Post War Experience*, Cambridge University Press, Cambridge, pp. 147–63.

Storer, D. (1985), *Ethnic Family Values in Australia*, Prentice Hall, Sydney.

Stromback, T. (1984), 'The earnings of migrants in Australia', BLMR Conference Paper, Canberra.

Stromback, T. & Williams, T. (1985), 'Do migrants earn what they should?', *Bulletin of Labour Market Research*, vol. 15.

Sweetser, F. L. (1982), *Urban Residential Areas in Australia*, Department of Sociology, Research School of Social Sciences, ANU, Canberra.

Terrill, R. (1987), *The Australians*, Transworld Publishers, London.

Vasta, E. (1990), *Australia's Post-War Immigration: Power, Identity and Resistance*, Ph. D. thesis, University of Queensland, Brisbane.

Webber, M., Morrison, P., Campbell, I. & Fincher, R. (1989), *Migrant Men and Women in Australian Manufacturing Labour Markets 1971–1986*, Report to the Office of Multicultural Affairs, University of Melbourne, Melbourne.

Whitelaw, J. S. & Humphreys, J. S. (1980), 'Migrant response to an unfamiliar environment', in I. H. Burnley, R. J. Pryor & D. T. Rowland (eds), *Mobility and Community Change in Australia*, University of Queensland Press, St Lucia, Qld.

Williams, T. (1987), *Participation in Education*, Australian Council for Educational Research, Hawthorn, Vic.

Wilton, J. and Bosworth, R. (1984), *Old Worlds and New Australia*, Penguin, Ringwood, Vic.

Wooden, M. (1990a), 'The economic impact of immigration', in M. Wooden, R. Holton, G. Hugo & J. Sloan, *Australian Immigration: A Survey of the Issues*, AGPS, Canberra.

—— (1990b), 'The labour market experience of immigrants', in M. Wooden, R. Holton, G. Hugo & J. Sloan, *Australian Immigration: A Survey of the Issues*, AGPS, Canberra.

Wooden, M. & Robertson, F. (1989), *Factors Associated With Migrant Labour Market Status*, AGPS, Canberra.

Wooden, M., Holton, R., Hugo, G. & Sloan, J. (1990), *Australian Immigration: A Survey of the Issues*, AGPS, Canberra.

Zubrzycki, J. (1960), *Immigrants in Australia*, Melbourne University Press, Melbourne.

—— (1977), 'Towards a multicultural society in Australia', in M. Bowen (ed.), *Australia 2000: The Ethnic Impact*, University of New England, Armidale, NSW.

—— (1978), 'Immigration and the family in a multicultural Australia', *Australia's Multicultural Society*, La Trobe University, Melbourne.

UNITED STATES

Archdeacon, T. J. (1983), *Becoming American: An Ethnic History*, The Free Press, New York.

Bach, R. L. (1978), 'Mexican immigration and the American state', *International Migration Review*, vol. 12, Winter, pp. 58–8.

—— (1990), 'Immigration and US foreign policy in Latin America and the Caribbean', in Robert W. Tucker, Charles B. Keely and Linda Wrigley (eds), *Immigration and US Foreign Policy*, Westview Press, Boulder, pp. 123–49.

Bach, R. L. & Argiros, R. (1991), 'Progress toward economic self-sufficiency among Southeast Asian refugees', Office of Refugee Resettlement, US Department of Health and Human Services, Washington DC.

Bach, R. & Meissner, D. (1990), *America's Labor Market in the 1990s: What Role Should Immigration Play?*, Carnegie Endowment for International Peace, Washington DC.

—— (1990), *Employment and Immigration Reform: Employer Sanctions Four Years Later*, Carnegie Endowment for International Peace, Washington DC.

Bailar, B. (1988), 'Finding those the Census missed', *Technology Review*, May/June.

Baker v. *Carr* (1962), 82 S. Ct., 691.

Barrera, M. (1979), *Race and Class in the Southwest*, Notre Dame University Press, South Bend, Indiana.

Barth, F. (ed.) (1969), *Ethnic Groups and Boundaries*, Allen & Unwin, London.

Barringer, F. (1991), 'Commerce Department declines to revise '90 Census counts', *New York Times*, 16 July, p. A1.

Bean, F. D. & de la Garza, R. (1988), 'Illegal aliens and Census counts', *Society*, March/April, p. 52.

Bean, F. D., Edmonston B. & Passel, J. (1990), *Undocumented Migration to the United States: IRCA and the Experience of the 1980s*, The Urban Institute Press, Washington DC.

Bean, F. D., Vernez, G. & Keely, C. (1989), *Opening and Closing the Doors: Evaluating Immigration Reform and Control*, The Urban Institute Press, Washington DC.

Bean, F. D., Schmandt, J. & Weintraub, S. (eds) (1989), *Mexican and Central American Population and US Population Policy*, University of Texas Press, Austin.

Bean, F. D., Espenshade, T., White, M. & Dymoski, R. (1990), 'Post-IRCA changes in the volume and flow of undocumented migration to the United States', in F. Bean, B. Edmonston & J. Passel (eds), *Undocumented Migration to the United States: IRCA and the Experience of the 1980s*, The Urban Institute Press, Washington DC, pp. 111–58.

Beard, C. (1913), *An Economic Interpretation of the Constitution of the United States*, Macmillan, New York.

Bernard, W. S. (1950), *American Immigration Policy: A Reappraisal*, Harper & Brothers, New York.

Billington, R. A. (1959), *The Westward Movement in the United States*, D. Van Nostrand, New York.

Borjas, G. (1990), *Friends or Strangers: The Impact of Immigrants on the US Economy*, Basic Books Inc., New York.

Briggs, V. (1984), *Immigration Policy and the American Labor Force*, The Johns

Hopkins University Press, Baltimore.

Burnham, W. D. (1981), 'The system of 1896: an analysis', in Kleppner et al. (eds), *The Evolution of American Electoral Systems,* Greenwood Press, Westport, CT.

Bustamante, J. A. (1990), 'Undocumented migration from Mexico to the United States: preliminary findings of the Zapata Canyon Project', in F. Bean, B. Edmonston & J. Passel (eds), *Undocumented Migration to the United States: IRCA and the Experience of the 1980s,* The Urban Institute Press, Washington DC, pp. 211–26.

Calavita, K. (1984), *US Immigration Law and the Control of Labor: 1820–1924,* Academic Press, London.

Carson, M. (1990), *Settlement Folk. Social Thought and the American Settlement Movement, 1885–1930,* University of Chicago Press, Chicago.

Carter, T. (1970), *Mexican Americans in Schools: A History of Educational Neglect,* College Entrance Examination Board, New York.

Chapman, L. (1976), 'Illegal aliens: time to call a halt', *Readers Digest,* October, pp. 188–92.

Charlton, R., Farley, L. T. & Kaye, R. (1988), 'Identifying the mainsprings of US policy', *Journal of Refugee Studies,* vol. 1, no. 3/4.

Chavez, L. (1990), 'Rainbow Collision', *New Republic,* 19 November.

Chiswick, B. R. (1978), 'The effects of Americanisation on the earnings of foreign-born men', *Journal of Political Economy,* 86, pp. 897–921.

—— (1988), *Illegal Aliens: Their Employment and Employers,* Upjohn Institute for Employment Research, Kalamazoo.

—— (1990), 'Opening the golden door', *Washington Post,* Sunday, 7 October, D3.

City of Mobile v. *Bolden* (1980), 446 US 55.

City of New York v. *US Department of Commerce* (1990), 739 F. Supp. 761.

Commission for the Study of International Migration and Cooperative Economic Development (1990), *Unauthorized Migration: An Economic Development Response,* Washington DC.

Congressional Quarterly (1990), Senate Votes, 21 July, Washington DC.

Cornelius, W. (1989), 'Impacts of the 1986 US immigration law on emigration from rural Mexican sending communities', *Population Development Review,* December, 15, pp. 689–706.

—— (1990), 'Impacts of the 1986 US immigration law on emigration from rural Mexican sending communities', in F. Bean, B. Edmonston and J. Passel (eds), *Undocumented Migration to the United States: IRCA and the Experience of the 1980s,* The Urban Institute Press, Washington DC, pp. 227–50.

Cox, O. C. (1948), *Caste, Class and Race,* Doubleday, Garden City, New York.

Craig, R. (1971), *The Bracero Program: Interest Groups and Foreign Policy,* University of Texas Press, Austin.

Crane, K., Asch, B. J., Heilbron, J. & Cullinane, D. C. (1990), *The Effect of Employer Sanctions on the Flow of Undocumented Immigrants to the United States,* Urban Institute Report, Program for Research on Immigration Policy JRI–03, Washington DC and Santa Monica, CA, pp. 90–8.

Cross, H., Kenney, G., Zummerman, W. & Mell, J. (1990), *A Hiring Audit of Employment Discrimination,* The Urban Institute Press, Washington DC.

Davidson, C. (1991), 'A comparison of alien admissions before and after IRCA',

Immigration Issues, Office of Plans and Analysis, Statistics Division, US Immigration and Naturalisation Service, Washington DC, Table 1.

de la Garza, R. (1982), *Public Policy of Chicano Élites,* Overseas Development Council, Washington DC.

—— (1985), 'Mexican Americans, Mexican immigrants, and immigration reform', in Nathan Glazer (ed.), *Clamor at the Gates,* Institute for Contemporary Studies, San Francisco.

—— (1989), 'Mexico, Mexicans and Mexican Americans in US-Mexican relations', *Texas Papers on Mexico,* no. 89–02, Institute of Latin American Studies, University of Texas, Austin, p. 12.

—— (forthcoming), 'Immigration reforms as a civil rights issue: a Mexican American perspective', in G. Perle and B. Cain (eds), *Developments in American Politics,* Oxford University Press, New York.

de la Garza, R. & DeSipio, L. (1990), 'The *Voting Rights Act* and Latino electoral participation', paper prepared for presentation at the Key to Empowerment? The Voting Rights Act of 1965 conference, American University, Washington DC.

Donato, K., Durand, J. & Massey, D. (1990), 'Stemming the tide? Assessing the deterrent effects of the Immigration Reform and Control Act', Population Studies Center Working Paper, University of Chicago, Chicago.

Eig, L. & Vialet, J. (1985), 'Comprehensive immigration reform: history and current status', *Georgetown Immigration Law Journal,* 1(1), pp. 27–59.

Espenshade, T. J. (1990), 'Undocumented migration to the United States: evidence from a repeated trials model', in F. Bean, B. Edmonston & J. Passel (eds), *Undocumented Migration to the United States: IRCA and the Experience of the 1980s,* The Urban Institute Press, Washington DC, pp. 159–82.

—— (1989), *A Short History of US Policy Toward Illegal Migration,* The Urban Institute Press, Washington DC.

Eyles, J. (1990), 'Group identity and urban space: the North American experience', in M. Chisholm & D. M. Smith (eds), *Shared Space: Divided Space,* Unwin Hyman, London, pp. 46–66.

Fair v. Klutznik (1980), 468 F. Supp 564 (DDC 1980, three judge court) appeal dismissed 447 US 916 (1980).

Fairchild, H. P. (1920), *Immigration,* MacMillan, New York.

Fix, M. & Passel, J. S. (1991), 'The door remains open: recent immigration to the United States and a preliminary analysis of the *Immigration Act* of 1990', Program for Research on Immigration Policy, PRIP–UI–14, The Urban Institute Press, Washington DC.

Fix, M. & Hill, P. (1990), *Enforcing Employer Sanctions,* The Urban Institute Press, Washington DC.

Fuchs, L. (1990a) 'The reactions of Black Americans to immigration', in V. Yans-McLaughlin (ed.), *Immigration Reconsidered: History, Sociology, and Politics,* Oxford University Press, New York.

—— (1990b), *The American Kaleidoscope: Race, Ethnicity, and the Civic Culture,* Wesleyan University Press, Hanover.

—— (1990c), 'The blood of all nations: the triumph of inclusivity in immigration policy', *Ethnicity and Public Policy,* vol. 1, no. 7.

Geary, P. & O'Grada, C. (1985), *Immigration and the Real Wage: Time Series Evidence from the United States, 1820–1977,* paper presented at joint

CEPR–RIIA Workshop on International Labour Migration.

General Accounting Office (1990), *Immigration Reform: Employer Sanctions and the Question of Discrimination,* Washington DC.

Glazer, N. (1990), 'New Rules of the Game', in R. Tucker et al. (eds), *Immigration and US Foreign Policy,* Westview Press, Boulder.

Gonzalez-Baker, S. (1990), *The Cautious Welcome: The Legalization Programs of the Immigration Reform and Control Act,* University Press of America, Lanham MD.

Gordon, M. M. (1964), *Assimilation in American Life,* Oxford University Press, New York.

Greenwood, M. & McDowell, J. (1986), 'The factor market consequences of US immigration', *Journal of Economic Literature,* XXIV, December, pp. 1738–72.

—— (1990), *The Labour Market Consequences of US Immigration: A Survey,* US Department of Labor, Washington DC.

Handlin, O. (1951), *The Uprooted: The Epic Story of the Great Migrations That Made the American People,* Little Brown, Boston.

Hartz, L. (1964), *The Founding of New Societies,* Harcourt Brace Jovanovich, New York.

Harwood, E. (1986), *In Liberty's Shadow: Illegal Aliens and Immigration Law Enforcement,* Hoover Institution, Stanford, California.

Higham, J. (1963), *Strangers in the Land: Patterns of American Nativism, 1860–1925,* Rutgers University Press, New Brunswick; republished (1977), Athenaeum, New York.

Hollifield, J. (forthcoming), *Immigrants, Markets, and the State,* Harvard University Press, Cambridge.

Hutchinson, E. P. (1981), *Legislative History of American Immigration Policy, 1798–1965,* University of Pennsylvania Press, Philadelphia.

Interpreter Releases (1990a), vol. 67, p. 1335.

Interpreter Releases (1990b), vol. 67, p. 1398.

Jacob, W. (1980), 'Lack of cash and poor coordination plague US refugee policies', *National Journal: The Weekly on Politics and Government,* 12, pp. 1234–7.

Jones, M. (1960), *American Immigration,* University of Chicago Press, Chicago.

Key, V. O. (1949), *Southern Politics in State and Nation,* Vintage, New York.

Kiser, G. & Kiser, M. (eds) (1979), *Mexican Workers in the United States,* University of New Mexico Press, Albuquerque.

Lau v. *Nichols* (1974), 414 US 563.

Levy, F. (1987), *Dollars and Dreams: The Changing American Income Distribution,* Russell Sage, New York.

Massey, D. S. & Denton, N. A. (1987), 'Trends in the residential segregation of Blacks, Hispanics and Asians', *American Sociological Review,* 52, pp. 802–25.

McCarthy, K. F. & Valdez, R. B. (1985), *Current and Future Effects of Immigration in California,* Rand, Santa Monica.

McDowell, L. (1983), 'Towards an understanding of the gender division of urban space', *Society and Space,* 1, pp. 59–72.

McHugh, L. B. (1990), *Migration and Refugee Assistance Budget: Problems and Prospects,* Congressional Research Services, Library of Congress, 20 July.

Miller, L. et al. (1984), 'Attitudes toward undocumented workers: the Mexican American perspective', *Social Science Quarterly,* 65/2, p. 844.

Mink, W. (1986), *Old Labor and New Immigrants in American Political Development: Union, Party, and State, 1875–1920,* Cornell University Press, Ithaca.

Montejano, D. (1987), *Anglos and Mexicans in the Making of Texas 1836–1986,* University of Texas Press, Austin.

Montero, D. (1979), *Vietnamese Americans: Patterns of Resettlement and Socioeconomic adaptation in the United States,* Westview Press, Boulder.

Moore, J. & Pachon, H. (1985), *Hispanics in the United States,* Prentice Hall, Englewood Cliffs, New Jersey.

Morris, M. D. (1985), *Immigration: The Beleaguered Bureaucracy,* The Brookings Institution, Washington DC.

Morse, A. (1990), 'United States immigration and refugee policy: federal policy and its impact on states', *State–Federal Issue Brief,* vol. 3, no. 2, June.

NALEO Education Fund (1985), *Proceedings of the First National Conference on Citizenship and the Hispanic Community,* Washington DC.

—— (1989), *National Latino Immigrant Survey,* Washington DC.

Nelson, B. A. (1984), *The Coming Triumph of Mexican Irredentism,* The American Control Foundation, Monterey VA.

North, D. S. (1985), *The Long Grey Welcome: A Study of the American Naturalization Program,* NALEO Education Fund, Washington DC.

Pachon, H. & DeSipio, L. (1991), *Administering Americanization: The INS and Naturalization,* NALEO Educational Fund, Washington DC.

Papademetriou, D., Bach, R., Johnson, K., Kramer, R., Lowell, B. & Smith, S. (1989), *The Effects of Immigration on the US Economy and Labor Market,* Immigration Policy and Research Report 1, US Department of Labor, Washington DC.

Papademetriou, D. G. & Muller, T. (1988), *Recent Immigration to New York: Labor Market and Social Policy Issues,* National Commission for Employment Policy, Washington DC.

Passel, J. S., Bean, F. D. & Edmonston, B. (1990), 'Undocumented migration since IRCA: an overall assessment', in F. Bean, B. Edmonston and J. Passel (eds), *Undocumented Migration to the United States: IRCA and the Experience of the 1980s,* The Urban Institute Press, Washington DC, pp. 251–26.

Pear, R. 'Major immigration bill is sent to Bush', *New York Times,* 29 October 1990.

Pedraza-Bailey, S. (1985), *Political and Economic Migrants in America: Cubans and Mexicans,* University of Texas Press, Austin.

Portes, A. & Bach, R. (1985), *Latin Journey: Cuban and Mexican Immigrants in the United States,* University of California Press, Berkeley.

Potter, D. M. (1954), *People of Plenty: Economic Abundance and the American Character,* University of Chicago Press, Chicago.

Reimers, C. W. (1984), 'The wage structure of Hispanic men: implications for policy', *Social Science Quarterly,* 65, pp. 401–16.

Reimers, D. (1985), *Still the Golden Door? The Third World Comes to America,* Columbia University Press, New York.

Reisler, M. (1976), *By the Sweat of Their Brow: Mexican Immigrant Labor in the United States, 1900–1940,* Greenwood Press, Westport.

Ridge v. *Verity* (1986), 715 F. Supp. 1308.

Rodriguez, C. E. (1989), *Puerto Ricans,* Unwin Hyman, New York.

Rosberg, G. (1977), 'Aliens and equal protection: why not the right to vote?',

Michigan Law Review, April/May, pp. 1092–1136.

San Miguel Jr, G. (1987), *'Let Them All Take Heed': Mexican Americans and the Campaign for Educational Equality in Texas, 1910–1981*, The University of Texas Press, Austin.

Sanger, C. (1987), 'Immigration reform and the control of the undocumented family', *Georgetown Immigration Law Journal*, 2(2), pp. 295–356.

Scanlan, J. & Loescher, G. (1983), 'US foreign policy, 1959–80: impact on refugee flow from Cuba', *Annals of the American Academy of Political and Social Science*, no. 467, May, pp. 116–37.

Schuck, P. (1990), 'The great immigration debate', *The American Prospect*, Fall, pp. 100–18.

Schuck, P. H. & Smith, R. M. (1985), *Citizenship Without Consent: Illegal Aliens in the American Polity*, Yale University Press, New Haven.

Schultz, B. & Schultz, R. (eds) (1989), *It Did Happen Here: Recollections of Political Repressions in America*, University of California Press, Berkeley.

Scott, A. J. (1985), 'Location processes, urbanisation and territorial development', *Environment and Planning*, A17, pp. 479–501.

Select Commission on Immigration and Refugee Policy (1981), *US Immigration Policy and the National Interest*, US GPO, Washington DC.

Seller, M. S. (1982), 'Historical perspectives on American immigration policy: case studies and current implications', *Law and Contemporary Problems*, vol. 45, no. 2, pp. 137–62.

Simon, R. (1987), 'Immigration and American attitudes', *Public Opinion*, July/August.

Skerry, P. (1989), 'Borders and quotas: immigration and the affirmative action state', *The Public Interest*, 96, pp. 86–102.

Smith, D. H. (1926), *The Bureau of Naturalization: Its History, Activities and Organization*, The Johns Hopkins University Press, Baltimore MD.

Stevenson, R. (1990), 'Selling a free-trade pact with Mexico', *New York Times*, 11 November.

Tabraham, B. & Rosenberg, H. (1990), *Family Fairness Guidelines Offer a Little More Certainty*, University of California Cooperative Extension, California.

Teitelbaum, M. (1985), *Latin Migration North*, Council on Foreign Relations, New York.

—— (1990), Letter to Hon. R. Dunne, Appendices, *Report and Recommendations of the Task Force on IRCA-Related Discrimination*, September 1990, VSPGO, Washington DC.

Thernstrom, A. (1987), *Whose Votes Count? Affirmative Action and Minority Voting Rights*, Harvard University Press, Cambridge.

Tillema, R. G. (1981), 'Starting over in a new land: resettling a refugee family', *Public Welfare*, 39(1), pp. 34–41.

Tocqueville, A. de (1969), *Democracy in America*, Anchor Books, New York.

Trolander, J. A. (1969), 'Twenty years at Hiram House', *Ohio History*, vol. 78.

—— (1975), *Settlement Houses and the Great Depression*, Wayne State University Press, Detroit.

Tucker, R. (1990), 'Immigration and foreign policy: general considerations', in R. Tucker et al. (eds), *Immigration and US Foreign Policy*, Westview Press, Boulder.

——, Tucker, R., Keely, C. & Wrigley, L. (eds) (1990), *Immigration and US Foreign Policy*, Westview Press, Boulder, CO.

Turner, Frederick Jackson (1962), *Rise of the New West: 1819–1829*, Collier, New York.

—— (1963), *The Significance of the Frontier in American History*, Frederick Unger Publishing Company, New York.

United States General Accounting Office (1990), *Immigration Reform: Employer Sanctions and the Question of Discrimination*, GAO/GGD, Washington, 90–62, 29 March.

United States Bureau of the Census (1983), *1980 Census of Population, Chapter D, Detailed Population Characteristics*, Washington DC, Table 254.

—— (1991), 'Census Bureau releases preliminary coverage estimates from the Post-Enumeration Survey Demographic Analysis', Press Release, 18 April.

United States Immigration and Naturalization Service (1990), *1989 Statistical Yearbook of the Immigration and Naturalization Service*, Washington DC.

United States Senate Committee on the Judiciary (1975), *Hearings on S. 407, S. 903, S. 1297, S. 1409 and S. 1443 Extension of the Voting Rights Act of 1965*, Washington DC.

—— (1980), *History of the Immigration and Naturalization Service*, The Congressional Research Service, Washington DC.

Vialet, J. (1980), *US Immigration Policy: The Western Hemisphere*, Congressional Research Service, Washington DC.

—— (1990), *Refugee Admissions and Resettlement Policy*, Congressional Research Service, Washington, DC, 18 July.

Warren, R. (1990), 'Annual estimates of non-immigrant overstayers in the United States: 1985 to 1988, in F. Bean, B. Edmonston and J. Passel (eds), *Undocumented Migration to the United States: IRCA and the Experience of the 1980s*, The Urban Institute Press, Washington DC, pp. 77–110.

Wattenberg, B. J. (1991), *The First Universal Nation: Leading Indicators and Ideas About the Surge of America in the 1990s*, The Free Press, New York.

White, M. J., Bean, F. D. & Espenshade, T. J. (1990), 'The US 1986 *Immigration Reform and Control Act* and undocumented migration to the United States', *Population Research and Policy Review*, 9, pp. 93–116.

Wilson, K. & Portes, A. (1981), 'Immigrant enclaves: an analysis of the labour market experience of Cubans in Miami', *American Sociological Review*, 86, pp. 296–318.

Woodrow, K. A. & Passel, J. S. (1990), 'Post-IRCA undocumented immigration to the United States: an assessment based on the June 1988 CPS', in F. Bean, B. Edmonston & J. Passel (eds), *Undocumented Migration to the United States: IRCA and the Experience of the 1980s*, The Urban Institute Press, Washington DC, pp. 33–76.

Woodward, C. Vann (1966), *The Strange Career of Jim Crow*, Oxford University Press, New York.

Zolberg, A. (1990a), 'The roots of US refugee policy', in R. Tucker et al. (eds), *Immigration and US Foreign Policy*, Westview Press, Boulder.

—— (1990b) 'Reforming the back door: the *Immigration Reform and Control Act of 1986* in historical perspective', V. Yans-McLaughlin (ed.), *Immigration Reconsidered: History, Sociology, Politics*, Oxford University Press, New York.

COMPARATIVE AND THEORETICAL

Bach, Robert L. (1985), 'Political frameworks for international migration', Steven E. Sandersen (ed.), *The Americas in the New International Division of Labor*, Holmes & Meier, New York, pp. 95–124.

Babcock, B. A. (1984), *Unfairly Structured Cities*, Blackwell, Oxford.

Berry, A. & Soligo, R. (1969), 'Some welfare aspects of international migration', *Journal of Political Economy*, vol. 77, pp. 778–94.

Borjas, G. (1988), *International Differences in the Labor Market Performance of Immigrants*, W. E. Upjohn Institute for Employment Research, Kalamazoo, Michigan.

Bourgeois-Pichat, J. (1989), 'From the 20th to the 21st century: Europe and its population after the year 2000', in L. Sergent (trans.), *Population: English Section*, no. 1.

Bovenkerk, F., Miles, R. & Verbunt, G. (1990), 'Racism, migration and the state in western Europe: a case for comparative analysis', *International Sociology*, vol. 5, no. 4, December, pp. 475–90.

Brubaker, W. R. (ed.) (1989), *Immigration and the Politics of Citizenship in Europe and North America*, University Press of America, Lanham, MD.

Carlson, L. A. & Swartz, C. (1988), 'The earnings of women and ethnic minorities, 1959–1979', *Industrial Labor Relations Review*, 41, pp. 530–46.

Castles, F. G. (1985), *The Working Class and Welfare*, Allen & Unwin, Sydney.

Castles, S. (1984), *Here for Good: Western Europe's New Ethnic Minorities*, Pluto Press, London.

Dahrendorf, R. (1988), *The Modern Social Conflict: An Essay on the Politics of Liberty*, Weidenfeld and Nicolson, London.

Demeny, P. (1988), 'Demography and the limits to growth', in M. Teitlebaum & J. Winter (eds), *Population and Resources in Western Intellectual Traditions. Population and Development Review*, supplement to vol. 4, The Population Council, New York.

DeSipio, L. (1987), 'Social science literature and the naturalization process', *International Migration Review*, vol. 21, summer, pp. 390–405.

Dowty, A. (1987), *Closed Borders: The Contemporary Assault on Freedom of Movement*, Yale University Press, New Haven.

Evans, P., Rueschemeyer, D. & Skocpol, T. (eds) (1985), *Bringing the State Back In*, Cambridge University Press, Cambridge.

Feagin, J. R. (1989), *Race and Ethnic Relations*, Prentice Hall, Englewood NJ.

Freeman, G. (1986), 'Migration and the political economy of the welfare state', *Annals*, AAPSS, vol. 487, pp. 51–63.

—— (1979), *Immigrant Labor and Racial Conflict in Industrial Societies: The French and British Experience, 1945–75*, Princeton University Press, Princeton.

Gregory, D. (1978), *Ideology, Science and Human Geography*, Hutchinson, London.

Hamilton, B. & Whalley, J. (1984), 'Efficiency and distributional implications of global restrictions on labour mobility: calculations and policy implications', *Journal of Development Economics*, vol. 14, pp. 61–75.

Hammar, T. (1985), *European Immigration Policy: A Comparative Study*, Cambridge University Press, London.

—— (1990), *Democracy and the Nation State: Denizens and Citizens in a World of*

International Migration, Gower, London.

Hartz, L. (1964), *The Founding of New Societies*, Harcourt Brace Jovanovich, New York.

Harvey, D. (1975), 'Class structure in a capitalist society and the theory of residential differentiation', in R. Peel, M. Chisholm & P. Hagett (eds), *Processes in Physical and Human Geography*, Heinemann, London, pp. 354–69.

Hawkins, F. (1989), *Critical Years in Immigration: Canada and Australia Compared*, New South Wales University Press, Sydney.

Hayden, D. (1986), 'What would a non-sexist city be like: speculations on housing, urban design and human work', in R. G. Bratt, C. Hartman & A. Meyerson, *Critical Perspectives on Housing*, Temple University Press, Philadelphia, pp. 230–46.

Higham, J. (1989), 'The Movement of Peoples: 1788–1989', G. Withers (ed.), Commonality and Difference: Australia and the United States, Allen & Unwin, Sydney.

Hollifield, J. F. (forthcoming), *Immigrants, Markets, and States*, Harvard University Press, Cambridge, Mass.

Katzenstein, P. J. (1985), *Small States in World Markets*, Cornell University Press, Ithaca.

Little, J., Peake, L. & Richardson, P. (eds) (1988), *Women in Cities*, Macmillan, London.

MacKenzie, S. (1988), 'Building women, building cities: toward gender sensitive theory in the environmental disciplines', in C. Andrew & B. M. Milroy, *Life Spaces: Gender, Household, Employment*, UBC Press, Vancouver, pp. 13–30.

Messina, A. M. (1990), 'Political impediments to the resumption of labour migration to western Europe', *West European Politics*, vol. 3, no. 1, January, pp. 31–46.

Miller, M. (1987), *Employer Sanctions in Western Europe*, Center for Migration Studies, New York.

Ministry of Labour, Sweden (1990), 'The pre-requisites for the direction of a comprehensive refugee and immigration policy', International Organization for Migration, December.

Mishra, R. (1990), *The Welfare State in Capitalist Society*, Harvester Wheatsheaf, New York.

Ong, P. (1987), 'Immigrant wives' labor force participation', *Industrial Relations*, 26, pp. 296–303.

Parkin, A. (1977), 'Ethnic politics: a comparative study of two immigrant societies, Australia and the United States', *Journal of Commonwealth & Comparative Politics*, 15/1, pp. 22–38.

Peck, J. (1989), 'Labour market segmentation theory', *Labour and Industry*, 2, pp. 119–44.

Plender, R. (1988), *International Migration Law*, Martinus Nijhoff, Dordrecht.

Power, M. (1975), 'Women's work is never done—by men: a socio-economic model of sex typing in occupations', *Journal of Industrial Relations*, 17, pp. 225–39.

Pratt, G. & Hanson, S. (1988), 'Gender, class and space', *Society and Space*, 6, pp. 15–35.

Price, C. A. (1974), *The Great White Walls Are Built: Restrictive Immigration to North America and Australasia 1836–1888*, ANU Press, Canberra.

Robinson, W. (1984), 'Illegal immigrants in Canada: recent developments', *International Migration Review*, vol. 18, no. 3.

Salt, J. (1989), 'A comparative overview of international trends and types, 1950–80', *International Migration Review*, 23/3, pp. 431–56.

Schoen, D. (1977), *Enoch Powell and the Powellites*, St Martin's Press, New York.

Simon, J. (1989), *The Economic Consequences of Immigration*, Basil Blackwell, New York.

—— (1990), *The Economics of Immigration*, The Free Press, New York.

Skocpol, T. (1985), 'Bringing the state back in: strategies of analysis in current research', in P. Evans, D. Rueschemeyer & T. Skocpol (eds), *Bringing the State Back In*, Cambridge University Press, Cambridge.

Soja, E. (1989), *Postmodern Geographies*, Verso, London.

van der Berghe, P. A. (1981), *The Ethnic Phenomenon*, Elsevier, New York.

Weir, M. & Skocpol, T. (1985), 'State structures and the possibilities for "Keynesian" responses to the Great Depression in Sweden, Britain and the United States', in P. Evans, D. Rueschemeyer & T. Skocpol (eds), *Bringing the State Back In*, Cambridge University Press, Cambridge, pp. 107–68.

Williamson, J. (1974), 'Migration to the new world: long term influences and impact', *Explorations in Economic History*, vol. 11(4), pp. 357–89.

Zolberg, A. (1989), 'The next waves: migration theory for a changing world', *International Migration Review*, 23, pp. 403–30.

ABBREVIATIONS AND ACRONYMS

AUSTRALIA

ACMA	Advisory Council on Multicultural Affairs
ACPEA	Australian Council on Population and Ethnic Affairs
ACTU	Australian Council of Trade Unions
AEAC	Australian Ethnic Affairs Council
AIMA	Australian Institute of Multicultural Affairs
ALP	Australian Labor Party
AMEP	Adult Migrant Education (now English) Programme
AWU	Australian Workers Union
CAAIP	Committee to Advise on Australia's Immigration Policies (FitzGerald)
COASIT	Italian Assistance Council
COPQ	Council on Overseas Professional Qualifications
DILGEA	Department of Immigration, Local Government and Ethnic Affairs
DORS	Determination of Refugee Status Committee
EAC	Ethnic Affairs Commission
ECC	Ethnic Communities' Council
ESB	English-speaking background
ESL	English as a Second Language
FECCA	Federation of Ethnic Communities' Councils of Australia
FILEF	Italian Federation of Immigrant Workers and their Families
IMP	An econometric model of the Australian economy
LGA	Local Government Area
NESB	Non-English-speaking background
NPC	National Population Council
OMA	Office of Multicultural Affairs
ORANI	An econometric model of the Australian economy

PNC	Prohibited Non-Citizen
ROMAMPAS	Review of Migrant and Multicultural Programmes and Services (Jupp)
TAFE	Technical and Further Education
TIS	Telephone Interpreter Service (now Translating and Interpreting Service)

UNITED STATES

AFL	American Federation of Labor
CIO	Congress of Industrial Organizations
CPS	Current Population Survey
FAIR	Federation for American Immigration Reform
FTA	Free Trade Agreement
GAO	General Accounting Office
INA	*Immigration and Nationality Act* (1952)
INS	Immigration and Naturalization Service
IRCA	*Immigration Reform and Control Act* (1986)
LULAC	League of United Latin American Citizens
MALDEF	Mexican American Legal Defense and Education Fund
NALEO	National Association of Latino Elected Officials
OMB	Office of Management and Budget
ORR	Office of Refugee Resettlement
RAW	Replenishment Agricultural Worker
SAVE	Systematic Alien Verification for Entitlements
SAW	Special Agricultural Workers
SCIRP	Select Commission on Immigration and Refugee Policy
SLIAG	State Legalization Impact Assistance Grants
VRA	*Voting Rights Act* (1965)

INDEX